THE CROSS AND THE ENSIGN

Peter Elliott has a long-standing interest in naval history and has been known as an author on the subject since just after the Second World War. He joined the Royal Navy straight from school in 1941 and served throughout the war, eventually becoming a lieutenant. His career was very varied and he served on destroyers, frigates, corvettes and fleet minesweepers. At the end of hostilities he went to Brasenose College, Oxford but found it too difficult to settle to the academic life after the hectic war years. He now lives in Somerset and, as well as holding a senior managerial post, devotes much of his time to writing.

PETER ELLIOTT

The Cross and the Ensign

A naval history of Malta 1798–1979

HarperCollins*Publishers*

HarperCollins*Publishers*
77–85 Fulham Palace Road,
Hammersmith, London W6 8JB

This paperback edition 1994
5 7 9 8 6 4

Previously published in paperback by Grafton Books 1982
Reprinted twice

First published in Great Britain by
Patrick Stephens Limited 1980

ISBN 0 586 05550 9

Set in Times

Printed and bound in Great Britain by
Omnia Books Ltd, Glasgow

Contents

Preface

'Malta — that tiny rock of history and romance.' In those few words Sir Winston Churchill summed up this island, which has had such a great influence on the history of the Mediterranean Sea, and on that of the nations which surround it.

This book describes the naval history of Malta over two centuries — the years during which the Royal Navy has been so closely associated with the island; and the book appears soon after the British finally withdrew from the island, after a long and friendly relationship with its people. Many books have been written about Malta, but this one links up those 178 years into a single story, with the benefit of original records from the Second World War which have recently been de-classified.

High on the landward end of Valletta, a vantage point in the Upper Barracca Gardens looks out over the expanse of Grand Harbour, and towards the ancient Fort St Angelo on the opposite shore. From these gardens the citizens of Valletta and the families of the ships' companies have watched the warships of many nations come and go below them during those two centuries, and with those ships have ebbed and flowed the fortunes of the island itself, and the balance of power in the Mediterranean.

The Knights of St John watched the French Fleet arrive in 1798, but Nelson's ships followed them two years later.

From here a Royal Naval force sailed against the Crimea in 1869, and then with the French against the Dardanelles in 1915. Two years later the convoy escorts wore the flags of Britain, America, France, Japan and Australia.

The fleet sailed on splendid cruises in the years of peace, with their Royal Marine bands playing on the quarter decks as they left harbour. When the bombers of Hitler and Mussolini came in 1941, the big ships left Grand Harbour to the destroyers and submarines. Here the aircraft carrier *Illustrious* was nearly sunk, the famous Force K sailed to strike against the Axis supply convoys, and the arrival of the surviving ships of the Pedestal convoy brought scenes of wild rejoicing.

The Americans came in 1943, only six months after the island's deliverance, to join the British in assaulting Sicily and the Italian mainland; here too the Italian Fleet came to surrender in that year – that was a great day for the Maltese people.

In 1956 the British and French forces sailed from Grand Harbour to assault the Suez Canal, and for many years the ships of other NATO forces (notably the United States Sixth Fleet) called regularly until Malta, first independent and then a republic, banned them all except the Royal Navy. In March 1979 they too withdrew, and the British bases closed down.

One of the main features of this book is its many photographs, and a special word is due about two collections which the author is privileged to highlight among them.

First is that of Mr Richard Ellis, which has not been published in this way before. Bombed in his house on Kingsway in Valletta and then flooded elsewhere, his photographs in this book are among the best that survive of a unique parade of ships, recorded on the heavy glass plates of yesteryear.

The second is that of Mr Anthony Pavia whose family, as that of Mr Ellis, has photographed the calling ships and provided prints for their crews over many generations. Between them these two have recorded a remarkable period of history, and the author is grateful to them for the use of their collections. Sadly the work of a third source, the Grand Studio, was destroyed in the bombing of Valletta.

The research for the book in both Malta and London was long and fascinating. Among other finds was the location of the original logs of Nelson's ships in the Public Record Office, and enthusiastic and valuable help has been provided by a number of private individuals.

It is hoped that this book will provide an important record of two centuries of naval warfare and peace-keeping in and around this mighty little island, standing proudly right in the centre of the tempestuous Mediterranean Sea.

Peter Elliott
Somerton, Somerset 1979

Acknowledgements

Grateful thanks to the following, for providing access to research facilities, information, or photographs: **Malta** Allied Newspapers Ltd, Valletta; British Forces Broadcasting Service, Floriana; Joseph Caruana, Senglea; Commander J L Duffett, RN, Commanding Officer, HMS *St Angelo;* Richard Ellis, Valletta; Chief Superintendent W. Landels, Admiralty Constabulary, Vittoriosa; Malta Drydocks, Cospicua; National War Museum, Fort St Elmo; National Tourist Organisation, Valletta; Anthony Pavia, Birkirkara. **South Africa** Peter Humphries, Sea Point. **United Kingdom** British Newspaper Library, Hendon; Imperial War Museum, Lambeth; Ministry of Defence (Navy), Whitehall; National Maritime Museum, Greenwich; Public Record Office, Kew; Lieutenant Commander Philip Ratcliffe, East Grinstead (Identification of old photographs); Royal Marines Museum, Eastney; Ian Sturton, Southampton, (drawings of *Ark Royals);* P.A. Vicary, Cromer.

Significant dates

1500	BC	Phoenicians in control
700		Greeks took over
650		Carthaginians captured Malta
216		Hamilcar surrendered Malta to the Romans
60	AD	St Paul shipwrecked on Malta
395		Malta absorbed into Byzantine Empire
870		Arabs captured Malta
1090		Count Roger the Norman took over
1450		Spain in control
1530		Knights of St John arrived
1565		The Great Siege
1571		Battle of Lepanto (Turks defeated)
1798	May 19	French Fleet sailed from Toulon
	June 11	Napoleon captured Malta
	June 22	British and French Fleets in 'near-miss' east of Malta
	August 1/2	Battle of the Nile
	October 12	Blockade of Malta commenced in earnest
	November	Menorca captured by British
1800	September 4	British captured Malta
1814		Treaty of Paris — Malta granted to England
1838		Dowager Queen Adelaide visited
1854		Crimean War
1848		First drydock opened
1869		Suez Canal opened
1871		Second drydock opened
1903		King Edward VII visited
1906		Breakwater completed
1912		Fort St Angelo commissioned as HMS *Egmont*

1914		The First World War began
1915		Assault on the Dardanelles
1921		Prince of Wales opened first parliament
1925		Turkish attack on Iraq threatened
1933		HMS *Egmont* renamed HMS *St Angelo*
1936		Italian-Abyssinian crisis and Spanish Civil War
1937	May	Admiral Sir Andrew Cunningham appointed Commander in Chief, Mediterranean Fleet
1939	May	Italian-Albanian crisis
	September	The Second World War began
1940	June 10	Italy declared war
	June 24	France surrendered to Germany
1941	January	*Illustrious* bombed at Malta
	February	German Afrika Korps formed in North Africa
	April	Force K operated for 1 month from Malta
	July	Operation Substance – convoy Gibraltar-Malta
		Italian attack on Grand Harbour
	September	Operation Halberd – convoy Gibraltar-Malta
	October	Force K returned
	November	Force B arrived
	December	Both Forces dissolved after losses
1942	March	Admiral Cunningham relieved by Admiral Harwood
	April 16	George Cross awarded to Malta
	May	10th Submarine Flotilla withdrew to Alexandria
	June	Operation Harpoon – convoy Gibraltar-Malta
	July	10th Submarine Flotilla returned to Malta
	August	Operation Pedestal – convoy Gibraltar-Malta
	October 26	Battle of El Alamein
	November	Operation Stoneage – convoy

		Alexandria-Malta
	December	Force K returned
		Operations Portcullis and Quadrangle – convoys Alexandria-Malta
		Operation Torch – invasion of North Africa
1943	January	Force B returned
	February	Admiral Sir Andrew Cunningham returned
	May 12	Axis forces in North Africa surrendered
	June 11	Assault on Pantellaria
	June 20	King George VI visited Malta
	July 10	Assault on Sicily
	September 3	Italy surrendered
	September 6	Assault on Salerno
	September 11	Italian Fleet surrendered at Malta
	October 16	Admiral Sir Andrew Cunningham relieved by Admiral Sir John Cunningham
1946		Palestine Patrol
	July	CinC Mediterranean returned to Malta as base
1947		British mine clearance in Mediterranean completed
1949		Princess Elizabeth visited Malta
1956	November 5	Assault on Suez Canal
1958		Malta dockyard changed to commercial basis
1964	September 21	Malta declared independent
1967	June	Last CinC Mediterranean left
1969	March	Last Royal Navy force based on Malta disbanded
1972		New defence agreement between Malta and Britain
1974	December 13	Malta declared a Republic
1979	March 12	Flag Officer Malta struck flag in HMS *St Angelo*
	March 31	Last British forces withdrew
1980		No 6 Dock due to be opened

CHAPTER 1

Island of destiny, 1500 BC — AD 1797

The history of the Maltese islands goes back at least to 3,500 BC, and recorded history starts around 1,500 BC. This short introduction aims to do no more than highlight the naval events which led from the arrival of the Phoenicians in that latter period, through to the arrival of the French in 1798.

There are two main islands — Malta, which is the largest, is only 17 miles long and nine miles wide, and Gozo to the north-west is roughly half that size. The islands have through all these centuries been a coveted possession of the ruling powers around the sea, as they lie right across the sea routes of the Mediterranean, about equally distant from Gibraltar and Alexandria, and so enjoy a remarkable strategic position. Their attraction has been greatly enhanced by one of the largest and finest of the natural harbours in the Mediterranean, and every battle, every invasion of the islands has centred upon possession of this remarkable base.

Around the harbour rise high promontories, and for centuries the Maltese and their overlords have built on them their cities, out of the soft golden limestone of the land. From the period of the Knights of St John especially there survive many fine buildings around this Grand Harbour, which still glow in the warm Mediterranean sunshine in all their glory, in spite of the worst that the bombers could do to them 35 years ago.

The people of Malta have watched traders and invaders come and go over many centuries. The earliest recorded history shows the Phoenicians in control of the islands from about 1,500 BC. They were the real architects of early Mediterranean history, for they founded Carthage and Marseilles, and penetrated to Cornwall where they established tin mines. Malta was a natural trading post for them, and they held the islands for 750 years until in 700 BC the Greeks took over. From their new masters the islands received the name 'Melita' ('the honeyed one'), but only 50 years later the Greeks gave up the islands to the Carthaginians.

For the next 400 years the fortunes of Malta followed those of Carthage. The islands suffered in the Punic Wars between the Carthaginians and the Romans; the harbour became a naval base and, at one stage, the Romans invaded the islands burning and pillaging as they went, but later the Carthaginians regained control. The harbour received many trading ships during the rule of Carthage, and the bright oars of galleys crossing the 140 miles of sea to the parent capital flashed in the sunlight off the coast.

The Romans started the Punic Wars with no navy, but they learned quickly, setting up rowing benches on shore to train their galley crews. In three bitter wars the two nations fought for power in the Mediterranean; eventually the Romans won, and in 216 BC Hamilcar surrendered the Maltese islands to the Roman consul Titus Sempronius.

The Roman occupation of Malta was to last for nearly 700 years. The islands prospered as an important trading station, and port facilities in the Marsa area of the harbour were much expanded.

The major event under the Romans, and now treasured by the Maltese, was the shipwreck of St Paul on the north coast of the island in AD 60. He was travelling under guard to Rome to appeal against a charge of heresy, when a great storm threw the vessel upon the island at the mouth of the bay which now bears his name. There is a vivid account of the shipwreck in the Acts of the Apostles. St Paul recorded that 'the barbarous people showed us no little kindness; for they kindled a fire, and received us every one, because of the present rain and because of the cold'. St Paul and his escort stayed in the island for three months as the guests of Publius, 'the chief man of the island', and legend has it that Paul converted his host who became the first Bishop of Malta.

St Paul and his companions boarded a ship on its way from Alexandria to Rome, and he continued his journey towards his martyrdom. The church in Malta every February celebrates the feast of 'St Paul Shipwrecked', both in pomp at the cathedral, and in the little church which bears his name, but is tucked away up a steep side street.

As Roman power waned in the fifth century AD, Malta was first raided by the Vandals, who had founded a kingdom in North Africa and from there sent expeditions against the islands; then it was absorbed into the Eastern Empire of Constantinople in AD 395. The Byzantines were succeeded in their turn by the Arabs, who took Malta in 870. There is little remaining evidence of their rule, though they built up a big empire, and used the islands as a base for their piratical raids to the north. The Islamic faith was proclaimed, though some Maltese, no doubt bravely, retained their Christian faith.

The Arabs controlled Malta for two centuries, until the Norman Count Roger I, Great Count of Sicily, threw them out in 1090. His victory was an easy one; he made a mock attack on St Paul's bay to attract the Arab army, while his real assault force was climbing the cliffs to the west, to take the defenders by surprise.

Five centuries followed which produced no eventful history, and little has been left in the way of records. Under the Aragon rule Moslems were expelled from the islands, the Christians re-established their faith, and today Malta remains a strong bastion of the Christian world. There was

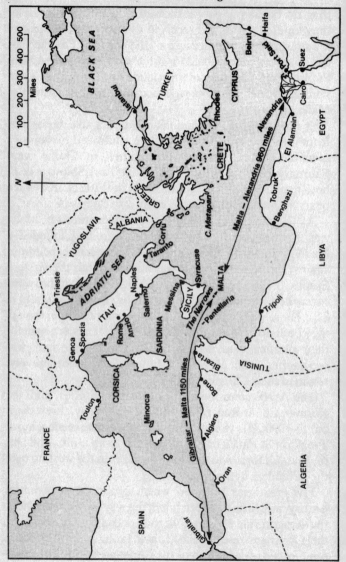

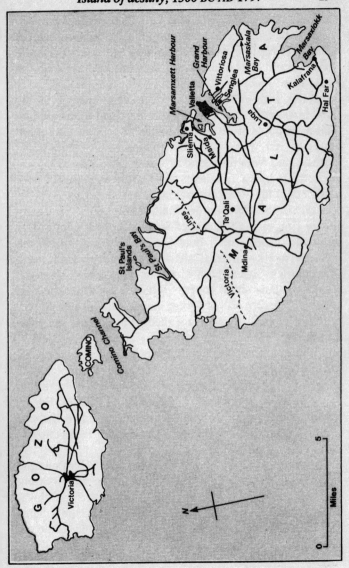

prosperity under Roger, but in 1283 Charles of Anjou used the islands as a naval base and as a springboard for his attempt to capture Sicily. His fleet was defeated in a battle inside Grand Harbour, and Malta reverted to the kingdom of Aragon.

In the 14th century there were many pirates in the Mediterranean, and no doubt some of them were based on Malta. Raiders from North Africa attacked Malta three times in ten years, and the Aragonese mounted a big reprisal raid from the island against the Moslems. This was successful, but a few years later the forces from North Africa counter-attacked, sacking Malta and Gozo.

Early in the 16th century Malta came under the control of the Emperor Charles I of Spain, who was overlord of most of Europe, other than France and England. In the same period the forces of Islam were advancing to the west, and Charles saw in Malta a frontier post beyond which the Turkish galleys could not pass. The war between the Cross and the Crescent was not going well for the Christians.

The Christian forces were thrown back from the Holy Land, and among them were the Knights Hospitallers of the Order of St John. The Knights were dedicated to the task of repelling the Islamic invaders, and to defending the pilgrims to the Holy Land; but when they had to retreat from there, they fell back to the island of Rhodes. For six months they held out against the Turks but in the end massive attacks overwhelmed them and the Turks allowed them to leave with honour.

Charles now saw a way of using Malta as a bastion, and he offered the islands to the Knights, who were not en-chanted by the prospect, but had little choice. Tripoli was included in Charles' gift, but after only 20 years the Knights relinquished their control of a port for which they could see little use.

The Knights arrived in Malta in 1530 and lost no time in

improving the fortifications of Grand Harbour. They had brought with them from Rhodes their fast galleys and, for their base, they took over what is now Vittoriosa, and a little fort which even then stood at the tip of St Angelo. A new fort was built on the peninsula and was to become the centrepiece of Grand Harbour; it stands today as impressive as it was then, even after receiving the full weight of the German air attacks four centuries later.

They also fortified St Elmo, at the tip of the peninsula on which would be built Valletta, and curtain walls were erected at the landward end of the two promontories which enclosed the galley base. To complete the defence, booms were thrown across the mouth of the creeks, the outer boom consisting of a heavy chain.

All this time the threat of a Turkish invasion was in their minds, but not until 1565 did the news arrive that a great invasion force was being prepared in Constantinople, to eliminate this Christian fortress. At dawn on May 18 the defenders looked out to sea and saw the horizon full of white sails, nearly 200 of them, and the Great Siege was on.

The Knights were led by a determined Grand Master, Jean de la Valette Parisot, and his courage and leadership had a big influence on the battle. There were only 600 Knights with some 7,000 auxiliary troops, few enough to resist an invading force of 35,000. The Turks did not have a great leader in their fleet, until the corsair Dragut took over, and his fiery personality nearly swung the battle in favour of the invaders.

The island's unique position and its grave danger were being watched by the rest of the Christian world. In England the recently-crowned Queen Elizabeth said: 'If the Turks should prevail against the Isle of Malta, it is uncertain what further peril might follow to the rest of Christendom'. She ordered prayers for Malta to be read in all the churches in England, three times a week for six weeks.

The Turkish fleet circled round Malta, then anchored in Marsaxlokk bay, and the great army with its guns was landed and spread out towards Grand Harbour.

A great assault was launched against St Elmo, which was defended by 52 Knights with 500 soldiers. They were ordered to resist the Turks to the last, and this they did heroically. As long as they held out, no Turkish ships could enter the harbour. The Turks had estimated five days for the capture of St Elmo, but it took them 31, and 60,000 cannonballs were fired in the fight. The defenders lost 1,500 men (reinforcements were run across Grand Harbour from St Angelo by night) but the Turks lost 8,000 men in the assault, including their leader Dragut. So bitter was the struggle that when on June 23 the Turkish flag was finally run up over St Elmo, four of the Knights who were captured were slaughtered, their bodies lashed to wooden crosses and floated up harbour past St Angelo, to frighten the defenders there. Tradition has it that in reply the Knights fired from their cannon towards the Turkish positions, the heads of every Turkish prisoner they held. It had been an expensive victory, and the attackers were exhausted and demoralised.

The Grand Master had in the meantime sent several pleas for help to the Viceroy of Sicily; it took some time to assemble the relieving force of 10,000 men, but on September 7 they landed on the north side of Malta; by a ruse the Turks were persuaded that the relieving force was much larger than it was, and they fled to their ships.

The following day the Turkish Fleet sailed away, and the siege was over. The Turks left 25,000 dead behind them from the four months' battle, and of the defenders half the Knights and 2,000 of the soldiers were dead, together with many of the Maltese people. It was little wonder that the battles of 1941 and 1942 were to be named the Second or Greater Seige. Ever since 1565 on September 8, the feast of

Our Lady of Victories, this great battle has been com-
memorated in the chapel of St Anne in the fortress of St
Angelo; and since 1943 there has been additional thanksgiving for the surrender of the Italian Fleet, also on
September 8.

The survivors lost no time in repairing their damaged
fortresses, and a great plan was launched to build a fortified
city on the peninsula which runs out to St Elmo. The
foundation stone was laid in March 1566 and the new city
was named Valletta, after the Grand Master who had so
nobly led his Knights through the Great Siege. The leading
architects and designers of fortifications of the day were
brought to Malta to supervise the building of the city, and
the great bastions which surround it. Magnificent new
auberges were built, one for each of the *langues* (or
nationalities) of the Knights, and these provided
communal living for them. Some of these *auberges* have
survived, and none is finer than the Auberge de Castille,
which now houses the offices of the Prime Minister of
Malta. A great cathedral was constructed, and the floor of
the nave was built of remarkable marble memorials to the
dead Knights.

Across the water new fortifications were built to the
landward side. The promontory on which St Angelo stands
had been named Vittoriosa in honour of the victory, and a
new curtain wall of gigantic proportions was built to protect
it and the next peninsula across the Dockyard Creek, and
this new wall was named the Cottonera Lines. New forts
were built at the mouths of the harbour and the new Fort
Manoel faced the entrance across Marsamxett harbour.

. Malta was soon much more secure, but the Knights had
little relaxation. Apart from the great labours of building,
the Turkish Fleet remained active, and the defenders had
to be constantly on their guard. Look-out towers were built
around the coasts to watch for invaders, and twice in the

17th century there were alarms. Once a strong Turkish raiding force landed at Marsaskala bay, but was forced back into the sea; on another occasion a fleet appeared off Marsaxlokk, but the guns of the defenders drove them off.

Gradually Turkish sea power declined. The battle of Lepanto in 1571 was the turning point, and thereafter Islam was not seen as a serious threat to Christianity in Europe. The eyes of the great powers turned towards the new lands discovered on the other side of the Atlantic, and Malta for a time lost some of its strategic importance.

The Knights also declined into a less effective fighting force; their life became somewhat dissolute, with drunkenness, brawling and disobedience, and the galleys sailing from Grand Harbour were no longer the up-to-date warships which they had been a century before. The Maltese people were in poverty, and there was despondency in the islands.

The scene was set for Napoleon.

CHAPTER 2

The great Mediterranean chase, 1798

So the scene was set for a further change of overlord in Malta, and it was not long in coming.

The storming of the Bastille in Paris in 1789 put events in motion. First a Decree of 1791 deprived the French Knights of their nationality and possessions; then in the following year the possessions of the Order were taken over, or subjected to heavy taxation, in Germany, Naples, Portugal, Sicily and Spain. The income of the Order in Malta fell disastrously, from three million livres in 1788 to just one million in 1797.

The Tsar of Russia, Paul I, was keen to extend his influence in the Mediterranean, and made overtures to Grand Master de Rohan in Valletta, seeking to become Protector of the Order. He offered a substantial gift for the foundation of an orthodox *langue* for Russian nobles, but Britain heard of this and, wanting to keep Russia out rather than having any ambitions of the kind for herself, she also entered into negotiations with the Grand Master.

Rather unwisely as it turned out, he took up the Tsar's offer. He in turn thought it wise to appease the British, and he awarded the Cross of Malta to Lady Hamilton in Naples, and the Knights gave her the title of Dame Petite Croix within their Order.

Britain was not in any position of strength just then. Her fleet had been withdrawn entirely from the Mediterranean in December 1796, as Pitt and the government in London regarded the risk of England being invaded by Napoleon as overriding, especially after his sweeping land victories in Italy. Earl Spencer, First Lord of the Admiralty, planned to hold the English Channel and the Atlantic approaches by pinning the invasion fleets in their home ports. With this objective a fleet of 30 sail of the line was blockading Brest, and a similar number under Admiral the Earl St Vincent was stationed off Cadiz.

The Mediterranean seemed wide open in the early months of 1798; and when word reached London that the French were gathering a great invasion force in Toulon, the Admiralty knew at once that it was essential to blockade that port as well. Napoleon could turn west from the south coast of France and invade Ireland on his way to England, or he could turn east to attack Egypt, and then British India. The British Fleet started the year stretched to its limits, and this was to have an important influence on the size of Nelson's squadron in the Mediterranean in the next few vital months.

The information reaching London from Toulon was not far from the truth. The Directorate in Paris had put the successful Napoleon (still only 29 years old) in charge of the expedition, and he was being briefed in Paris early in May, before embarking in Toulon. The original intention of the Directorate had in fact been an invasion of England by this fleet, as yet unblockaded by the British; but Napoleon persuaded them that this was not the best plan — rather they should attack Egypt, and pass on to the British possessions in the East, and bring England to her knees later.

Only Nelson and his squadron, with their victory at Aboukir Bay, were to frustrate that plan; just as in 1942, 144 years later, it was to be the Royal Navy, with the Maltese people, who held out against the German forces, and who were instrumental in halting General Rommel's drive on Egypt, and so in frustrating Hitler's plan, which had closely followed that of Napoleon Bonaparte.

The French invasion force assembling in Toulon was indeed a big one. There were 13 French sail of the line, and two Venetian 64-gun ships. They were supported by eight frigates, with a further six frigates armed *en flute,* or with reduced crews. There were 400 sail of transports, carrying some 36,000 troops, and the crews of the warships numbered a further 10,000 men.

The Commander-in-Chief of the fleet, under Napoleon as overall commander, was Vice-Admiral Brueys d'Aigalliers, a most experienced officer, and he had with him Rear-Admirals Villeneuve, Blanquet and Decrès. The Commander-in-Chief's flag was flying in the three-deck, 120-gun ship of the line *Orient;* her previous name was *Sans Culotte,* and she had been significantly renamed for this expedition. Rear-Admiral Villeneuve was flying his flag in the 80-gun *Guillaume Tell,* and his ship was to play a big part later in the blockade of Malta.

Meanwhile Horatio Nelson, now a Rear-Admiral of the Red, and just turned 40 years of age, had been recuperating in England from the amputated arm which he had suffered in his last action. But he was anxious to get back to sea, and was appointed to fly his flag in the 74-gun *Vanguard,* then completing, and with Edward Berry remaining with him as his Flag Captain.

Vanguard joined the blockading fleet off Cadiz on April 29 1798, and Nelson was immediately detached as an independent commander to proceed into the Mediterranean, 'to endeavour to ascertain the real object of the preparations making by the French'. Earl St Vincent still had a high regard for Nelson, from his previous successful adventures in the Mediterranean, and this free-roving assignment was ideal for Nelson himself.

He was given as his squadron for this mission two more 74-gun ships of the line, *Alexander* (Captain Alexander Ball) and *Orion* (Captain Sir James Saumarez). With them were two 32-gun frigates, *Emerald* and *Terpsichore,* a sloop captured from the French, *La Bonne Citoyenne,* and the

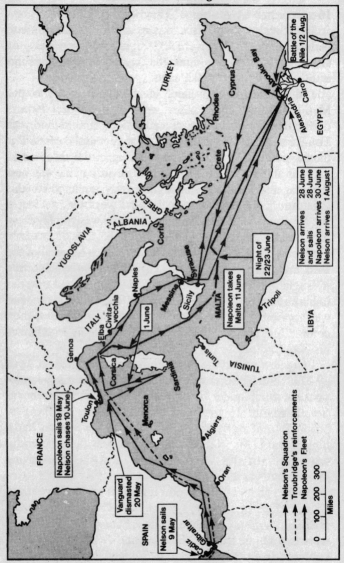

Napoleon sails 19 May
Nelson chases 10 June

Vanguard dismasted 20 May

Nelson sails 9 May

FRANCE
SPAIN
Cadiz
Gibraltar
Oran
Algiers
Toulon
Menorca
Sardinia
Corsica
Genoa
Elba
Civita-vecchia
ITALY
Naples
Messina
Sicily
Syracuse
Corfu
ALBANIA
GREECE
YUGOSLAVIA
TURKEY
Crete
Rhodes
Cyprus
Aboukir Bay
Battle of the Nile 1/2 Aug.
Alexandria
Cairo
EGYPT
LIBYA
Tripoli
Tunis
TUNISIA

1 June

MALTA
Napoleon takes Malta 11 June

Night of 22/23 June

Nelson arrives 28 June
Nelson arrives and sails 28 June
Napoleon arrives 30 June
Nelson arrives 1 August

Nelson's Squadron
Troubridge's reinforcements
Napoleon's Fleet

0   100 200 300
Miles

16-gun brig-sloop *Mutine* (Captain T.M. Hardy).

Signalling to these ships to conform to his movements, Nelson moved off on May 2 towards the Straits of Gibraltar. The squadron arrived there two days later, and after taking on stores and water (depleted by their blockade duty) the ships sailed again on May 9 into the Mediterranean.

The British squadron took up its surveillance station off Toulon on May 17, and on that very day Nelson heard from the Captain of a privateer that there were 19 French sail of the line in the harbour, that 15 were all ready for sea, and that Napoleon Bonaparte was on his way south to embark.

However, to the frustration of the British Captains, a strong north-westerly wind sprang up which forced them off station, and it was all they could do to prevent their ships being damaged by the storm. The following night, with Napoleon safely embarked, the great French Fleet

Critical factors in Nelson's chase of Napoleon 1 *Excellent appreciation of strategic situation by the Admiralty, and by Admiral Lord St Vincent off Cadiz.* **2** *Good timing of Nelson's despatch to blockade Toulon, and on Troubridge's reinforcing squadron from Cadiz.* **3** *Nelson's misfortune in being dismasted off Toulon, just as Napoleon's fleet was departing from there.* **4** *On return to the blockade of Toulon, Nelson only realised a week later that Napoleon had left, one day before the French took Malta.* **5** *The British did not appear to appreciate the full importance of Malta, until Napoleon had taken it.* **6** *Nelson had no frigates throughout the chase, though the French were well provided.* **7** *The incredible near-miss of the two fleets east of Malta, on the morning of June 22, and again that night.* **8** *The sailing efficiency of the British squadron, compared with the slowness of the French Fleet.* **9** *Nelson's decision to leave Alexandria, when in fact the French Fleet was only just over the horizon.* **10** *The fighting efficiency of the British. Nelson's ships had been at sea for three months, while the French had had a week in Malta, and a month in Egypt.* **11** *All the subsequent moves of the British ships, and of the surviving French ships, revolved around the occupation of Malta.*

slipped out of Toulon, and turning east before the strong wind, was quickly away into the mists of the Mediterranean.

Of all this, Nelson knew nothing; for his squadron had run 25 leagues (75 miles) before the wind and to the south of the islands of Hyêres, where at midnight the wind gusted to gale force, and the British Captains needed all their seamanship just to keep in touch with one another. All sails were furled in each ship, only a small storm trysail being carried on the mainmast, but it was to no avail.

At two o'clock in the morning *Vanguard*'s main topmast went over the side with a great crack; the topsail yard was crowded with men struggling with the wet and heavy canvas, but miraculously few of them were lost. Half an hour later the mizzen topmast went the same way, and the foremast gave out a loud cracking noise. A few minutes later it too went over the side 'with a most tremendous crash'.

'The situation was then really alarming,' recorded Edward Berry. The wreckage of the topmasts and rigging was hanging over the side of the ship and beating against the hull in the steep seas. The main topmast was swinging violently against the main rigging, threatening to bring the mainmast down with it, with every roll of the groaning hull, and the long bowsprit was sprung, so that it could take little weight from a sail.

On top of it all, the ships were still running before the strong wind and driving down on to a lee shore. Something had to be done, and fast. In *Vanguard*, a torn piece of the spritsail was still usable, and a jury sail was rigged from it, so that the great ship could be gently nursed over on to the other tack in an effort to clear the islands to the south of them.

In this way they struggled against the wind for a day and a half, while the squadron was scattered, and only the faithful Ball managed to keep in touch with Nelson and Berry. Then, as suddenly as it arose, the wind died away, leaving *Vanguard* and *Alexander* rolling violently in the big swell raised by the storm and drifting helplessly down upon the shores of Sardinia.

'Leave me,' Nelson signalled to Ball, 'Better to lose one ship than two.' But Ball would not leave his beloved Admiral that easily and continued his endeavours to pass a towline, though with little enough breeze to keep steerage way. Then just as the situation looked hopeless, cat's paws of wind appeared on the smooth surfaces of the heaving waves and a little breeze sprang up in the nick of time.

Alexander managed then to pass her towrope over to *Vanguard*, and with great seamanship Ball carefully nursed the badly-damaged flagship round the point of land which was now so dangerously close under their lee bows, until at last on May 22 they were able to anchor in the harbour of San Pietro in Sardinia.

The crews of *Vanguard*, *Alexander* and *Orion* (which had just managed to rejoin) worked feverishly to repair the flagship, knowing full well that only their watch on Toulon could keep track of the French Fleet. They managed by their own efforts to hoist and rig jury masts, they 'fished' (or spliced) the bowsprit, and triumphantly though wearily they struggled back on station off the French coast by June 3.

Reinforcements were at hand. At home the Admiralty, equally concerned about Napoleon's intentions, sailed eight ships of the line from the Channel Fleet off Brest to join St Vincent off Cadiz. He in turn despatched ten of his 'choice' ships from the Inshore Squadron under Captain Troubridge, to join Nelson off Toulon. These ten left their blockading stations as soon as the Channel Fleet reinforcements hove in sight over the northern horizon on May 24, and the latter had replaced them on the inshore blockade before dawn, so that the watchers on shore should see no change.

On June 5 the brig-sloop *Mutine* came flying from Gibraltar with the news that Troubridge's ships were on the way. Nelson was worried about making the rendezvous with them, for the two frigates and the sloop had lost touch with the squadron during the storm, and thinking that the Admiral had run for Gibraltar to find shelter, went there themselves, and so missed the subsequent actions. Nelson was to lament bitterly that the lack of frigates would 'be found engraved on his heart', and their absence during the great chase across the Mediterranean which was to follow may well have altered the course of history.

Now Nelson spread his three big 74-gun ships and the one smaller ship as far apart as visual signalling would allow, and they all kept a sharp lookout for Troubridge's squadron. In the process the British ships sighted 15 sail of richly laden Spanish merchantmen, and *Alexander* and *Orion* each captured one.

On June 7 the two squadrons were united, and at last Nelson had a fleet with which he could challenge the French. Details of his ships appear later in the blockade of Malta; the majority of the Captains were of his devoted 'band of brothers', and the golden memory of those days retained over the years by the Royal Navy is shown by the fact that in World War 2, British warships proudly carried the names of 12 Captains out of the 15 ships then under Nelson's command.

Troubridge brought with him fresh orders from St Vincent, which were after Nelson's own heart: 'Pursue and attack the enemy', they said, 'wherever he may be found'. Admiral Sir Andrew Cunningham, sailing in those same waters 145 years later, was to issue the same order to his cruisers and destroyers as the Axis forces attempted to retreat from Libya to Italy.

By June 12 Nelson realised that Napoleon with his fleet had eluded him and had sailed from Toulon while *Vanguard* had been struggling against the storm. Nelson's previous encounters with the French had given him experience in analysing their intentions and now he was convinced that Napoleon was heading for Egypt and, having taken that land, would pass on to invade British India.

Nelson knew that the French ships had left Toulon with a north-west wind behind them and had achieved a flying start up the Mediterranean. So his squadron steered first for Corsica; the next leg of his search took him to Elba, and then *Mutine* was sent into Civita Vecchia for news. But none was available there, so the squadron sailed on along the coast of Tuscany, where a Moorish vessel gave them the false news that the French Fleet had arrived in Syracuse in Sicily.

On June 17 Nelson's ships stood into the bay of Naples, where the British ambassador told him that the French were probably making for Malta. The British ships turned south again and, after two frustrating days of light breezes, passed through the Straits of Messina on June 22. There the consul told them that Malta and Gozo had been captured, so Nelson turned south for the islands, running at last before a freshening north-westerly breeze.

They were off Cape Passero in Sicily at dawn on June 22, when a Genoese brig told *Mutine* that the French had sailed from Malta on June 16, running before the same wind.

The French did not in fact leave Grand Harbour until June 19, but the news was good enough for Nelson, who could see that Napoleon must now be heading for Alexandria. So the British ships altered course once more, and crowding on all possible sail they steered south-east to catch up with the French in the waters east of Malta.

We may leave them plunging onwards through the blue

seas in bright sunshine, while we retrace our steps to follow Napoleon's movements after leaving Toulon on May 19.

The strong north-west wind carried the great French Fleet quickly along the coast of Provence to Genoa, where a further division of troop transports sailed out to join them. Moving onwards the ships had Corsica in sight from May 23 to May 30, and there they beat back and forth, awaiting the sailing of another convoy from Civita Vecchia on May 28.

Napoleon received intelligence from ashore on June 3 that three British ships of the line and two frigates had been seen off Cagliari; he sent a division of ships in that direction to check, but they saw nothing. The convoy had still not arrived, however, and the French then sailed on without it, rather than risk an encounter with the British squadron.

The great fleet passed west of Sicily and was within gunshot of the port of Mazara on June 5. The following day one of the French scouting frigates captured a British brig, whose crew told their captors that Nelson's ships were not far astern. Although this was a false report, it worried the French Admiral, and the fleet left the coast of Sicily and moved off to the south-east.

At dawn on June 9 they sighted the islands of Malta and Gozo and approached the land in the golden morning sunshine. The convoy of 70 sail from Civita Vecchia joined forces with them just then, and the Knights of St John and the Maltese saw the frightening spectacle of nearly 500 ships approaching them, with 13 ships of the line as escorts.

The French sent squadrons to take soundings all round the main island, looking for suitable places to land troops. Admiral Brueys sent a pinnace into Grand Harbour, asking permission for the French Fleet to enter to take on water. This in fact was no more than a ruse by which to gain entry by force.

The Knights held a debate for two days, heated and despairing, and while they did so the French made landings in seven different places during the night. The French General Vaubois, who had already been designated as Governor of Malta, landed at St Julian's bay without opposition, and marched his men to Mdina, the ancient inland capital, where he dined with the Archbishop. General Desaix landed at Marsa Scirocco in the east, also without fighting, while Generals Lannes and Marmont, later to become famous marshals, occupied Marsamxett and Fort Tigne.

However, the Grand Master, von Hompesch, had no wish for a fight, and by June 11 he was suing for peace. In this thinking he had been encouraged by a Monsieur Poussielgue, the secretary to the French legation in Genoa, who had been sent on ahead of the fleet, to sound out the French Knights and to help start an insurrection in Valletta.

The Knights surrendered on June 11, and the French ships of the line entered Grand Harbour, taking as prizes two 64-gun ships, one frigate and three of the traditional Maltese galleys, now entirely outclassed by the newer sailing ships of the line. The following day Napoleon landed at Custom House Steps from the flagship *Orient*, and walked in triumph up the steep Merchants' Street in Valletta.

Von Hompesch was given three days to leave the island, and in that time the Knights packed up and departed with some indignity, leaving to the French the great fortress which their predecessors had fortified so well.

The Maltese received their new masters as liberators, not as despots, but they were quickly to learn their mistake as Napoleon swept into action. He installed himself in the house of a noble Maltese lady; this house, the Parisio Palace, on Merchants' Street, is now used as the General

Post Office. He set himself with enormous energy to republicanise the islands; a new code of laws based on the French one was promulgated, the Knights' escutcheons on buildings were defaced and the Order's palaces were looted, to the sum of three million francs. Jewellery, tapestries, paintings and plate were plundered freely, while the Maltese looked on in silent amazement. New taxes were imposed on the inhabitants, who were already poor, and every day brought new and oppressive decrees. French became the official language overnight, and some streets received strange-sounding new names, such as rue des Droits de l'Homme. Palace Square, in front of the Grand Master's Palace, became Place de la Liberté, but the Maltese felt that these were empty names.

Then, abruptly, seven days after he had landed, Napoleon re-embarked in *Orient,* with all the looted treasure, and on June 19 the great fleet departed, heading for Egypt.

As he left he made one bad mistake. He had misjudged the spirit of the Maltese people and left General Vaubois with a small garrison of only three thousand men; though, in the ensuing blockade of Valletta, that small force showed by its heroic resistance how undignified had been the hasty surrender of the Knights.

Now came the most dramatic moments of this great Mediterranean chase. Napoleon with the French Fleet had sailed eastward from Malta on June 19. The north-west breeze was fresh and the ships were able to lay a direct course for Alexandria. Frigates were stationed on the horizon ahead of them, stopping every vessel encountered in the search for news of Nelson's ships.

The British squadron had also turned eastward before the same wind, leaving the coast of Sicily on June 22. But while the French ships were moving at a comfortable speed, keeping the great fleet in formation, Nelson's ships had crowded on every possible stitch of canvas and they were moving much faster. An additional factor was that Nelson and his ships' companies were in good form, enjoying their squadron's new and independent mission, whereas the French ships had been too long in harbour and their crews were slower at their sail drill.

On the morning of June 22 three sail were sighted from the British squadron; Nelson sent the swift 50-gun *Leander* to chase them and soon Captain Thompson was signalling back from the horizon that they were French frigates. But just then Captain Hardy in *Mutine* chased and captured a brig, whose Captain told him that after capturing Malta, Napoleon and his great fleet had sailed from Grand Harbour on June 17.

Nelson called a conference of his Captains aboard *Vanguard* to assess this rather puzzling information, and they concluded that Napoleon had already headed east. So Nelson hoisted signals recalling *Leander* from her pursuit of the three French frigates; Captain Saumarez recorded that the French ships were not thought important enough to warrant the splitting up of the British squadron.

Those French frigates were actually part of the outer scouting screen of the great French Fleet itself, which had left Malta two days later than the brig had reported. Napoleon and his 472 sail were only just over the horizon to the southward, and if *Leander* had gone after the frigates just an hour or two earlier, or better still, if Nelson's fast frigates had only remained with him when *Vanguard* had been dismasted, then there would have been a tremendous naval battle that day.

More dramatic still, during the hours of darkness that were to follow, the two fleets passed very close to one another — so close that the French could hear the sound of the minute guns from the British ships rolling across to them over the misty water. Nelson's squadron was steering south-east at full speed, Admiral Brueys was heading east, and when he heard the British guns he altered course away to the northward — in itself a remarkable feat in the darkness, with nearly 500 ships to control.

Historians should not, perhaps, speculate too much on what might have been, but here was a momentous near-miss. If Nelson had detected and caught Napoleon and his fleet on either of those two occasions, the whole course of history would really have been altered. Napoleon would not have reached Egypt, the Battle of the Nile would not have been fought, nor — had Nelson been victorious — would the battles of Trafalgar and Waterloo have been necessary. As an historian of the 19th century was to record: 'This escape was to cost Britain and the civilised world 17 more years of war, waste, and destruction'.

Nelson pressed on with all speed, but Napoleon did not have as big a start as he thought, so that the British squadron simply increased its lead ahead of the French Fleet. For six days they made good progress, speaking to only three vessels on the way, but they could find no news of the French.

The British ships carried out intensive gunnery exercises each day and three times, when the weather permitted, the ships were hove to while the Captains were rowed over to *Vanguard* for planning conferences. It was agreed that the prime objective of the British squadron on joining action with the French Fleet at sea must be to destroy the transports full of troops. For this purpose the British force was split up into three divisions, one of five ships of the line, the others of four each, with the larger division detailed to engage the French ships of the line, while the others went for the soft-skinned transports.

Nelson was feeling acutely the absence of any frigates to scout ahead of the big ships for the enemy. On June 28 the British force sighted the great Pharos lighthouse at the entrance to Alexandria's harbour, and could see that the French Fleet was not there. *Mutine* went in for news but found none, so the squadron turned north-east and headed towards the Greek islands and Corfu, to see if the French Fleet had gone there to take on water, or even headed back to Sicily or Naples.

From Alexandria Nelson wrote a despatch to Lord St Vincent, on his blockading station off Cadiz, which he sent off by *Mutine;* in it he spoke again of his lack of frigates, 'to which I shall ever attribute my ignorance of the situation of the French Fleet'.

Nelson's sweep into the north-east corner of the Mediterranean drew another blank, so he headed quickly for Syracuse to take on stores and water. Arriving there on July 19, the ships entered by a different channel from the usual one, due to the prevailing wind, but with good seamanship they all arrived safely in the harbour.

The squadron sailed again on July 24 for the Greek islands; here Nelson received further confirmation that Napoleon's destination was Alexandria after all, so the British ships, weary and frustrated, crowded on all sail yet again and steered at full speed for Egypt.

In the meantime the French Fleet arrived off Alexandria on June 30, and the French consul hastened out to tell them of Nelson's reconnaissance of only three days before. Once again Nelson's hunch had been correct, and he had hardly left the area before the sails of Admiral Brueys' armada appeared over the western horizon.

The troops were put ashore in haste, in case the British ships returned, and there was an alarm on July 1 when a sail came up over the horizon; but it turned out to be the frigate *Justice*, catching up after a delayed departure from Malta.

Napoleon landed with the army and captured Alexandria on July 2. The following day Admiral Brueys moved the ships of the line up the coast to Aboukir Bay, 'where they could present their resistance to the best advantage'. Heavy guns were landed from the transports and batteries were sited at strategic positions ashore in both anchorages.

Napoleon himself pressed on to Cairo with the army, capturing the city on July 22, and then went on to assault Suez. Contemporary history books say that Napoleon even then was planning a canal from the Mediterranean through to the Red Sea; whether or not this was so, this operation was an interesting parallel to the Anglo-French assault on Alexandria in 1956.

By this time the British squadron was once more approaching Alexandria. At dawn on August 1 the British forward look-out ships *Alexander* and *Swiftsure* signalled that they could see the harbour, and it was 'a wood of masts', but with no ships of the line. French tricolours were flying from every ship and from every flagstaff ashore. Then *Zealous* and *Goliath* which were searching further up the coast reported in excitement that they had spotted the French ships of the line, moored in Aboukir Bay.

Nelson recalled the four scouting ships, and *Culloden,* which was astern of the squadron towing a captured wine brig; and together his squadron responded to his signals, ordering action with the French Fleet. The battle began that evening and raged all night. The French line was held together by cables, to prevent the British ships from breaking through. Nelson's force pressed on inshore of the French ships, and by some daring manoeuvres and courageous gunnery battles at short range, they decimated the French Fleet.

The flagship *Orient,* of 120 guns, exploded during the action, carrying with her the gallant Admiral Brueys, and all of the treasure plundered in Malta. As dawn broke over the battle scene, the French had been clearly defeated; of the 13 French ships of the line ten had been captured, though three had burned out. One of the four frigates had been sunk, and another burned. No British ship was lost and only five suffered casualties; of these *Bellerophon* and *Majestic* suffered the worst. But British killed and wounded numbered no more than 450, against an estimated 4,000 French casualties.

Of the five ships which attempted to escape from the British gunfire, the 74-gun *Timoleon* was quickly caught and destroyed. But two ships of the line, *Généreux* of 74 guns and *Guillaume Tell* of 80 guns (the latter with Rear-Admiral Villeneuve still on board) and two frigates, *Diane* of 40 guns (with Rear-Admiral Decrès on board) and *Justice* of 36 guns got away. They all appear again in the story of Malta. The French army was marooned ashore in Egypt. Napoleon marched north-east through the country that now is Israel and embarked in a frigate in which he slipped back into France. By this battle the British Fleet regained its dominant position in the Mediterranean and was not to lose it again until 1941. This dominance was to be quickly reinforced by the capture of two vital naval bases. First to fall was Malta in 1800, and then Menorca was recaptured, and Port Mahon once more became a main fleet base for the Royal Navy.

CHAPTER 3

Nelson captures Malta, 1799-1800

Meanwhile there was much discontent in Malta among the islanders. They liked their new masters no better than the outgoing Knights and their grievances were growing daily. The wives and children of the men who had been pressed into the service of the French Fleet had been left to starve; all civil pensions had been suspended, and more heavy taxes had been imposed, to pay for the French troops stationed there. But all of these irritations faded into the background when the French took what proved to be their fatal step, by starting to plunder the very churches themselves. They outraged the feelings of a deeply religious people, and made the situation worse by introducing civil marriage as well.

Towards the end of August, when the feelings of the Maltese were running especially high, there limped into Grand Harbour three broken and blackened ships. They were *Guillaume Tell, Diane* and *Justice,* three of the four French ships which had survived from the battle of the Nile; and the sight of them gladdened Maltese hearts.

The breaking point came on September 3, when the French held a public sale of the treasures of the church of Our Lady of Mount Carmel, in the ancient capital of Mdina. The people rose in revolt, and the small French garrison there was slaughtered. The main French garrison was driven back into Valletta and surrounded by the rebellious islanders, led by a canon of the cathedral, Xavier Carnova, who later became Archbishop of Malta.

However, the walled city seemed impregnable. It was known to have supplies for seven months and the Maltese

had few arms and little ammunition. Help was badly
needed,..when in mid-September sails were seen to the
south of the island. A deputation of the principal islanders
put out in boats and found Captain Sir James Saumarez in
Orion; his squadron had sailed from Alexandria on August
6, and had six British ships of the line, escorting six of the
French ships captured at Aboukir Bay, on their way back to
England. Now all these ships were detained off the islands
by light airs and calms. The islanders tried to persuade
Saumarez to stay at Malta, and to help them in throwing
out the French garrison; but this he could not do, as the
prizes were badly needed to reinforce the British Fleet at
home. But Saumarez did send in a flag of truce to General
Vaubois in Valletta, calling on him to surrender.

The proud French garrison was in no mood to give in so
easily. The French General sent him back a note saying:
'You have clearly forgotten that it is Frenchmen who hold
Malta'. So Saumarez had to content himself with landing
1,200 muskets with a good supply of ammunition from the
captured French ships, for the Maltese to use in their siege
of Valletta. This gesture had much to do with the success of
the Maltese in their fight against the French, and Saumarez
also promised to ask the Earl of St Vincent, on his arrival at
Gibraltar, if ships could be sent to blockade the French
from the sea.

Saumarez and his ships continued to meet frustrating
light breezes and did not reach Gibraltar until mid-
September. In the meantime the Maltese sent out another
delegation, this time to the north, to seek aid from Sicily or
Naples. The King of Naples gave a ready and helpful response, which took a strange form. The Earl of St Vincent
had sent further reinforcements from the fleet off Cadiz to
support Nelson in his search for Napoleon's fleet; these
ships were mainly Portuguese, four 74-gun ships of the line,
with the British 74-gun *Lion* in support and with the British

fire-ship *Incendiary,* and a brig. This force was under the command of the Portuguese Rear-Admiral the Marquess de Niza, and a contemporary historian comments that, 'it was lucky for Nelson that the force did not get to the Nile in time!' Now it was diverted to blockade Malta, as an aid to the islanders.

When Nelson arrived with some of his victorious ships at Naples, they were badly in need of refits to repair the damage sustained at Aboukir Bay; but he quickly detached Captain Alexander Ball with a small squadron, to go to Malta and give what help he could. His force comprised: *Alexander,* 74 guns, Captain Alexander Ball; *Colossus,* 74 guns, Captain George Murray; *Culloden,* 74 guns, Captain Thomas Troubridge.

Ball arrived off Valletta on October 12 and relieved the Portuguese ships, and the blockade became effective. Inside Grand Harbour were *Guillaume Tell, Diane* and *Justice,* from the Nile battle, under Rear-Admiral Villeneuve, and Rear-Admiral Decrès was now in charge of the ships captured from the Knights earlier in the year — the 64-gun *Athénien* and *Dego,* and the 36-gun frigate *Carthagénaise.*

A demand for surrender was sent in to General Vaubois, who rejected it angrily, and the siege of Malta was on in earnest. It was to last almost two years from that point.

There were 10,000 Maltese in arms against the French; they had declared themselves to be subjects of the King of Naples and gay Neapolitan flags were flying from the old outer city walls of Valletta. The islanders had under their control 23 pieces of cannon of which 12 were mounted, and from commanding positions on Fort Manoel and Fort Tigne they were able to keep up an almost continuous fire into the city. They also had two armed galleys and four gunboats. The civil population inside the walls were on the side of the besiegers and carried out acts of sabotage and civil disobedience. But General Vaubois was a gallant soldier and an inspiring leader. He and his officers were still imbued with revolutionary fervour and they mounted successful punitive sorties from the city gates from time to time.

Captain Alexander Ball did not have enough strength with him with which to mount a seaborne attack, but he could and did maintain an effective blockade. On October 24 Admiral Lord Nelson arrived with *Vanguard* and *Minotaur,* to have a look at the situation. During his visit Ball staged a landing on the smaller island of Gozo and the commander of the 217 French troops there gladly signed a surrender. Nelson left the next day for Naples, bearing the French flags captured at Gozo as trophies for his friends the King and Queen of Naples, and for Emma Lady Hamilton the wife of the British Ambassador to the Neapolitan court. Nelson was despondent about the blockade of Malta; writing back to St Vincent he said: 'Malta is in our thoughts day and night. We shall lose it, I am afraid, past redemption. If we lose this opportunity, it will be impossible to recall it'. He was still recovering from a headwound received at Aboukir Bay, and was not to spend too long with the blockading squadron off Malta.

Meanwhile another drama had been unfolding away to the north-east. *Leander,* under the command of Captain Thomas Boulden Thompson, had sailed from Alexandria on August 6 with Nelson's despatches for the Commander-in-Chief covering the Battle of the Nile. On August 18 at dawn while lying becalmed, Thompson saw a strange sail in the south-east quarter, still carrying a fair breeze. This turned out to be the French *Généreux,* which after escaping from Aboukir Bay and licking her wounds had parted company the previous day from *Guillaume Tell, Diane* and *Justice,* which were on their way to Malta.

A fierce and prolonged gunfight followed, with the

inevitable result that *Généreux* captured *Leander*. The Frenchman had a broadside of 40 guns to *Leander's* 26, and the latter had only 282 crew on board, being 80 men short, while the French ship carried 936. *Leander* had put up an honourable and famous defence.

While *Généreux* was proceeding on her way with her prize, the British brig-sloop *Mutine* approached; but her Captain, the Hon T.B. Capel, thought the ships were *Généreux* and *Guillaume Tell,* and kept his distance, as he was carrying back to Gibraltar duplicate copies of Nelson's report on the Battle of the Nile. So *Généreux* and her prize reached Corfu in safety, and the former will re-enter the story of the Malta blockade.

November saw a successful attack on the Spanish island of Menorca by a British squadron under Commodore Thomas Duckworth, in *Leviathan* with a squadron of seven ships of the line, and with transports full of troops. Ball with *Alexander* was called to assist in the assault, since the island was important to British naval strategy in the Mediterranean, and it was unlikely that the French could muster a strong enough force to relieve Malta at that time.

The great natural harbour of Port Mahon in Menorca is complementary to the naval history of Malta, as the second really important island naval base in the Mediterranean. The natural harbour is three and a half miles long, and on two islands in the anchorage stand a great 18th century British naval hospital, and a big quarantine station. A peninsula 256 feet high guards the entrance, and in Nelson's day was thick with gun batteries.

At the top of the harbour lies the town on one side, full of British architecture of the period, and the Royal Naval dockyard on the other, still today in its original state, and in use by the Spanish Navy. Facing each other on hills beside the harbour are two magnificent red-painted villas; one was used by Lord Nelson during his visits, and the other was the home in that period of Admiral Collingwood, who was Admiral in charge of the Mediterranean until his death in Mahon in 1810.

Port Mahon will appear regularly in the story of Malta over the next 45 years, and again in 1943.

Life on the British naval blockade of Malta was an invigorating one, and activity was usually brisk. Whilst Malta enjoys a sunny climate, with blue skies as the normal scene, the wind can blow strongly in the winter months, and even in the summer the *gregale,* the local version of the French *mistral,* can spring up quickly, and become a tearing gale in just a few minutes.

The blockading ships often needed to make repairs to their masts and rigging, and storeships bringing meat, bread, wine and water met them in the quiet bays of St Paul, St Julian, and Marsa Scirocco. The reader wishing to follow the life of the blockading squadron more closely will find a wealth of detail in the daily logs of the British ships – *Alexander, Foudroyant, Success,* and *Vanguard* have all left logs which, in the unemotive wording of their Captains, disclose drama, fine seamanship and constant movement.

In the early months of 1799 *Alexander* was constantly on patrol off the islands. At the new year fresh gales were blowing and with three other sail, she ran before the wind through the channel between Gozo and Malta. When the gales eased, she beat back to the squadron's main anchorage in St Paul's bay, where she found her consorts anchored, and water being taken on by the transfer of barrels. The frigate *Emerald,* freshly arrived, passed over to her two live oxen weighing 604 lb. Later in the month there were more gales, and while manoeuvring off Valletta *Alexander* parted three of her starboard mizzen shrouds with a loud crack. Preventer rigging had to be fitted while the ship was under way, with the deck pitching and rolling violently, and while the seamen were busy on this task the fore topsail split with a bang. More seamen raced up the foremast, unbent the wildly flapping sail, and bent on another, while clinging to their precarious toeholds on the upper boom.

Small vessels were still attempting to slip into Grand Harbour from time to time, carrying provisions and mails from France. On February 2 *Alexander* fired a shot across the bows of a strange vessel, sent a boarding party across to her, and took her into St Paul's bay, where she was found to be full of live oxen and hogsheads of wine for the French garrison. The cargo became just as welcome to their blockaders. A week later the frigate *Minerve* chased another strange sail at dawn, but before she could be caught, she slipped into the safety of Grand Harbour, cheekily hoisting her French tricolour as she rounded Fort St Elmo.

The blockade ashore needed the assistance of the British ships too. During the night of February 16 flashes were seen ashore on the outskirts of Valletta; assuming it was the Maltese attacking the garrison, Captain Ball landed a party of marines, with three Lieutenants, to assist them. The ship's log barely mentions that a gale was blowing, and although the ship was safely anchored in St Julian's bay, both anchor cables appeared about to part at the time.

In March, with the Maltese attacking more aggressively, Ball landed from *Alexander* two of her lower deck guns with 100 shot, for the use of the Maltese, and on two further occasions he landed more of his ship's big guns, which then had to be manhandled across the country to the Maltese forces. The strong winds continued throughout March, with the ships of the blockading squadron maintaining their station between three and 20 miles offshore. One small prize taken by *Alexander* was fitted out with two of the carronades from the 74-gun ship, to act as an armed inshore tender; a night or two later *Alexander* fired on another strange sail, and brought the vessel into the squadron anchorage at St Paul's bay, though with great difficulty in the heavy weather. She turned out to be a French prize, taken off Genoa, and trying to run the blockade into Malta with provisions.

The ships of the squadron came in one by one into the bays, to rest at anchor and to take on fresh water, meat, bread, and lemons. Supply ships came and went for this purpose, and now and again a cutter came in from Gibraltar with despatches and mail. Every third month each ship would return to Sicily or to the Italian mainland, to refit her masts and rigging (usually carried out by the ship's company themselves) and for a longer rest. It was certainly active duty, in the golden days of the Royal Navy.

The French Government, the Directorate, was not going to let Malta go without a fight. During the winter months Admiral Bruix prepared a relieving force in Brest; with 25 ships of the line and ten frigates it was a formidable expedition, and on May 5 1799 it sailed from Brest, eluded the blockading British squadron, and then pressed through the Straits of Gibraltar under the helpless eyes of Lord St Vincent, ashore on the Rock, and with his fleet pinned in harbour by an unfavourable wind.

It seemed that all the Mediterranean, let alone the valuable Malta, could be within Bruix's grasp, and St Vincent reacted strongly. He summoned Admiral Lord Keith and his squadron from their blockade position off Cadiz, and set sail as soon as he could with the combined fleet for Port Mahon, to protect that vital base, and to be in a position to move quickly to Malta if needed. Ball's squadron was also summoned away to Port Mahon, so that the most powerful British Fleet possible was ready to do battle with the French force. But Admiral Bruix put into Toulon, and there he stayed until mid-August, when he returned westwards through the Straits of Gibraltar, carefully shadowed by British frigates, and he passed safely back into Brest.

The French in Valletta took advantage of Ball's absence to attack their annoying besiegers. Three of the ships bottled up in Grand Harbour promptly emerged, and proceeded to blockade the Maltese positions in their turn, in Marsa Scirocco and in St Paul's bay. Then it was the turn of the Maltese to get hungry and thirsty.

Ball returned with his squadron in June, when Bruix' fleet seemed determined to stay in Toulon. The three French ships quickly retreated into Grand Harbour, and the close blockade was resumed.

Alexander and her consorts now kept an ever closer watch on the French garrison, often anchoring within three miles of Valletta, with a frigate anchored even further inshore, just out of gunnery range. The Maltese insurgents were also increasing their pressure outside the city walls, and Captain Ball was careful to reinforce them as much as he could. In successive weeks, in September and October he landed four of his main deck guns and two 18-pounder carronades, with a good supply of shot for the Maltese to use.

On the first day of November 1799 Rear-Admiral Lord Nelson arrived off Valletta in the 80-gun *Foudroyant,* with *Audacious* and *Minotaur* in company, to see how the blockade was progressing. Impatient to capture the island, he sent in a further demand for surrender. But the French General Vaubois was not yet ready to haul down the tricolour; his reply was a courteous but stirring one:

'*Jaloux de mériter l'estime de votre nation, comme vous recherchez celle de la nôtre, nous sommes résolus de défendre cette forteresse jusqu' à l'extrémité.*'

'Mindful of being worthy of the respect of your country, as you are with our own, we are resolved to defend this fortress to the last.'

Nelson ordered Ball to go ashore, to lead and encourage the Maltese in their fight, and from this time Ball started to win their respect, resulting later in his appointment as Governor after the island had fallen to the British. *Foudroyant* remained at Malta for the last two months of the year, taking full part in the activities of the blockading squadron. Under her Captain, Edward Berry, she normally maintained her station under way, between ten and 20 miles off the islands, and like *Alexander* and other ships of the line, she experienced weather damage at sea to her masts and sails. On the night of November 4, while off Gozo, her fore topmast and topgallant mast were 'shivered to pieces' by lightning, and killed one seaman and injured several others. Berry and his men carried out all the repairs at sea, without leaving their blockading station. During another long night *Foudroyant's* mainsail split, and the hard-worked seamen unrove it in the darkness, and bent on a fresh new sail.

On December 5 at long last some fresh British troops arrived to take part in the seige. Two Infantry regiments, the 30th and 89th provided 1,300 troops to support the 1,500 tired Maltese with their 1,000 irregulars. From Naples 1,200 more soldiers arrived, but General Thomas Graham, in charge of the combined force, knew he still had too few men with which to take Valletta by storm. The besiegers mounted raids to wear down the morale of the French and by this time General Vaubois' men were in poor shape. Food was in increasingly short supply, and food prices were rising sharply, multiplying three and four times in the course of only a few weeks. But still the French had no intention of surrendering.

So the siege carried on, as the first days of 1800 dawned. At the end of January a schooner darted into Valletta, hugging the coastline in mist. She brought food and stores from Ancona and next day, a small *aviso* arrived from

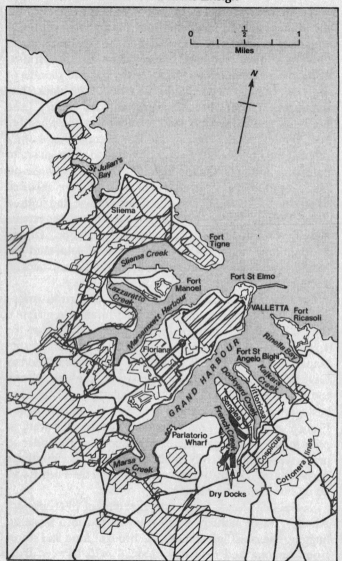

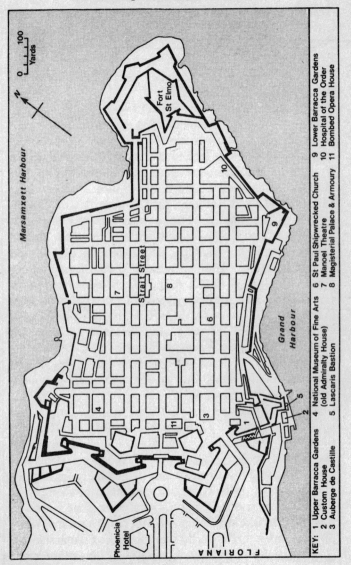

KEY: 1 Upper Barracca Gardens
2 Custom House
3 Auberge de Castille
4 National Museum of Fine Arts (old Admiralty House)
5 Lascaris Bastion
6 St Paul Shipwrecked Church
7 Manoel Theatre
8 Magisterial Palace & Armoury
9 Lower Barracca Gardens
10 Hospital of the Order
11 Bombed Opera House

Toulon. This vessel brought despatches from the new government in France, and news of the appointment of Napoleon Bonaparte as Chief Consul. The French garrison of Valletta was overjoyed, their revolutionary fervour flourished once more, and they swore that they would never yield to their besiegers.

Early in February a big French frigate, *Boudeuse,* also managed to elude the blockading squadron, and to the renewed joy of the garrison unloaded big quantities of stores of all kinds. It looked as though the chances of the French in Valletta were getting brighter, but in fact *Boudeuse* was the last French ship to succeed in breaking through to Grand Harbour. As if to underline their isolation from Metropolitan France, soon after the arrival of *Boudeuse* Lord Keith, Vice-Admiral of the Red, arrived off Valletta in his flagship *Queen Charlotte,* of 100 guns (Captain Andrew Todd): He had with him Lord Nelson, Rear-Admiral of the Red, in the 80-gun *Foudroyant* (Captain Sir Edward Berry), three 74-gun ships of the line, *Audacious* (Captain Davidge Gould), *Northumberland* (Captain George Martin) and *Alexander* (Lieutenant William Harrington, acting in command in Captain Ball's absence ashore). The 64-gun *Lion* (Captain Marley Dixon) was also in the squadron, as was *Sirena,* a Neapolitan frigate, and three sloops.

Alexander was on patrol to the north of the main squadron on February 13 when the frigate *Success* (Captain Sheldham Peard) came running before the wind from the north-west, with the news that a French squadron was approaching, consisting of a ship of the line, four frigates and some transports, clearly with the intention of breaking the blockade and relieving Valletta. *Alexander* ran down towards the island to warn the other British ships, while *Success* stayed to the north, shadowing the French ships.

Admiral Keith quickly organised his ships to intercept

the enemy. In his flagship *Queen Charlotte* he anchored as close to Valletta as the French guns would allow him, and with him he kept Nelson in *Foudroyant, Audacious* and *Northumberland;* the first two were to be ready to get under way quickly to chase to the windward, if the enemy appeared there, and *Northumberland* was to cover the south-east sector. *Lion* was sent to the westward to guard the passage between Gozo and Malta, and *Alexander* kept under way to the northward of the anchored ships, to act as a look-out. Once again the lack of frigates affected the British battle plan; they were forced in their place to use 74-gun ships as scouting vessels.

At dawn on February 18 *Alexander* sighted four ships to windward, and then more; they were undoubtedly the enemy, so Leiutenant Harrington fired a gun and made the appropriate 'enemy in sight' flag signal, to warn the squadron to the southward. He then chased the French ships, in full sight of Lord Nelson in *Foudroyant,* and by fast sailing and good manoeuvring caught up with them, and at 0800 hours fired at an armed store ship, *Ville de Marseille,* and brought her to, when she surrendered. A boarding party went quickly over by cutter, and *Alexander* continued the chase. By this time the main squadron could be seen approaching from the southward. On hearing gun-fire in the dawn, Nelson had got *Foudroyant* quickly under way, and making all possible sail joined the chase, with *Northumberland* hard on his heels. They soon overhauled *Alexander,* and together the three British ships gradually drew closer to the French squadron. By 1330 hours they were nine miles off the north-west point of Gozo, when the smaller French ships tacked together, and managed to pass to windward out of gunshot of the British ships; they turned out to be the 28-gun frigate *Badina* with two corvettes and several transports, carrying some 3,000 troops fresh out of Toulon, and now they managed to make good their escape.

But the big French ship of the line could not follow their example, or she would have come within gun range of *Alexander,* so she bore up closer to the wind. Now the frigate *Success* made her move; with good judgement and great gallantry Captain Peard altered course towards the enemy, and put his ship across the path of the Frenchman. At 1100 hours he opened fire, and raked her with several broadsides, but the French ship got near enough to fire her heavier broadside at *Success,* and the frigate was damaged and had to bear away.

It took a while longer for the heavier British ships to close the range, but at 1630 hours *Foudroyant* came within gunshot, and Nelson ordered two rounds to be fired at the French ship, to see if she still wanted to fight such a superior force. The British now had an overwhelming advantage in numbers and after firing one broadside to preserve her honour, the French ship struck her colours.

She turned out to be the 74-gun *Généreux,* which was one of the four ships which had escaped from Aboukir Bay, and earlier she had captured *Leander.* On board was Rear-Admiral Perrée, who had received a splinter wound in his right eye, and then had his right thigh torn off, in the battle with *Success;* this had affected the fighting spirit of the ship.

Northumberland came up at speed, and Nelson put Captain Martin in charge of the prize, and with *Alexander* the three ships set course for Syracuse at 1800 hours. Lieutenant Harrington put 270 of his men aboard the prize for the passage, and received on board from her 147 French prisoners of war. *Audacious* caught up with them, and together they arrived at Syracuse on February 21, where the prisoners were landed.

By March 1 *Alexander* was back off Valletta in the blockading squadron, and the siege went on. In her absence the other British ships had been fighting one more gale; they took refuge in St Paul's bay, but even there

Foudroyant's main topsail split, and part of it blew away just as they were anchoring. An hour later, as the anchored ships plunged up and down, and the wind was blowing very hard with violent squalls of rain, *Foudroyant's* best bower anchor cable broke under the strain.

As soon as the wind eased the squadron was back off Valletta; this time Nelson took his flagship right in towards Fort St Elmo, and anchored in 55 fathoms only two miles off the fort. During the night the ship dragged her anchor under the force of the wind, and at daylight the batteries on the fort fired several shots at her, one of which struck the fore topmast As the wind was foul, all the ship's boats were lowered, and the big ship was slowly warped out of reach of the French guns.

Foudroyant returned to Palermo during March for rest and repairs, and Lord Nelson went ashore for a while, as he was indisposed. He was not to return to the Malta blockade. Under her Captain, Sir Edward Berry, the ship returned to the blockade at the end of the month, and en route from Palermo she spoke to the sloops *Perseus* and *La Bonne Citoyenne* off Gozo, and learned from them that the French ships in Grand Harbour were expected to break out that night. Captain Berry proceeded to rejoin the squadron, which was anchored off Valletta, and *Foudroyant* dropped her own anchor in 48 fathoms only three miles from the lighthouse on Fort St Elmo. She found *Alexander* and *Lion* there; the flagship of the squadron which was now *Culloden* (Captain Troubridge) was away under repairs after grounding in the approaches to Valletta, and the 36-gun frigate *Penelope* (Captain Henry Blackwood) was on patrol to the northward.

During the night, which was a very dark one with no moon, Lieutenant Harrington in *Alexander* saw many gun-flashes and the firing of rockets from Grand Harbour, and heard much gunfire; but in the darkness they saw nothing, and at dawn they found that *Foudroyant* and *Lion* had disappeared, and their only companion was the little sloop *La Bonne Citoyenne*. For once breaking the calm official language of his daily log, Lieutenant Harrington recorded that they felt very lonely and exposed at that moment.

Something had indeed occurred during the night. General Vaubois knew that his food supplies were down to a critical level and he had ordered Rear-Admiral Decrès to leave in the 80-gun ship of the line *Guillaume Tell* and try to break through the British blockade, to tell Napoleon that Valletta could not hold out longer than June.

That night (March 30) Captain Saulnier in command of the big French ship waited until the night was at its blackest and then took advantage of the southerly gale and at 2300 hours slipped out of Grand Harbour. But the British blockade was a tight one, and sharp eyes were watching for him. The frigate *Penelope* was under way between the harbour mouth and *Lion,* the nearest anchored ship of the line. At 2355 hours she suddenly saw *Guillaume Tell* looming up at her out of the blackness, under a full press of sail. She immediately fired a gun to warn the squadron and despatched the brig *Menorca* (Captain George Miller) to warn the others. As soon as the big Frenchman had passed by her the British frigate tacked, and stood after her.

Menorca first warned *Lion,* and that ship quickly got under way to follow *Penelope;* the brig went on to tell *Foudroyant* close by, but Captain Sir Edward Berry had seen the gunflashes and rockets on shore, and at midnight slipped his cable and made all sail to the northward. He then heard the guns and signals from *Penelope,* as she took off after *Guillaume Tell.* It took the frigate just half an hour to catch up with the heavier Frenchman; *Penelope* then luffed under her stern and poured in her larboard broadside, then bore up into the wind under Captain Saulnier's larboard quarter and gave him the starboard broadside as well. So expertly did Captain Blackwood position his ship that the only reply the big Frenchman could give him was from his stern chasers.

By this time the first light of dawn was showing on the eastern horizon, and Rear-Admiral Decrès could see the other British ships closing in; so he kept on going, altering course first to the north, and then to the east. But he had reckoned without *Penelope*. Her Captain was a practised seaman and using his superior speed, he kept his frigate darting about *Guillaume Tell* like a terrier, pouring in raking broadsides whenever opportunity offered.

So good was the aim of his gunners that at 0400 hours Captain Saulnier's main and mizzen topmasts came tumbling down, and with them the main yard. Only the mizzen and the headsails were left pulling, and these were much damaged by shot from the frigate's guns. The French ship was suffering heavy casualties too, while *Penelope* had only slight damage to her rigging and sails, though her master had been killed and three seamen wounded.

Lion meantime had slipped her cable and was sailing as fast as she could in the direction of the firing, showing a rocket and a blue light every half hour, as a signal to *Foudroyant* and – hopefully, but in vain – to *Alexander*, who should have been following astern. Catching up with the damaged *Guillaume Tell* and the swooping *Penelope* at 0500 hours, *Lion* steered between the two, passing so close to the crippled Frenchman that the yardarms of the two ships barely passed clear of each other. She sailed up the starboard side of Captain Saulnier's ship, and poured in a destructive broadside of three round shot to a gun. Then she luffed up into the wind across the bows of *Guillaume Tell*, so close that the Frenchman's jib boom passed between *Lion's* main and mizzen shrouds. *Lion* had only two thirds of her full crew on board, and for a few minutes she had to be desperately manoeuvred to avoid either being boarded by the French crew, or being in a position where she would have to board the French ship.

Eventually the jib boom of *Guillaume Tell* carried away, and *Lion* broke free and took up a position across her bows. From here, aided by *Penelope*, she kept up a steady cannonade into the wallowing Frenchman; but *Lion* had herself been badly damaged and she became unmanageable, and dropped down astern of the French ship, though she kept up her gunfire as she did so. Half an hour later *Foudroyant* arrived on the scene. She passed so close to the French ship that her spare anchor only just passed clear of *Guillaume Tell's* mizzen chains. Edward Berry called on Captain Saulnier to strike his colours, and made his point with a treble-shotted broadside; but the French Captain replied in like manner, and this broadside cut away much of *Foudroyant's* rigging. A second broadside from the wallowing French ship carried away Berry's fore topmast and main spritsail yard, the jib boom and the main topsail yard, *Foudroyant's* foresail, mainsail, and staysails were cut in ribbons by the hail of shot, and the ship dropped away from alongside the Frenchman.

Here an error in ship handling helped Berry; for he had arrived at full speed, with every stitch of canvas set, but he did not reduce sail in time, so that *Foudroyant* shot past *Guillaume Tell* as these broadsides were exchanged. The extra speed which the British ship was carrying gave Berry's crew an unexpected relief from the shattering effect of the incoming French shot. For an hour the firing became sporadic, while both crews worked frantically to cut away the wreckage of the masts and rigging. But *Guillaume Tell* was not finished yet; amid the smoke and the tangled and broken spars a French sailor was seen to climb the stump of the shattered mizzen mast, and nail to it a fresh tricolour, to fly proudly in the breeze.

By 0630 hours *Foudroyant* was under way again and

reeling like a heavyweight boxer, she again closed with *Guillaume Tell* and renewed her broadsides, but she was nearly unmanageable still, and at one point 'nearly fell on board of the French ship'. But her opponent was in even worse shape; at 0805 hours the British shot brought down her foremast and she was then nothing but a hulk, rolling helplessly in the seas, with the wreckage of her masts and rigging masking most of the guns which could still be worked on her engaged side. Her violent rolling caused her lower deck gun ports to be shut, to save flooding the ship, and ten minutes later Rear-Admiral Decrès hauled down his colours.

Both *Foudroyant* and *Lion* were too badly damaged to lay alongside *Guillaume Tell* to accept the French surrender, so it was left to the frigate *Penelope* to do this, and Captain Blackwood accepted this honour with alacrity. As soon as the ships had recovered sufficiently *Penelope* took *Guillaume Tell* in tow, and they struggled slowly north to Syracuse. There the French ship was repaired and then sailed home to Portsmouth; after a full refit she was re-commissioned as HMS *Malta*, and became the largest two-decked ship in the Royal Navy, other than the *Tonnant*, which had also been captured at the Battle of the Nile.

The French defence of *Guillaume Tell* was one of the most heroic actions of the war, and compared with the British defence of *Leander* against *Généreux* in these same waters only a few weeks earlier.

If *Foudroyant* and *Guillaume Tell* had fought alone, it would have been a contest between two of the most powerful ships that had ever so met; and yet the French ship fought off *Lion* and *Penelope* as well. Here are their comparative sizes:

	Length of first deck	Extreme breadth	Tons
Foudroyant	183ft 8½ in	50ft 7¾ in	2,062
Guillaume Tell	194ft 4in	51ft 7½ in	2,265

The casualties on the British side were light. Of her complement of 719 *Foudroyant* lost eight killed and 64 wounded; *Lion* lost eight killed and 38 wounded out of 300; and *Penelope* had one man killed and three wounded. But for the French ship it was a different matter — 207 killed, and many wounded (including both the Rear-Admiral and Captain Saulnier) out of a complement of 919.

Foudroyant's log faithfully records her expenditure of gunner's stores during the action:

Gunpowder		162 barrels
Round shot	32-pr	1,200 barrels
	24-pr	1,240 barrels
	18-pr	100 barrels
	12-pr	200 barrels
Other shot	32-pr	30 barrels
	24-pr	32 barrels
	12-pr	18 barrels
Ball cartridges		700 barrels

Captain Sir Edward Berry performed divine service on the deck of *Foudroyant,* to give thanks to Almighty God for the victory; but a few minutes later the damaged mizzen mast suddenly fell and wounded seven more men. The mainmast was then examined and it was found to be 'shot and wounded' in several places, so the main yard and topmast were hurriedly lowered to take the strain off the mast.

Foudroyant called up *Lion* to tow her, and kept company with *Penelope,* which was towing the prize. It took two days to clear away all the wreckage in Berry's ship, so that jury sails could be hoisted on the stumps of the masts, but on April 2 she was able to cast off the tow. When they reached Syracuse *Foudroyant* and *Lion* went alongside *Guillaume Tell*, one on each side, to assist in making her seaworthy to be sailed to England. Jury masts were hoisted by a purchase from *Foudroyant's* fore yard, and sheerlegs were rigged to hoist them into place. The ships had to be largely self-reliant for their own repairs of weather and battle damage in those days; skilled work on masts, rigging and sails was always a major part of the running on any operational warship. So ended one of the most heroic sea-fights in the long naval history of Malta.

The French garrison in Valletta was very depressed by the loss of *Guillaume Tell*; soon all beasts of burden, dogs, cats, fowls and rabbits had been eaten, disease was becoming rampant, and the troops were dying at the rate of 100 to 130 each day. The frigate *Boudeuse,* which had arrived so providentially earlier in the year, was broken up for firewood, and the water cisterns were fast drying up.

The British forces outside the city walls twice sent in further demands for surrender (on the second occasion saying falsely that a Russian Fleet had arrived at Messina, and was going to join in the blockade); but each time Vaubois rejected the demand, though he knew he had not much time before his garrison must surrender. His last gamble to conserve supplies, in August, was to reduce the civilian population of Valletta from 45,000 to 9,000, by ordering the citizens out through the gates, to be taken care of by the besieging forces.

On August 24 he sent the two frigates *Diane* and *Justice* out of Grand Harbour, to try to break through to France, rather than surrender them. They sailed on a very dark night, with a fair wind, but they were sighted just outside the harbour by the 32-gun frigate *Success,* still commanded by Captain Sheldham Peard. He was joined by Captain

George Martin in *Northumberland,* who was by now in command of the blockading squadron, and by *Généreux,* now repaired and in commission as one of His Majesty's ships — a cruel coincidence for the two frigate Captains. There was a short running fight, but *Diane* had a crew on board of only 114, and she soon hauled down her colours. *Justice* slipped away from the fight under cover of the darkness, and eventually arrived safely at Toulon.

Time had now clearly run out for the French garrison of Malta. On September 3 General Vaubois held a council of war with his officers, and in a very different mood from that of only weeks before, they agreed to surrender to the British forces. Simultaneously the British landed a further 1,300 fresh troops, just to underline the situation. The following day a flag of truce was sent out from the gates of Valletta to General Graham, now commanding the British and Maltese land forces, and to Commodore Martin, the senior British naval officer present. Terms were agreed which were honourable to both parties, but included the immediate surrender of the French. The garrison, which had defended its position nobly, marched out with the honours of war, and 'with their personal property secured to its owners'; they were quickly shipped back to Marseilles, to ease the food problems in the islands. No reprisals were taken against some French inhabitants of Valletta, but in Maltese eyes the victory was a little marred when the newly-arrived British commander allowed the French to leave with their spoils intact.

So ended a siege which had been withstood by the French for two years and two days; only the shortage of food and water had finally reduced the garrison, but they had amply demonstrated that there had not been a need for the last Grand Master, von Hompesch, to surrender to them so quickly, on Napoloen's arrival two years later.

Now Sir Alexander Ball retraced the footsteps of

Napoleon, and in his turn walked in triumph up Merchants Street in Valletta. Now, too, he began his civilian governorship of Malta which was to be so impressive. A few years later it was recorded that, 'the warmth of his attachment, no less than the wisdom of his measures, endeared him to the Maltese people.' When he died in 1810 he was given the great honour of burial under the Abercrombie Curtain of Fort St Elmo, and his memory is still kept alive by the little Greek-style temple which was erected in his memory in the Lower Barracca Gardens. Amazingly untouched by all the bombs of the Second World War, this little temple was the backdrop for the final departure of the Royal Navy from Malta in March 1979.

In Grand Harbour the victorious British Forces found two 64-gun ships, but only one was in a seaworthy state, the *Athénien*, a fine ship of 1,404 tons. The other large ship, *Dego*, and the frigate *Carthagénaise* had been so neglected, and so much wood had been removed from them for firewood, that they were not worth salving.

CHAPTER 4

Bargaining counter of the peace, 1801-15

The capture of Malta by the British and Maltese forces was followed by the Treaty of Amiens. This was to be a complicated affair, since Napoleon used the negotiations to further his own plans, while the British people were only wanting peace, and an assurance against a French invasion. The British Government was keen to restore the fallen monarchies of Europe, and had no ambition to gain more colonies, to be a drain on the country's resources. Nearly all of France's pre-war possessions were restored to her, including her West Indian islands and forts and trading posts in British India. Only Ceylon and Trinidad were retained from the war, and Egypt was restored to Turkey.

For his part Napoleon promised to withdraw the French troops from the central Italian ports, and also that he would refrain from attacking Portugal. But he needed time to consolidate his gains, and to prepare for his true objective, the invasion of England. Thus Malta was used as a bargaining counter in the negotiations leading up to the Treaty of Amiens, and this suited Napoleon very well. He proposed that the victorious British troops should withdraw from Malta after a period of three months, and that the islands should be handed back to the Knights of the Order of St John. In the meantime he wanted Neapolitan troops to replace the British, and he suggested that in the longer term Malta's independence and neutrality should be guaranteed by a rather vague collection of European monarchies.

He was by now First Consul of France, and he played his cards cunningly, he had never intended to lose Malta as it was the strategic centre of the Mediterranean. The British went along with his proposals in the early stages, but they soon saw his game, and when the Treaty was about to be signed in Paris in the early hours of March 25 1801, the clause covering Napoloen's proposals for Malta was cut out by Lord Cornwallis, the British signatory, and Malta's future was once more in the balance.

The negotiations continued, but made no progress. At one point Napoleon said frankly to the British Ambassador in Paris: 'Peace or war depends on Malta. It is vain to speak of the Netherlands and Switzerland, they are but trifles. For myself, I would put you in possession of the heights of Montmartre rather than of Malta'. But his further proposal, that the Pope should elect a new Grand Master of the Knights, produced riots in Malta.

A big delegation from the islands hastened to London early in 1801, to petition King George III for protection. The Maltese knew their own minds, and received news of the negotiations with horror and indignation. They said that they wanted to remain under the British Crown, as the British had already shown their understanding of the brave spirit of the Maltese people, and they thought that the British were efficient and fair, compared with their recent experiences in Valletta. They asked the king not to withdraw Captain Alexander Ball, nor to give the islands to the French, which they rightly saw as the real plan behind Napoleon's proposals. They believed that the Knights would continue to be powerless to protect them against the French.

In the autumn of 1801 the British organised an expedition to drive the French out of Egypt. The assault force (as it would be called today) sailed from England early in September and after rests at Gibraltar and at Port Mahon in Menorca, it arrived at Grand Harbour late in the month.

The naval force was under the command of Admiral

Lord Keith, and the land force was under General Abercromby. Among the warships included were *Minotaur* (wearing the flag of Rear-Admiral of the White, Sir Richard Bickerton), *Ajax, Kent, Northumberland, Swiftsure* and *Tiger*.

The expedition pressed onwards from Malta in December. The log of *Alexander* records that when she returned to Grand Harbour on December 6 and warped her way up harbour to her berth, she found the naval force there together with the troopships and transports. A week later *Minotaur* sailed with the first division of the troopships and their escort; *Northumberland* and the second division sailed on December 20, and *Foudroyant* (now Vice-Admiral Keith's flagship) with the third division followed two days after them. But *Alexander,* as part of the Malta Force, stayed behind in Grand Harbour.

Napoleon heard that the force had reached Malta on its way to Egypt, but he was hard put to it to get reinforcements through to Alexandria. Eventually two fast French frigates arrived there on February 3, just ahead of the British Fleet – *Justice,* which had escaped from the British blockade of Malta in 1800, and which now slipped into Alexandria while the British Fleet was in full sight of it, and *Régénérée,* carrying 200 troops and a company of artillery. A contemporary account tells how *Régénérée,* kept close company with the British Fleet for a whole day, answering every signal that was made; but this seems a little doubtful (without being too partisan) since French accounts of the time do not appear to mention it. A small French brig, *Lodi,* also managed to slip into Alexandria at that time, after a fast run from Toulon. Egypt fell to the British in the following spring. Suez being captured on April 21.

Captain Alexander Ball had been appointed a British Knight for his part in the capture of Malta. During this period his calm and efficient figure played a significant part in the story. He had been returned to active duty at sea in February 1801, but in June 1802 in deference to the request of the Maltese people he was brought back to Valletta as His Majesty's Plenipotentiary to the Order of St John, charged with the official policy of handing the islands back to the Order. The Treaty said that the Pope was empowered to nominate a new Grand Master, to return to Malta. On May 16 1802 *Maidstone* arrived in Grand Harbour with a copy of the Definitive Treaty of Amiens, which specified that this was to happen. But Ball delayed the Grand Master's return, saying that he was unable to vacate the Magisterial Palace in Valletta for him, but that the Verdala Palace towards the western end of the island was awaiting him, if he wished to live there. Ball was not only a popular ruler in Malta, he was also delaying the hand-over to the Knights, in order to keep Malta for his own country. The new Grand Master apparently got the message, for he never did arrive in the islands.

In 1803 Napoleon declared that his patience over Malta was exhausted (rather were his further warlike preparations well advanced), and he told Britain that if she wanted war and not peace, she could have it. So he tore up the Treaty of Amiens, such as it was, and embarked on the long war that was to lead to the Battle of Waterloo and his exile. Ball, by now a Rear-Admiral, was in charge of Malta when the new war with France broke out, and he renewed the spirits of the Maltese. On the very day that the new war was declared, Lord Nelson was despatched from England in a frigate, to take up command in the Mediterranean; for by now the Royal Navy fully appreciated the strategic importance of Malta, and it was even more important that it should then be retained than it had been in the uneasy years of peace.

On his arrival in Grand Harbour in June Nelson wrote to London: 'I now declare that I consider Malta as a most important outwork to India, and that it will give us great influence in the Levant, and indeed in all the southern parts of Italy. In this view, I hope we shall never give it up'. Two years later Admiral Lord Keith was to reinforce this appreciation, when the Admiralty asked for his opinion. 'Malta has this advantage over all other ports in the Mediterranean, Mahon, Elba and Sardinia, that the whole harbour is covered by its wonderful fortifications, and that in the hands of Great Britain, no enemy would presume to land upon it.'

It was important to the Admiralty that British trade in the Mediterranean should be protected, and Malta was the best port available. Privateers were ranging the coasts of Spain and Italy, and constituted a further threat to British shipping, in addition to French warships. So Nelson organised a convoy system, with the escorts based on Malta and Gibraltar, and Grand Harbour became the pivot for all naval operations east of Tunis. But the distance from Malta to the fleet's blockading position off Toulon (600 miles) was too great for comfort; Nelson complained: 'When I am forced to send a ship there, I never see her under two months.'

He himself watched outside Toulon with six ships of the line, while his other heavy units with all the frigates were widely dispersed on convoy protection duties. This is an interesting comparison with the similar problems experienced by the Royal Navy in both the World Wars of the 20th century. For nearly two years Nelson's blockading ships did not enter a port; with relief ships of the line simply not available, storeships were sent up from Malta to unfrequented roadsteads near the blockading force, for replenishment of stores and ammunition. Here was the antecedent of the great fleet trains of the Pacific war of 1944-5.

Then the war started moving again. Napoleon was proclaimed Emperor of France, Prime Minister Pitt of Britain negotiated with the Tsar of Russia, and in July 1805 an Anglo-Russian Treaty was ratified. In June of that year the French Fleet in Brest broke out of the British blockade, and headed across the Atlantic. Nelson's squadron moved quickly out of the Mediterranean, to assist the Channel Fleet in chasing the French ships. The war moved away from Malta, but we should recall that the Battle of Trafalgar was fought in 1805 to prevent the French Admiral Villeneuve from moving to Cadiz and into the Mediterranean, where he had orders to recapture Malta, and if possible to take Sicily as well.

During the renewed hostilities the Maltese people prospered by running a profitable contraband trade with the blockaded countries of Europe, while the Royal Navy continued to use Grand Harbour as a main naval base. From its central position in the sea, the island was well suited to the sailing capabilities of ships from all parts of the Mediterranean, and it became an ideal rendezvous for licensed traders and smugglers of all nationalities. Better than that, all ships trading with Europe were virtually obliged to call at Grand Harbour to obtain clearance from the Royal Navy. The warehouses in Malta were bulging with goods, and merchandise was filtered into Europe 'through every crevice'. French and English alike conspired to travesty the system of official blockade, and licences were freely granted to dealers, provided that they traded mainly in British goods. Grand Harbour was declared a free port for customs purposes and exports from Britain to Malta rose to £250,000 in the year 1806, and quadrupled to the million pound mark by 1808. This remarkable economic progress was to be maintained until 1813, when a very bad outbreak of plague almost closed the port, and from untold prosperity Malta was then plunged quickly into economic disaster.

In the archives in London are the hand-written records of all vessels admitted to *pratique* (granted entry) in Malta during those years, and there was an average of ten arrivals each day, or a total of 3,500 vessels a year. Most of these ships, remarkably, bore the Maltese flag, though there were a few Sicilian ships, some from Greece, some American ships with cotton, and just a few British merchantmen. These latter increased as the years went by, mainly employed in maintaining the British garrison in the islands. On January 29 1812, for example, the Valletta newspaper *Giornale di Malta* announced the arrival of a convoy of 23 ships from Britain, escorted by HMS *Havannah*. They were 33 days out of Portsmouth, including 17 days on the last leg of their journey from Gibraltar.

So the British continued to occupy Malta during the long-lasting war, and to build up a relationship with the islanders. When Nelson first visited Valletta on his arrival back in the Mediterranean, he noted that, 'they hope sincerely never to be separated from England.'

As the second war against Napoleon drew to its successful conclusion, Britain's tenure of the islands was officially recognised by the Treaty of Paris in 1814, which laid down that, 'the Island of Malta and its dependencies shall belong in full right and sovereignty to His Britannic Majesty'. In the following year, after the Battle of Waterloo, the Congress of Vienna legalised Britain's retention of Malta as a colony. But now, as it was to be throughout the 178 years of their relationship with Britain, the Maltese began to feel that their aspirations had been misunderstood in London. They had hoped not just to be 'a colony of Britain', but to work in partnership and development with them. The Maltese were hurt that they had not been included in the surrender negotiations with the French garrison in 1800, and found that it was to be the same with the subsequent British administrations. The Royal Navy quickly developed the Knights' small shipyard into a useful repair base for their ships (Ball's own previous command, the 74-gun *Alexander,* spent 26 weeks there in 1802, refitting), but development of the island's civil facilities, laws and trade did not appear to concern London very much. Ball himself well understood their problems and feelings but was unable to persuade London to his way of thinking.

In Valletta an inscription was placed in stone over the Main Guard, opposite the Magisterial Palace, in 1814. It is still there today, after all the bombing of 1942, and it reads:

> *To Great and Unconquered Britain*
> *The Love of the Maltese and the Voice of Europe*
> *Confirms these Islands.*

Reflecting the spirit of Ball's governorship, those words must have been comforting to the citizens of Valletta during the dark days of the Second World War, but their authors would be astonished to see Malta as it is today.

CHAPTER 5

Victorian and Edwardian calm, 1816-1913

The Treaty of Paris ushered in what was to be virtually a century of peace for Malta. It was not, however, to be an easy century, for the British found that they had taken over an island which was ideal as a naval base, but also a people which had remarkable economic problems of its own. The Maltese in their turn were to come to the view that their new overlords were mainly interested in the naval base, and were not doing enough to develop the islands. In one form or another, this friendly but distant relationship was to persist throughout the 178 years in which the Royal Navy was to use Grand Harbour as a base.

The opening years of British rule were not happy ones. Following on the plague of 1813, the islands were placed in quarantine for a full 14 years, and this had a disastrous effect on Malta's economy. The new-found prosperity of the people had been based on the growing naval dockyard, and on providing services for the British Fleet; but much of the wealth had also come from the new *entrepôt* trade, and this just about disappeared when the plague arrived. From the peak of 7,000 ships entering *pratique* in 1802, the total fell to 3,000 in 1812 and by 1825 the numbers were down to less than 1,000. In that year the Greek war of independence put a stop to most trade in the eastern Mediterranean, which made matters worse. A further outbreak of cholera in 1837 added to the islanders' troubles, and in 1840 there was a severe drought. Already the islands were over-crowded — in 1833 there were over 1,000 people to the square mile — the highest population density in the world at that time, though the figure was to double again in the following century. The agricultural industry had fallen into the doldrums, and the disappearance of the sailing trade had reduced the foreign exchange available to import food.

On the other hand, political developments in the Mediterranean caused the Admiralty to increase the size of the fleet considerably. In 1816 one first-rate ship of the line and seven smaller ships were seen as adequate, but just 12 years later the fleet had grown to three first rates and 27 supporting ships. With all its troubles, Malta was now a part of the British Empire, and so attracted visitors. The most distinguished of these was the Dowager Queen Adelaide, who made a long visit to the island in 1838. She entered Grand Harbour in HMS *Hastings,* which was under the tow of *Rhadamanthus,* and the ships were surrounded by cutters with their crews tossing their oars, while the yards of the warships in harbour were manned by seamen, the ships were dressed overall, the gun salutes were fired in unison. In Valletta stands a great monument to commemorate her visit; she gave £100,000 for the building of the Anglican cathedral, which was brought within the diocese of Gibraltar, where it still remains. The Queen's visit encouraged other British travellers to include Malta in their itinerary, and during the first half of the century Valletta welcomed Sir Walter Scott, William Thackeray, Edward Lear and Rudyard Kipling. A Union Club was opened in the old *Auberge de Provence,* following the British Empire tradition, and we have been left a picture by numerous writers of that period of the aloof British, keeping to themselves and not mixing with the Maltese on an equal basis, if they could avoid it.

The Royal Navy was quick to appreciate the value of its new base. Grand Harbour offers one of the finest natural harbours in the Mediterranean, and the dockyard and service facilities were expanded to meet the needs of the fleet. The first of the five drydocks was opened in 1848, and the dockyard established its position as the single largest employer in the islands.

The army understandably examined the extensive fortifications with some awe, but did not spend much money on them in the first half of the century. In 1854 however the Crimean War erupted, and Grand Harbour was the assembly point for the allied fleet, before the assault got under way. Then the convenience of the islands as a hospital area was also appreciated for the first time, and the wounded were brought back to Malta to recuperate. The hostilities brought some prosperity to the islanders in their wake, as naval and military spending rose quickly from £200,000 in 1852 to four times that figure in the war years.

A further boost to the economy came from the American Civil War; Malta had a good capacity to grow and ship cotton, and the upheaval in America gave the Maltese a chance to get into this trade. A good-quality heavy cotton sailcloth was also produced, and this was not only a resource for the Royal Navy, it also provided an export trade to the whole of Europe.

All this activity caused the War Office in London to have an examination made of the island's defences, and the result of this was published in 1859, after a visit to Malta by Colonel J.H. Lefroy of the Royal Artillery, and Lieutenant Colonel H.C. Owen of the Royal Engineers. The garrison at that time totalled 5,400 men, with four regiments of foot and five batteries of artillery. All of this force was earmarked in war to defend Valletta and the areas around Grand Harbour; the rest of the islands lay undefended. 'As long as we hold Valletta,' the report proclaims, 'the Harbour does not belong to the enemy.' Much effort was devoted to identifying points in the defences where an invading force might seek to scale the walls, and alarm posts were established at frequent intervals. The inspectors found to their surprise that liaison between the army and the navy was not all that it might be. The army units stationed at the harbour entrance had no instructions to challenge approaching squadrons, so that an enemy could enter easily without being challenged by guns of the forts.

Additional gun batteries were installed at strategic points around Grand Harbour – in St Angelo, Floriana, Fort Manoel, Fort Ricasoli and in the Cottonera Lines. The new rifled guns were gradually replacing the old smooth-bore variety – seven 68-pounders were quickly shipped out from England, and a total of 332 guns were authorised – one third more than those defending Gibraltar at that time. Finally the powder magazines were found to be vulnerable to mortar bombs, and needed much strengthening.

To that time an attack on Grand Harbour from the landward side had been assumed to be such a 'gigantic undertaking' that it would hardly be attempted; but the authors of this report recommended that Britain must be prepared to oppose such a landing (remembering, perhaps, how the French had captured Menorca from the British in the previous century). The final outcome of this idea was to be the new Victoria Lines, which enter our story a little later.

Other events were now taking place which re-emphasised the valuable position of Malta. Iron-hulled ships, both naval and merchant, began to replace the old wooden-hulled vessels, and this at first had an adverse effect on Malta's trade; these new ships were far more expensive, and beyond the islanders' means. In 1861 the population totalled 135,000; but there was a serious imbalance, since there was too much industry round the shores of Grand Harbour, and Valletta and the Three Cities suffered from a great deal of squalor, while outside in the country there was much poverty. Some of the calling trade was lost; the P & O lines were lured to call at Messina, where Italy's commercial progress was to be seen. Eventually Britain agreed to spend more on Malta, paying half the cost of a big drainage project, improving the streets in the cities and raising the standards of education.

The opening of the Suez Canal in 1869 soon changed this gloomy picture; Grand Harbour became an essential coaling station for the steam-powered ships which were beginning to take over from sail, and the creeks were again frequented by ships. The armed forces also saw Malta in a new light once the canal was open, and it became an important staging post for warships, troops and stores on their way to and from British possessions east of Suez. There were some minor campaigns which required this role to be fulfilled efficiently, not least in Abyssinia and in Egypt, and during the capture of Cyprus. The dockyard continued to receive new buildings and equipment, and another large new drydock was opened in 1871.

While the fleet was away, the dockyard employees were often under-employed, so the Admiralty experimented with the building of a small sloop at Malta, to be called *Melita* (the Greek name for the islands). A slipway was specially constructed, and the sloop was laid down in 1883. Construction was very slow, as it stopped whenever ships needed repair, and four years later even the hull was a long way from completion. Then Admiral Douglas, a new Admiral Superintendent for Malta, arrived with the specific instruction to 'get that ship afloat'. She was finally launched in 1888 by Princess Victoria-Melita, daughter of the Duke of Edinburgh, who was then Commander-in-Chief of the Mediterranean Fleet. The building of *Melita* was a disappointment to the Admiralty; she took over six years to build, compared with the average of two and a half years for the other ships of the class built in Britain. Warship construction at Malta was abandoned, except for barges and similar craft; but the slip is still there, and called the Melita Slip, and ships are constructed there today.

In parallel with this warlike activity, life in Malta did make some progress, reflecting the values of the Victorian age. A railway was built from Valletta to the inland capital of Mdina, using second-hand coaches and engines from the Isle of Wight in England; but it did not flourish and was finally abandoned between the two World Wars. A more promising enterprise was the building of the new opera house near the gates of Valletta; a grandiose building, it was opened in 1866, and had to be re-built seven years later after a bad fire. It was finally levelled by the German bombers in 1942, and its ruins are still one of the sights of the city.

So fast was military technology moving in those days, that a further inspection of the defences of Malta was ordered and in December 1877 the Inspector General of Forts, General J. J. A. Simmons, produced a report with far-reaching consequences. He came out with a statement which was unequivocal: 'Malta's strategic position is such that it is scarcely possible to conceive of one of greater importance. The difficulty in maintaining a fleet in the Mediterranean without the possession of Malta would be almost insurmountable, and if it were in other hands, would be a most dangerous point, from which the commercial route to Suez and the Levant could be obstructed. No expense, within reasonable limits, should be spared to make it as strong as art can render it'.

Previously the sea defence of Grand Harbour had only been designed to resist wooden ships and smooth-bored artillery. It was now decided to protect the harbour against enemy ships taking up positions beyond the range of the shore defence guns, and then bombarding the harbour with impunity. To quote the report: 'Shell fired at very high angles may be projected very great distances – say 6,000 or 7,000 yards'.

New armour-piercing guns were ordered, weighing up to

23 tons each. There were new Italian armoured ships under construction of the *Duilio* Class, which would have steel plates 22 in thick, and the heaviest gun previously mounted ashore in Malta would have been powerless to penetrate their sides.

The size of the garrison needed to man the new fortifications was doubled to 12,000 men, and four guns capable of dealing with these new Italian ships were rushed out from England and mounted on the sea front near the Grand Harbour entrances. Also following this report, a new line of foritifications was commenced on the high ground towards the western end of the island. Half a dozen detached forts were built there, of a low silhouette but mounting a punch, with 38-ton guns. This new line of defence would bring most of the inhabitants of Malta and all of their water supplies within the perimeter, whereas before only the cities around the harbour had been protected.

Finished in 1897, this new defence work was inevitably christened the Victoria Lines, at the time of the queen's jubilee. In the same year a statue of the queen was erected in a little square beside the Grand Master's Palace; despite all that the German and Italian bombers could do, that statue has survived to the present day.

An interesting aspect of Simmons' report was that he picked up the aloofness of the British to the Maltese, and saw it as a potential danger. 'There is an almost absolute estrangement in Society of the purely British and native elements. This is very much to be regretted, but is exceedingly marked. Maltese officers and gentlemen are not admitted to the English club, and the result is that strong anti-British feelings may be engendered in secret, almost unknown to the British community.' He recommended that a Maltese section of the garrison should be formed, to give them a greater interest in defending their island against the threat at that time of the Italians. As a result the 'Malta Fencibles' were introduced in 1873, and grew to include six batteries of artillery. Their successors were to perform nobly in the Second World War, just as their forebears had done in the siege of the French garrison in 1798.

Despite these efforts, the economic position of Malta had not improved. Algiers and Tunis set themselves up as competing coaling stations for the ships passing through the Mediterranean, and with larger ships which had longer ranges, coaling stops in Grand Harbour were no longer necessary. The entrepôt trade had declined again, and it was just as well that Britain saw increasingly the strategic importance of the island, and contributed by defence spending; exports were by this time no more than one twentieth of the cost of the food and materials which Malta needed to import, and still the population continued to grow – by 1891 the total was 165,000, or 1,500 to the square mile.

Meanwhile British strategy in the Mediterranean was being regularly debated and modified. Britain adopted the 'two-power standard' in 1894, which meant that at any time the British Fleet must have at least a marginal superiority over the next two strongest naval powers, which at that time were seen to be France and Russia. The British naval construction programme was drastically speeded up, since the fleet at that time came nowhere near to meeting this standard. It was thought in London that there was a great risk to the fleet in the Mediterranean in 1895, and consideration was even given to withdrawing it and sealing off the sea at both ends. This raised a grave question over the importance and security of Malta, and a clear statement on this was made in the British Parliament:

'The value of Malta to England lies in its being a fort-base for the Navy, and a main link in the chain of command with India by the Suez Canal, and a base of operations for any service the government may require of the Navy in the central or eastern Mediterranean. It cannot be too clearly stated that except in the sense of the fleet covering the enemy, and thereby preventing any serious attack upon the Island, the Navy is *not* required for the defence of Malta.'

This statement may be compared with that of Admiral Sir Andrew Cunningham in 1942, when Malta was under severe threat of invasion by the Germans, and the Admiral stated equally clearly that in that event, he would immediately lead the Mediterranean Fleet to the defence of Malta from its base in Alexandria.

The policy of the day was however a real one. The fleet was divided between Malta and Gibraltar, with the intention that if Britain were to be at war with France, then the fleet would concentrate on Gibraltar, there it would combine with the Channel Fleet, and together they would make expeditions into the Mediterranean, as might be appropriate. Once again history seemed to be repeating itself, for this had been the British policy in 1796, when the fleet was withdrawn from the Mediterranean, in spite of Nelson's heroic efforts. Much had happened since the early days of the century, when the Mediterranean was so dominated by Britain's naval power that nothing could happen in it without her consent.

It said much for the resolution of the Board of Admiralty of the day that it pressed on nevertheless with the development of the base at Malta, while new warships were being constructed at home as quickly as possible. The dockyard had enlargements carried out to it twice in the period of 20 years, and although Britain's undisputed superiority in the sea was now in question, the Admiralty was resolved that the Royal Navy should yet again become the greatest naval force there, if it could be done.

As a demonstration of the British resolve, in April 1903,

King Edward VII made a ceremonial visit to Malta, the first reigning monarch to do so since Nelson's ships captured the islands just over a century before. The fleet was there in full strength, dressed overall and gun salutes were fired as the royal yacht *Victoria and Albert* entered, and again as the king landed in an impressive parade of barges and cutters, moving in perfect precision towards the Custom House Steps. Whilst he was there he laid the foundation stone of the new breakwater, which was to be built with two arms to protect the entrance to Grand Harbour. Up to that time, a storm-driven sea from the north and east could roll straight in, causing great discomfort to the fleet; and at the turn of the century, the new torpedoes put the fleet in harbour at risk of attack, until the solid stone breakwater prevented direct sighting shots into the fleet anchorage.

The breakwater took three years to construct, and provided a welcome boost to employment in the cities around the harbour; but when it was completed in 1906, the boom in spending was replaced by yet another period of economic depression. All the time the number of mouths to feed was growing larger. The population rose by one third in the period of 20 years just ended, and in 1911 totalled 212,000.

As the pace of naval construction quickened, the debate in London on naval policy in the Mediterranean also became more heated. The years 1912 to 1914 were especially tense, with Winston Churchill installed as First Lord of the Admiralty, and supervising the preparations for war.

Again the comparisons with 1798 were striking, and some of the pronouncements of the leaders of the day were almost interchangeable with those of Napoleon, Nelson and Pitt in those earlier days. Churchill firmly took the line that the squadron of six battleships based on Malta should be brought back to England; he saw the German threat in the North Sea as the critical factor, especially in the first two weeks of any war. He went so far as to say that if Britain got through those first two weeks in safety, then the squadron could thereafter be sent back to Malta if required. Outlining his thoughts in a note to the naval staff in February 1912, he directed them to draw up plans to this effect without delay.

Public debate in Britain was also focused on this issue. In the same year Mr Julian Corbett brought out a book which set forth persuasively the arguments for maintaining the battle squadron in Malta:

'Our Mediterranean fleet,' he wrote, 'stands to-day in the eyes of Europe as the symbol and measure of British power.'

Another argument put forward at that time was that not just the balance of naval power would be affected by withdrawing the battleships, but there would be a resultant change in the attitudes of the strongest nations around the sea. Only a cruiser squadron would be left for observation purposes, and there would be severe criticism for the maritime trading community; insurance would rise on the ships and their cargoes, and there would be a general feeling of insecurity.

Without the support of the Malta squadron, the destroyer flotillas at Alexandria would not be able to protect the Suez Canal, or to mask the Dardanelles. There was no fortified naval base in Egypt, and the torpedo craft there would be rendered powerless by an enemy who had undisputed control of the sea.

One broadside in the Press declared that to cover the British possessions in the Mediterranean, 12 rather than six battleships were needed at Malta. With such a force there, no hostile expedition would dare set out for Egypt or Cyprus, for fear of incurring the fate of Napoleon's army in 1798.

Winston Churchill was not going to be persuaded that easily. He arranged for a meeting in Malta of the powerful Committee of Imperial Defence, which took place in May 1912. The Committee included Lord Kitchener, made its journey out and back by cruiser, and made a full inspection of the island. The arguments on each side were forceful, and the debate in Valletta was a heated one. Admiral Troubridge argued strongly that Malta must be retained; Italy and Austria, in the Triple Alliance with Germany, would attack Malta, if compelled by Germany to do so, to keep the battleships there and out of the North Sea conflict. Churchill came back with another strong paper to make his point of view. He argued that it was all about the numbers of battleships in commission; the new German Navy Law provided for 25 battleships with four more in reserve, while Britain had a maximum of 33 battleships in commission with a further eight in reserve. In his view there was a need to have all these ships in home waters, for the defence of Britain; even the eight stationed at Gibraltar should be brought home, and the return of the Malta squadron was indispensable. Italy and Austria were building new dreadnoughts, and the six British ships at Malta would in any case be outclassed by 1915.

The plan was put forward that without the battleships, Malta should have a nest of hard-hitting destroyers and submarines. Italy would not attack, if Grand Harbour were known to have a strong striking force; once more the reader will draw a parallel with the forces stationed at Malta during 1942.

In his arguments Churchill was supported by the First Sea Lord, the famous Admiral Sir John Fisher; and so it was that as the threat of war approached, the 4th Battle Squadron moved west to Gibraltar, where they were five days' steaming time closer to the North Sea than they had been at Malta. Four armoured cruisers were based on

Grand Harbour, and the destroyers were built up in numbers to 15, with more modern units coming out as the flow of new ships from the British shipyards increased. The dockyard at Malta was maintained on its existing scale, and two depot ships for the destroyers were moored in French Creek.

In 1912 a significant change was made in the Royal Navy's use of the ancient Fort St Angelo. The need for a depot ship to be based on Grand Harbour, and to supply spare ratings to make up shortages in the fleet, had been recognised as far back as the early years of the 19th century. Various sailing warships had been used, but in 1855 HMS *Hibernia*, a first rate ship of 110 guns, was specially fitted out at Portsmouth as the 'Receiving and Guard Ship' for Malta, replacing *Ceylon;* another first rate which had been performing the duty.

Hibernia continued in service in Grand Harbour until 1909, when she was broken up locally. Her successor was *Achilles*, a first class armoured cruiser built in Chatham in 1863, and she in turn was specially fitted out for service in Malta. At first re-named *Hibernia*, she was re-christened *Egmont* in 1904 and she had three other ships as tenders, *Cruiser, Bulldog* and *Firefly*.

Egmont was towed back to England in 1912, and the fort took on her name as the base ship for the fleet. During the First World War, when the French Fleet was also to be based on Malta, an old French three-masted sailing ship, *Tourville,* was moored at the foot of St Angelo to provide depot facilities for the French warships.

A further and happier change was to come in 1933, when Admiral Sir William Fisher changed the fort's name back to HMS *St Angelo,* a more fitting link with the past.

Since 1912 the White Ensign has flown from the tall flagstaff above the outer end of the fort, and it only came down in March 1979. To conform to the British Naval

Discipline Act, the commissioning pendant of the Captain of *St Angelo* must be flown afloat; in the early years of the century this was proudly carried by a small brass-funnelled picket boat moored in Kalkara Creek, and after 1945 a motor fishing vessel did the honours.

The figureheads of the old *Hibernia* and *Cruiser* were placed ashore in the fort, when the hulks were finally towed away between two World Wars, that of *Cruiser* was damaged in the bombing in 1942, but both were proud trophies of the Mediterranean Fleet, and have been returned to Britain during the rundown in 1978, no doubt to be placed beside the many other figureheads from the golden days of the sailing navy, which now grace the entrances of the three naval dockyards.

So Malta approached the first major war in 100 years in which it might be directly involved; and it seemed to be the strategic importance of the island which was the prime consideration, rather than the safety of its inhabitants. Admiral Troubridge wrote in a report that, 'they were excitable, and unreliable in war'. It was to be another 30 years before the Maltese people themselves were to disprove such thinking, under the weight of an attack heavier than the British people were to know.

CHAPTER 6

Rumbles of war, 1914-18

The First World War was to keep Malta busy, but the main events of the war in the Mediterranean took place far from the island's shores, and they escaped any real fighting. Indeed, had the grand strategy of the Allies worked out as they had intended, Malta would have had an even quieter time, but the German U-boats were able to tear a big hole in those plans.

In 1914 the battle line-up was seen as Britain and France (probably with Russia) versus Germany and Austria (possibly with Italy). The Admiralty in London had been growing increasingly worried about the big German naval construction programme, and it looked as though the Mediterranean might be a quiet backwater. So Britain and France agreed that the former would cover the North Sea, and the fast-growing German Fleet, while France's warships would be concentrated in the Mediterranean, to watch the Austrians and the Italians.

The French asked that their Commander-in-Chief in the Mediterranean should be in overall command in that theatre, and to this the British agreed. Before this could properly be put into effect, however, there was a major problem to be taken care of in that sea. This was the German battle-cruiser *Goeben*, which had been sent out there on her completion in 1912 together with the light cruiser *Breslau*, as one of Germany's far-flung squadrons. The strategy was that on the outbreak of war this independent squadron should cause as much damage as possible, before being destroyed by superior enemy forces. This gave Britain and France a dilemma, for *Goeben* was

faster and better armed than any of the French battleships.
So three British battle-cruisers, *Inflexible, Indefatigable*
and *Indomitable* with the cruiser *Black Prince* were
stationed in the Mediterranean before the outbreak of war,
to take care of the German ships. In addition there were
four British light cruisers based at Alexandria, and three
submarines at Malta. All were under the command of
Admiral Sir Berkeley Milne, with Rear-Admiral
Troubridge to support him.

France declared war first, and Admiral Milne followed
his orders and concentrated his forces on Malta. *Goeben*
and *Breslau* under the command of Rear-Admiral Wilhelm
Souchon were at Messina, and on August 3 they sailed at
once for the French Algerian coast, to bombard the towns
and, it was hoped, to intercept the French transports which
were to carry the 19th Army Corps from North Africa to
Marseilles, on their way to the western front; after that the
German ships were to proceed to the Dardanelles, where
neutral Turkey was expecting them.

Britain had not yet declared war, but two of the battle-
cruisers from Malta, *Indomitable* and *Indefatigable* were
escorting some French transports from North Africa while
the French Fleet was watching the Austrians in the
Adriatic. Suddenly the two German ships hove in sight,
coming from their shore bombardments. The British and
German naval commanders watched each other warily as
the distance between them narrowed, and each had a
problem. International courtesy demanded that each
salute the other's Admiral's flag, but *Goeben*'s guns were
all loaded with live ammunition, while the British did not
wish to be misunderstood, and start the war by mistake.
The two British battle-cruisers placed themselves between
the French transports and the German ships, but Admiral
Souchon made sure that his flag was not flying, and there
was no Admiral aboard the British ships, so honour was

satisfied. All the British could do at that moment was to turn and chase after the Germans as they passed; after several further incidents the *Goeben* and *Breslau* escaped to the Dardanelles, and so pass out of our story. A result of this escape was that Admiral Milne was recalled to London, and Rear-Admiral Troubridge was put in command of the British ships, under the French Commander-in-Chief, Admiral Boué de Lapéyrère. The British armoured ships were withdrawn to the North Sea, leaving Troubridge with only his flagship *Defence* and some smaller ships.

On August 11 the French Fleet was ordered to concentrate on Malta, and the following day Britain declared war on Austria. A strong British and French naval force went off to cover the Dardanelles against a break-out by the German ships, sailing from Malta in company the day after the French Fleet arrived in Grand Harbour. The battles of Nelson and Napoleon in 1798 seemed very long ago.

The war in the Mediterranean then became quiet for a few months, until the assault on the Dardanelles in the opening months of 1915 again focused attention on Malta as the vital advanced naval base. The British naval commander was by then Vice-Admiral S.H. Carden, with Rear-Admiral J. M. de Robeck as his Chief-of-Staff, and Commodore Roger Keyes was there also. There was a new Admiral Superintendent in Malta, Vice-Admiral J. A. Limpus, and he did much to make the base more efficient, and to draw attention to the inadequate defences.

The British Mediterranean Fleet grew rapidly in size as the assault forces gathered in Grand Harbour. By April there were 15 battleships, five heavy cruisers, 16 light cruisers, 16 monitors, 36 destroyers and 16 submarines. The base facilities had to be heavily reinforced, and before long there were five depot ships, two repair ships, two salvage ships and a survey ship in Grand Harbour to support the fleet units. Also there was the seaplane carrier *Ark Royal,* establishing the link between Malta and the Royal Navy ships of that name which was to stretch through to 1978; she was based on Malta for the rest of this war.

In April Admiral de Robeck was promoted to be Vice-Admiral commanding the British naval forces, flying his flag in the battleship *Lord Nelson.* The French Commander-in-Chief, still using Malta as his advance base, had with him the French battleships, some armoured cruisers and two divisions of light cruisers. Rear-Admiral Stuart Nicholson was second in command to Admiral de Robeck, flying his flag in *Prince of Wales,* and Rear-Admiral C.F. Thursby also joined the team, with his flagship the battleship *Queen.*

1916 opened with Gallipoli over, the Allied naval forces were able to catch their breath, and they tried hard to settle down and work effectively together. This was not as easy as it looked. Certainly the common objective was the defeat of the enemy, but each ally had its own preoccupation. The French and Italians were concerned lest the Austrian Fleet bombard their coastal towns, while Britain was more concerned with the safety of her two vital sea routes through the Mediterranean — the military one leading to the theatres of operations, and the commercial one to the Suez Canal.

These divergent aims were never really sorted out, and the inevitable compromise did not work too well. The British Admiralty had acceded to the French claim that their Admiral should be in overall command in the sea; this meant that London could claim that it was not responsible for Mediterranean policy, but the French policy equally had to be accepted in that situation.

In April 1916 a council of Admirals was held round a table in the French battleship *Provence,* moored in Grand Harbour, to try to work out tactics which would take care of all these operational needs. The result was excellent for the watch on the Austrian and Turkish Fleets, but could hardly have been worse for the protection of the shipping routes against submarine attack. The sea was divided up into 'zones of responsibility', with one nation being in charge of each. Fixed routes were laid down for the passage of all shipping, and armed trawlers were to patrol these routes. Far from leading to the destruction of submarines, this system even helped them; all they had to do was to find the shipping routes by detecting the trawlers' presence, and then wait for fat merchant ships to pass by. The only defence they needed was to submerge while the patrolling trawlers were in sight.

Luckily German submarines did not appear in any numbers before mid-1916, but they started making their presence felt. In September Admiral G.A. Ballard came out to relieve Admiral Limpus as Admiral, Malta, and he at once started stressing the dangers, and pressed for a convoy system to be instituted. He could get no support from the Admiralty, who insisted that the French were in charge. The French Admiral replied politely that he did not think that any combined movement of merchant ships was possible.

During 1917 the losses to the German U-boats became so serious that both the Admiralty and the French Ministry of Marine finally became alarmed. A fresh conference of the Allied Admirals was called to seek a better solution, but politics took over again. The French Admiral in the Mediterranean wanted to hold the meeting in Malta, so that Admiral Ballard could be present, but the French Ministry of Marine insisted that it be held at the French base in Corfu, as they did not like to see the British island becoming the centre of naval policy in the sea.

The result of the meeting was, in fact, constructive. The French Admiral was left to watch the hostile battle squadrons to the north, while a British Admiral was appointed and based in Malta, to work towards establishing a convoy system for the shipping routes. At first more patrols were to be provided, and later convoys were introduced. The British Admiral appointed was Vice-Admiral Sir Gough Calthorpe, and on his arrival he put the cat among the pigeons by insisting that the right answer was a net barrage across the Straits of Otranto, where the enemy submarines were based. Great effort was devoted to this barrage, but in the end it only destroyed one submarine.

The escort forces in the Mediterranean were greatly strengthened to take care of the requirements for convoy escorts, the Otranto barrage and the fleet needs to the north and east. From 15 destroyers in 1915 the force grew to 37, and then to 42 in 1918. Some of the excellent new *Flower* Class sloops being built in Britain were sent out — there were 11 based on Malta in 1916, but they also grew rapidly to 19 in 1917 and 31 in 1918. *Ark Royal* was joined by a second seaplane carrier, *Manxman,* (yet another name to appear in the defence of Malta in 1942) and in 1918 a third carrier, *Engadine* also came out. There was a total of 106 seaplanes operating out of Malta in those years; 36 from the three carriers, and the rest from the newly-opened Malta Naval Air Station.

The last 18 months of the war brought frightening losses from U-boat attacks, and there was a constant battle by the British Admiral in Malta to obtain enough escorts — a familiar cry down the centuries. From Cattaro, a base to the northward of Malta, 20 U-boats were operating, and their successes in the Mediterranean were at times greater than those in the Atlantic; one commander sank 50 Allied steamers in 1917.

The Otranto net barrage continued to absorb much of the escort capability, even though it was not producing results in U-boats destroyed. Admiral Calthorpe was by this time becoming much less enthusiastic about it, and more inclined towards the convoy system, but the French and the Italians still wanted the net barrage, so work on it continued. The Otranto Barrage Force in the summer of 1917 typically included: 30 destroyers, 36 American submarine chasers, 15 submarines, 30 hydrophone trawlers, 20 ordinary trawlers, 109 drifters, 4 kite balloon ships and 40 motor launches.

The British and French Navies supplied this considerable force, but the contribution by the American ships was of the greatest assistance. In spite of this drain on their escort resources, the Allies steadily increased the number of convoy routes inside the Mediterranean, until in June 1918 there were 18 of them; all of them touched on Malta, and sinkings by the U-boats were gradually reduced by half.

At the end of 1916 the Admiralty ordered that all transports should have a destroyer escort; but they had overlooked the fact that there were only four of these ships based at Malta. On being pressed, four more destroyers were somewhat grudgingly sent out, but this was not enough, so a force of Japanese destroyers was brought in. Designated the 'Second Detached Squadron', it consisted of the crusier *Idzumo* (Rear-Admiral K. Sato) with 14 destroyers, and they quickly established a reputation for efficiency.

During 1917 and 1918 there were on average two or three convoys each of about 20 ships, run in each direction in each month, and all of them called in at Malta. In the year from October 1917 to October 1918, seven ships were lost in 24 outward convoys, out of a total of 285 ships in convoy; the same number of ships were lost inwards, out of a total of 329 ships.

On March 21 1918 the major German offensive opened on the western front, and the Allies began throwing in troop reinforcements from other theatres of war. The Mediterranean escort forces were called on to cover big convoys of troopships in addition to the normal convoys of cargo ships. Rear-Admiral J.A. Fergusson had taken up the new post of British Admiral of Patrols, based on Malta, and his ships were worked very hard. That they were able to escort all the convoys adequately was in part due to the arrival of American warships at Gibraltar, and they worked from there in backing up the British escorts in the Mediterranean. The United States Navy contributed two light cruisers, five destroyers, six revenue cutters, five gunboats and an armed yacht. Later six Australian destroyers arrived, and the escort forces working in and out of Grand Harbour were made up of five nationalities.

One of the greatest dangers to shipping lay in the harbours of Malta itself. Only Grand Harbour had antitorpedo nets across its mouth, and it was so congested with the flood of shipping of all kinds that soon only warships, transports and colliers were allowed to berth there. All other ships had to go to St Paul's Bay or Marsa Scirocco, where there were no nets, booms, hydrophones, air defence or anti-submarine mines. The only defences in those two bays were an old drifter and a couple of motor launches, and a line of buoys to bluff the U-boats into thinking that there really was a minefield. When Admiral Calthorpe arrived in Malta, he was astonished to find 14 large steamers, fully loaded, lying in Marsa Scirocco where any U-boat could have remained comfortably out to sea, and picked them off at will with torpedoes.

The Admiralty apparently thought only of the Grand Harbour defences, and could not believe that half the ships were lying in these unprotected anchorages; it was as well that the Germans assumed that there were strong local patrols, and that submarines could only approach during the hours of darkness. Admiral Ballard found that the lighthouses on two of the large outer headlands were left burning all night, so they were hastily switched off; this left the U-boats able to approach only on bright moonlit nights, and then the local defence flotilla was put on special alert. As it was, the main German effort in 1916 concentrated on minelaying, and only in February 1917 did they intensify their U-boat campaign with torpedo attacks, and by that time they were desperate. The mines were usually laid in deep water, and caused serious casualties. A French transport was sunk almost in the entrance to Grand Harbour, while the hospital ship *Ghurka* was hit in 74 fathoms, beyond the end of the swept channel. She was carrying 800 wounded from Gallipoli, and this could have been one of the worst disasters of the war; but two destroyers dashed out from Grand Harbour followed by all the dockyard tugs, and they managed to get her safely into port. There was a flotilla of war-built minesweepers at Malta, and they had up to that time only swept out as far as the 50-fathom line; this mining casualty caused their sweeping area to be greatly extended, and although they worked hard, they never really managed to cover the danger area thoroughly and continuously. The battleship *Russell* (Admiral Fremantle's flagship, of 14,000 tons) was mined and sunk off Malta, while her sister ship *Cornwallis* was torpedoed 60 miles south-east of the island.

While all these naval operations were taking place, Malta was functioning as efficiently as ever as the fleet base. During the war the dockyard and supply facilities were supporting not one navy, but several; for in addition to the rapidly-growing British Fleet, the French Fleet was using Malta as its advanced base and repair facility, and the Japanese and American anti-submarine flotillas were calling in for replenishment and rest. There were even a few ships from the Russian, Italian and Greek Navies.

There was never less than one British and one French

capital ship in the drydocks, and often two of each. It was commonplace for warships of four different navies to be in Malta dockyard hands at the same time. An indication of the growth of the British naval forces was that Admiral Calthorpe flew his flag ashore, as Commander-in-Chief of the Mediterranean Fleet; Rear-Admiral S.R. Fremantle was in command of the British Aegean Squadron, flying his flag in *Lord Nelson;* Commodore A.W. Heneage flew his broad pendant in *Queen* and was in command of the British Adriatic Force, and there were three other Rear-Admirals and a Commodore on the strength of the fleet in Malta. Nearly all the hospital ships and troop transports, both British and French, called in at Malta on their way to and from the battle areas, Salonika, Egypt and Palestine; all the colliers for the fleets in the eastern Mediterranean sailed from there, and all tankers moving to and from the oilfields beyond the Suez Canal also came into the island's ports. It was the port of call for the entire eastbound Allied merchant shipping traffic − no wonder that only half the ships could get into the harbours around Valletta itself. A normal daily movement sheet would show not less than 25 arrivals and departures in each day. Surely no other port in the British Empire could have fulfilled Malta's triple role in this First World War − fleet base, main dockyard and major shipping port as well. Another service provided was communications. From September 1916 Malta became the focal point of most of the transmissions of reports and intelligence for the entire Mediterranean war theatre. The island's central position, its powerful wireless installations and good cable facilities enabled it to handle hundreds of messages every day. Yet one more main function of the island was to receive and look after most of the wounded being brought out of the battlefields. New hospitals were built, 15 of them, many well out into the countryside, and 25,000 beds were made available in this way. A fleet of

CHAPTER 7

The great inter-war years, 1919-39

There followed 20 years of welcome peace; but they were years in which Europe watched the renewed growth of German military power, and in the 1930s, the inexorable build up to the Second World War. In its home waters life for the Royal Navy followed a peacetime routine with a few real interruptions. For the Mediterranean Fleet, however, based on Malta, life was rather different. There were four distinct crisis periods, each of which left its mark on this great naval force. 1925 – a threatened Turkish attack on Iraq; 1935 – the Italo-Abyssinian War; 1936-1939 – the Spanish Civil War; 1939 – the Italian-Albanian crisis.

It is easy to forget now that those were difficult years of peace in which to live; the mix of constant training and readiness for war, combined with the social round of those gay years, made for a busy but pleasant life for the many British ships which served commissions based on Malta.

There is a further message to be found in the records of that era. The fleet was for too long before 1939 denied enough new ships of the right quality; but the standard of training was very high, and coupled with the fighting traditions of the Royal Navy, this was to stand the Mediterranean Fleet in good stead when the final crisis came in 1939. The records of Taranto, Matapan and the Malta Striking Forces show how clear an ascendancy in trained seamen the Royal Navy had achieved; and when at last enough new warships were available, and later still when the Spitfires arrived in Malta, the men of the Mediterranean Fleet were once again the masters of the Mediterranean.

Here is an outline of those 20 years in Malta.

An early highlight was the opening of the first Parliament of Malta in November 1921; the Prince of Wales made a ceremonial visit to mark the occasion.

The Mediterranean Fleet was quickly reduced to its peacetime level. The Commander-in-Chief, Admiral Sir John de Robeck, flew his flag in *Iron Duke,* and with him was the 4th Battle Squadron – *Ajax, Benbow, Centurion, Emperor of India* and *King George V*. Six *C* Class cruisers formed a squadron, and one large destroyer flotilla included two leaders and 21 ships.

The old depot ship *Egmont* was moored near St Angelo, and flew the flag of the Admiral commanding Malta. There were some American ships in the area; the cruiser *Olympia* flew the flag of the Admiral commanding in the eastern Mediterranean, and his 19 destroyers with two tankers made a formidable squadron.

1925 brought the first crisis after six quiet years, in which mine clearance had been completed. The ships of the fleet were still those of the latter years of the war; *Queen Elizabeth* Class battleships, *C* and *D* Class cruisers, and the numerous *V* and *W* Class destroyers. The minesweepers had been paid off, and a dozen of the *Town* Class lay together in reserve in Marsamxett harbour.

Late in 1925 Turkey appeared to be threatening an attack on Iraq, following on the frontier award made by the Council of the League of Nations. If this were to take place, then Britain would be the designated arm of the League in forcing Turkey back behind the frontier, and the Mediterranean Fleet would be the spearhead. In November Malta became the scene of feverish preparations for an expedition against Turkey. The plan would be to occupy the Turkish islands, enter the Sea of Marmora and blockade Constantinople by sea.

It was expected that the Turks would mine the

Dardanelles, so full minesweeping coverage would be needed. The sweepers lying in reserve in Malta were re-commissioned, ostensibly to take part in fleet manoeuvres; the 1st Minesweeping Flotilla was similarly brought forward from reserve in England, manned by reducing the crews of some of the larger warships, and hastily despatched to join the fleet in Malta; extra colliers were also sailed to the island to support the sweeping force in its planned sweep to the north-east ahead of the main fleet. The 3rd Destroyer Flotilla at Malta was fitted with paravanes, since the speed of the fleet once in Turkish waters would leave the *Town* Class minesweepers well astern.

The fleet crowded the creeks of Malta's harbours, and was re-organised into four forces for this operation:

Force A: the fleet flagship, *Queen Elizabeth,* two *Iron Duke* Class battleships, the aircraft carrier *Eagle,* three cruisers, one flotilla of destroyers, and four minesweepers. Its mission would be to proceed direct to Constantinople, sending its aircraft ahead to swoop over the city.

Force B: two *Iron Duke* battleships, the aircraft carrier *Hermes,* one flotilla of destroyers, and five minesweepers. This force was to reconnoitre and then blockade two Turkish naval ports.

Force C: one cruiser, one flotilla of destroyers, two oilers and one collier. The mission: to patrol the Turkish islands and guarantee their non-involvement in the operation, and to fuel the fleet – one of the earlier Fleet Train operations.

Force D: one *Queen Elizabeth* Class battleship, the aircraft carrier *Furious,* the 1st Cruiser Squadron, one flotilla of destroyers. This force was to patrol the Dardanelles, and attack any Turkish naval forces approaching them.

Fortunately the threatened Turkish attack did not materialise; but the Mediterranean Fleet, supported by its base in Malta, had been in full readiness.

The crisis over, the fleet returned to its peacetime routine in 1926 and especially to its Summer Cruise from Malta — an annual event which on the surface was a pleasant affair, with groups of Royal Navy ships in immaculate condition visiting colourful and friendly ports, and taking part in a hectic round of social engagements.

In fact the ports were chosen with great care, in close consultation with the Admiralty and the Foreign Office, to have the maximum beneficial effect on political relationships in eastern Europe. This was 'flag waving' at its most effective, and the reports of proceedings of the Captains of the ships show how much care and effort were put into making these cruises a success.

That year the main body of the fleet visited the south coast of France, and especially Toulon, Nice and Villefranche; other squadrons made their way to Tangier, Trieste and the Turkish ports (though they predictably received a pretty cool reception in the latter); and ships called in at many of the delightful Greek islands, at Crete, Cyprus and some Italian ports. The great fleet sailed from Grand Harbour with Royal Marine bands playing on the quarterdecks of the big ships, the sailors at attention forward and aft, flags streaming in the breeze, and with the families and many Maltese crowding the Upper and Lower Barracca Gardens to watch them pass below.

The fleet split up outside the harbour into five squadrons for the cruise, and most of the visits went well, some spectacularly. The Commander-in-Chief, now Admiral Sir Roger Keyes, threw a great ball in his flagship *Queen Elizabeth* in the picturesque harbour at Villefranche, *Valiant* came alongside the flagship, bridges were built between the spacious quarterdecks, special canvas awnings were made to cover the entire area, and a combined Royal Marine orchestra played on staging rigged between the two ships. A colourful throng danced the night away in a snap-

shot of the gay 1920s. Admiral Keyes featured the ceremony of 'beating the retreat' when visiting foreign ports;
the massed Royal Marine band on the fleet marched up and
down in immaculate drill, and the White Ensign was lowered
at sunset to the lingering notes of the trumpets.

Barham went to Trieste with *Hermes* and *Dauntless*, but
had a strange experience. Ashore the sailors visited the
outdoor cafes lining the Piazza di Unite, while the
municipal band played in the centre of the square. On the
last night of their stay an excited crowd of young fascists
strode about the Piazza singing patriotic songs; and near
them, a British bluejacket who thought he had been short-
changed by a waiter, was rash enough to spit on a lire note.
The crowd in the square quickly became abusive, shouting
'Abassa Inglaterra', while the band broke into the fascist
march, playing it over and over again. In this scene of rising
tension the British libertymen started moving quietly
towards their boats, smiles of amused tolerance on their
faces, while the shore patrol of *Hermes*, quite unruffled,
kept the crowd at bay.

At Tangier the destroyer *Splendid* saw a warehouse burst
into flames on June 19, and landed a fire-fighting party in
her whaler, led by her Captain. This unscheduled exhi-
bition drew forth cheers of appreciation from the watching
crowd.

Dauntless at Bourgas had another delicate situation to
handle, when the Greek and Italian consuls attending a
party on board demanded special boats to take them
ashore, and had to be politely refused.

Their visits completed, the squadrons returned to Malta,
welcomed back from the ramparts by the families and the
Maltese, and glad to relax again in the friendly environ-
ment of the island. Peacetime routine in Grand Harbour
was pleasant, but not idle. Pulling and sailing regattas were
often held on the sparkling water of the creeks, overlooked

by the high ramparts, and brass-funnelled picket boats sped everywhere upon their errands. In the evenings libertymen came ashore in their hundreds, in picket boats and the slower drifters, to spread out to their favourite bars in the cities around the harbour − bars with traditional names, 'The British Bar', 'Aunty's', the 'Britannia', 'Harry's' and many others. Over on the west side of Valletta, below Kingsway, was a long and very narrow street which ran the length of the city; its real name was − and still is − Strait Street, but to generations of British sailors it was known as 'The Gut', and here lining the steps which carried the street up from St Elmo to the summit of Valletta were innumerable bars which came to life at night, and equally numerous ladies of pleasure. An ancient scribe once said that such a street should always be provided in every great seaport, and that it should lie close to the main street, but be hidden from it. Strait Street admirably filled that description. It has lost some of its former glamour now that the fleet has gone, but still, when a big warship is in harbour overnight, the lights come on and 'The Gut' comes back into its own.

For the officers there were endless cocktail parties, with formal guest lists and precedence by seniority − especially among the senior officers' wives − needing to be closely watched. The Opera House up near the gates of Valletta was another draw, while connoisseurs would visit the magnificent Manoel Theatre, built in 1731 after the lines of a Palermo theatre, and looking like a miniature of London's Covent Garden. In the shining sun of the following morning the inspections of the warships would be started again, the parades led by the Royal Marine bands would bring life and colour to the streets, and the drills to keep the ships' companies prepared for war never ceased. This mixture of drills, regattas, shore leave and cruises continued for a few years with little external disturbance; during this period the fleet was instrumental in restoring

Anglo-Turkish relationships, following the crisis of 1925.

There were, however, bound to be some internal frictions within a fleet such as this, operating in peacetime with all the social pleasures and sporting challenges, but also with the requirement for intensive exercises and continual training.

The Commander-in-Chief, Admiral Sir Roger Keyes, found himself in the spring of 1928 with such an internal problem on his hands, which did not resolve itself without difficulty and publicity. There was an incident on the quarterdeck of the battleship *Royal Oak* during an evening dance, in which Rear-Admiral Bernard Collard, the junior Admiral in the First Battle Squadron, was reported to have insulted the Royal Marine bandmaster. The official report of the incident is closed to the public until the year 2005, but it would appear from contemporary reports that Captain K.G.B. Dewar, in command of *Royal Oak*, and his second in command, Commander H.M. Daniel, protested to the point where the incident escalated into court martials for the latter two, and all three being posted elsewhere.

The incident quickly became public, as word about the dispute spread among the ships' companies and families in Malta, and it was widely reported in the Press. The Mediterranean Fleet was about to sail on extended and important exercises when it all happened, and the ships were held back for 40 hours, while a court of enquiry was hastily called at the Commander-in-Chief's headquarters in the *Auberge de Castile*. By the time that Admiral Keyes hoisted the signals in his flagship, *Queen Elizabeth,* for the fleet to proceed to sea, rumour was rife; headlines in some newspapers even ran to 'Mutiny in the *Royal Oak*'. It needed some months before the incident faded into history.

Rear-Admiral Andrew Cunningham came to Malta in January 1934; he had last been there as Captain of the destroyer *Scorpion* in the last war, and now he was to renew his association with the island, and then to become its champion through the next world war. He was a colourful figure and had a pleasant but strong personality, and his arrival as Rear-Admiral (Destroyers) soon made its mark. In his command was the 1st Destroyer Flotilla of the *V and W* Class, led by Captain the Earl Mountbatten in *Wishart;* Cunningham's headquarters were on Manoel Island, near the destroyer trots in Sliema Creek, and he soon decided that the old cruiser *Despatch* was too slow to be his flagship, and with the support of his Commander-in-Chief, the popular Admiral Sir William Fisher, he took over the new light cruiser *Galatea*.

In the winter of 1935-6 the fleet carried out a winter cruise, in addition to its normal summer excursions. The 1st Cruiser Squadron led by the Vice-Admiral in *London* visited Turkey and the Black Sea in January, with mixed results. *London* opened the innings by her arrival at Varna in Bulgaria. She gave a salute of 21 guns, which was answered by a field battery hidden in the hills. The Admiral called on the commanding General and was received by a large guard and band, who showed their independence by giving him a loud cheer in the middle of the salute. The Admiral was invited to Sofia to see King Boris; he was received cordially, and invited the king to visit *London,* which he did, accompanied by a large retinue of staff. He witnessed the catapulting and recovery of the cruiser's Walrus seaplane, and sent a message of greetings by radio to King George V in London. *London* was visited by 2,000 people there in two days; and to show that diplomatic relations were never far removed from cruises, two Turkish cruisers with five accompanying destroyers arrived and carried out exercises close to the shore, as a counter-demonstration to *London's* visit.

Devonshire with the destroyer *Searcher* in attendance

visited the Dardanelles beaches, then moved on to Istanbul where a Turkish destroyer manned ship for her, and she returned the compliment in kind. Then she went on through the Black Sea to Constanza in Roumania, streaming her paravanes en route, as this water had still not been declared free from mines. She had to plough her way through sea ice as she approached the port, but once there King Carol and Queen Marie visited the ship, and *Devonshire* was examined closely as an example of the latest British naval design; even then ships of the Royal Navy were influencing foreign governments in placing warship orders for export from Britain. During her stay there, the cruiser received the impressive total of 30,000 visitors, including the entire British colony of 25.

Ships of the same cruiser squadron went to Cyprus in April, *Delhi* and *Durban* celebrating the Silver Jubilee of King George V by illuminating ship, searchlight displays, whaler races and a naval march past ending in the singing of sea shanties in the main square of Larnaca. The battleship *Ramillies* went to Nice and Villefranche, and received 500 visitors a day. She landed an armed detachment of 280 men with a Royal Marine band, and homage was paid to the dead at the city war memorial, and a suitable wreath was laid on Queen Victoria's monument. Such events were often celebrated by the fleet, both in Malta and when cruising. The 1st Destroyer Flotilla was on passage from Singapore to Malta in February, and stopped in the Red Sea to mark the wedding of the Duke of Kent; in the blazing heat the Captains repaired on board *Duncan*, the flotilla leader, to celebrate.

In the same month the Commander-in-Chief visited Toulon again in *Queen Elizabeth,* to return a recent French official visit to Malta. The flagship was accompanied by the destroyer *Basilisk,* and was greeted at sea by three French destroyers; during the visit, *Basilisk's* football team was —

either soundly or tactfully — beaten by the second French Navy team.

Back at their base in Malta in mid-summer, the officers and men of the fleet were making efforts to keep close to the people of Malta. One large ship was open to the public each week, and during a visit by a squadron to the island of Gozo, 2,000 people a day went afloat to visit the ships.

The Times of Malta was by this time in regular production, and its headlines showed the important things of life in Grand Harbour. When the battleship *Revenge* won a cricket match, it made headlines on the front page, and naval appointments and new construction programmes were printed in full.

Then a cloud came over the horizon in the form of the Italian-Abyssinian crisis, and the Mediterranean Fleet (and Malta with it) went immediately on the alert. Once again Britain was seen as the active arm of the League of Nations, and it seemed inevitable that Italy would attack Malta, where the fleet represented the main obstacle to her ambitions. Early in August contingency plans for the fleet were put into effect. Visits to Italian ports were quickly cancelled, and the cruise programme changed to look as normal as possible, in view of hostile attacks in the Italian press. In fact, the fleet was being quickly reinforced from British waters.

When the crisis broke, the Mediterranean Fleet totalled 49 major warships, including the flagship *Queen Elizabeth*, and five *R* Class battleships, five cruisers, 27 destroyers and seven submarines. Just four weeks later the strength of the force at Malta had risen to 67 ships, including the battle cruisers *Hood, Renown* and *Repulse,* the aircraft carriers *Courageous* and *Glorious,* a further nine cruisers and a flotilla of fleet minesweepers. Reinforcements came to Malta from all over the world. In addition to the ships from home, two cruisers hurried from South America, two more from China, and destroyers from all directions. The anti-aircraft defences of the island were strengthened, but only in guns, not in fighters, and the grand total of those guns was 12. Admiral Fisher clashed with the Admiralty in London, where the air force and the army seemed to be winning their argument that Malta could not be defended in war. The Blue Funnel cargo ship *Bellerophon* was chartered to take the extra guns out, and the gun crews steamed out in parallel in the troopship *Neuralia*.

Then — a pointer to 1942 — to take away from the Italians the main temptation to attack Malta, the heavy units of the fleet left for Alexandria, which was by then established as an alternative fleet base, but without Malta's dockyard or leisure facilities. Left at Grand Harbour was a force of 20 destroyers, eight sloops and minesweepers, and a flotilla of submarines with their depot ship — the same type of balanced striking force that was to be based there in the coming World War.

In the crisis the support of the French Fleet was seen as vital, but when the League's negotiations in Paris failed in late August, the British Fleet was strengthened still further. Australia and New Zealand sent supporting cruisers, and the fleet took on stores to make it self-sufficient for four months. It was also decided — and here again the strategy for Malta of 1942 came through — that in the event of war it would not be practicable to operate a convoy system safely in the sea, and all merchant ships would need to be diverted round the Cape.

Britain urged Italy to reduce her large army in Libya, as the dispute was with the League of Nations, and not with her; but Italy in reply demanded that the fleet reinforcements be withdrawn from Malta. In the end one division of troops was withdrawn from Libya, but enough were still left to constitute a threat to Egypt. Once again the crisis passed and the world breathed a sigh of relief — and none more so than the people of Malta, who had been in the spotlight more than on any occasion since the British overcame the French there in 1800. Soon after the crisis passed, Admiral Fisher was relieved as Commander-in-Chief by Admiral Sir Dudley Pound. Fisher was given a great farewell dinner by his senior officers, and afterwards was pulled back to his ship in a galley entirely crewed by admirals, and escorted by a cutter manned by Captains. Fisher left harbour next morning standing on the fore turret of *Queen Elizabeth,* to the cheers of a grateful fleet.

Thoughts in Malta now turned more actively to preparations against war. There was a fear that poison gas might be used against the island in such an event, and on October 16 a dummy air raid was carried out on Valletta, to impress upon the people the need for precautions. It was a bizarre event; vans toured the streets, and thunderflashes thrown from them simulated exploding bombs, while water mains were turned on to indicate damage. There was a massive display of searchlight beams, and the church bells were rung to signify the order to extinguish all cigarettes. The people turned out to cheer.

Recent events had demonstrated rather publicly the view held by the army and the air force in Britain that Malta could not be defended from attack; in December the Prime Minister of Malta pleaded in the British House of Commons for the speeding up of the construction of airfields ('landing grounds for aeroplanes with wheels') as well as for defensive seaplane bases, which could not be put out of action by bombing.

Now life in Malta became a mixture of the old peacetime routines, and the overtones of war. Mock air raids became a regular feature of life in the cities around Grand Harbour, and the increasing naval construction programme in Britain was anxiously watched. In 1936 24 cruising liners visited Malta, and Valletta and Sliema were full of fun-loving passengers; and in February of that year, to loud applause, a Miles Falcon monoplane actually flew from England to Malta in ten hours. The new Governor of Malta, General Sir Charles Bonham-Carter, arrived splendidly in the P&O liner *Strathmore,* escorted by the destroyers *Wren* and *Wishart.*

The fleet cruises went on as well, though the political implications became ever more obvious. The autumn cruise of 1936 suffered from an acute shortage of friendly ports — Italian ports were out of the question, and while Athens could be visited, this could not be at the same time as the city was receiving the Turkish Fleet, as this might be misinterpreted in Italy. Another constraint was that the fleet should never be too far from Malta.

The Spanish Civil War broke out in the same year, and ships of the Mediterranean Fleet became heavily involved, operating at long distances from Grand Harbour, and their work was in evacuating refugees and keeping watch over British citizens. This was arduous work. The 3rd Destroyer Flotilla led by *Codrington* only met together as a flotilla for the first time, eight months after they had commissioned — and then only for two hours. They had 25 days together in the whole of their commission, and in 20 months they spent only four of them in Malta. In that first year *Codrington* herself was under way for 105 days, and steamed 15,780 miles — heavy work for a peacetime commission. The ships' companies of the destroyers cleaned their own boilers, and in general just stayed at sea on patrol.

Later the 2nd Destroyer flotilla carried out a patrol of 37 days off the Spanish coast, and each of its ships steamed a greater number of miles than a destroyer normally covered in peacetime in six months. There were some dramatic incidents. *Havock* and *Gipsy* of the 2nd Flotilla were bombed by insurgent aircraft on February 22 1937, and although they hoisted large White Ensigns to their mast-

heads and spread a Union Flag over their torpedo tubes,
two attacks were made on them — though without damage.
Gallant was attacked on April 6 by aircraft based at Palma;
two three-engined Junkers carried out deliberate bombing
runs but — a far cry from the coming raids of 1942 in which
this ship was to be lost in Grand Harbour — all the bombs
missed. The cruiser *Shropshire* rushed to her assistance.

A few days later *Hardy*, the leader of the 2nd Flotilla,
arrived at Palma in the middle of an air raid, and was
near-missed. Then *Havock* on patrol nearby was attacked
by a submarine, and saw the torpedo pass just a few feet
astern of her. The alarm was raised and the light cruiser
Galatea, with the Rear-Admiral (Destroyers) on board,
hurried to the scene with *Hotspur, Hereward* and *Active*.
Galatea's Walrus aircraft went up to spot for oil slicks, and
Havock dropped depth charges on one contact, then felt a
slight bump under her, as the submarine touched her
bottom; then it surfaced on her port bow and 'went por-
poising off into the distance'. The light cruiser *Penelope*
and more destroyers joined the hunt, but they did not sight
their quarry again.

After these bombing attacks, large red and blue stripes
were painted across the white B turrets of the British warships as distinguishing marks, and these show up clearly in
many photographs taken in Grand Harbour in those days.

The destroyers were thought to be too valuable to risk on
this duty, and two flotillas of the *Town* Class minesweepers
were hastily commissioned and based on Malta, to take
over this work. Then came the most serious casualty of the
Civil War for the Royal Navy. The destroyer *Hunter* was
mined on May 15 1937 five miles off Almeria. She was
badly damaged; the forward boiler burst and the ship was
badly flooded forward. The Spanish Government
destroyer *Lazaga* stood by her until British ships came to
the rescue.

The battleship *Africa* steams past the Upper Barracca Gardens, probably 1909
(Richard Ellis).

Alexander towing *Vanguard* (with Nelson aboard) off a lee shore on Sardinia, 1798
(National Maritime Museum).

The French flagship *Orient* blows up during the Battle of the Nile, August 1 1798. Much Maltese plunder went with her (National Maritime Museum).

Formidable being careened in Malta dockyard, 1873 (National Maritime Museum

...amemnon, an early iron and steel turret ship, carrying out boat drill in 1886
...ational Maritime Museum).

...dustan, Africa and *Hibernia* celebrating, about 1907 (Richard Ellis).

A French full-rigged ship in Malta, about 1875. Note the forest of masts in the background (Richard Ellis).

The breakwater under construction in June 1905, starting from the St Elmo end (Richard Ellis)

The British and French Fleets in Grand Harbour early in the First World War. In the background are *Indefatigable* and *Inflexible* (Richard Ellis).

Sunflower, a *Flower* Class sloop fitted for minesweeping, in Dockyard Creek in 1917 (Richard Ellis).

Emperor of India was in the battle squadron based at Malta after 1918. High wireless masts stand above St Angelo (Richard Ellis).

The destroyer *Wishart* entering in 1936, with Captain the Earl Mountbatten in command (Anthony Pavia).

The new aircraft carrier *Ark Royal* turns off St Angelo in January 1939 (Anthony Pavia).

The aircraft carrier *Illustrious* under dive-bombing attack in December 1941. She is berthed at Parlatorio Wharf (Imperial War Museum).

The bridge at St Elmo destroyed by Italian explosive motor boats in July 1941 ('The Times of Malta').

Clearing away a large unexploded bomb in 1941 ('The Times of Malta').

The Opera House near the gates of Valletta, destroyed by bombing in 1942 ('The Times of Malta').

he destroyer *Lance* down by the stern, after bombing damage in dry-dock in April 42 (Imperial War Museum).

ord Gort presenting the George Cross to the people of Malta in April 1942 The Times of Malta').

The fast minelayer *Welshman* passing St Angelo at dawn, bringing stores and, on this occasion, disguised as a French destroyer (Imperial War Museum).

Cargo from the later convoys was unloaded by floodlight, to save time (Imperial War Museum).

Submarines of the 10th Flotilla under way in Marsamxett Harbour. *Taku* in the foreground, boats of the U Class behind, and bomb damage ashore (Imperial War Museum).

King George VI touring the streets of Valletta, escorted by the Archbishop of Malta, June 1943 ('The Times of Malta').

Strange craft in the harbour; a Landing Ship, Tank, with its bow doors open, befo
the assault on Sicily ('The Times of Malta').

The cruiser *Uganda* berthed in French Creek, after bringing Admiral Cunningham
back to Malta in July 1943 (Imperial War Museum).

e escort carrier *Puncher* moored off Floriana in September 1943; *Illustrious* lies
ind her at Pariatorio Wharf (P A Vicary).

e frigate *Loch Scavaig* passing British and Italian ships moored in Sliema Creek
er a NATO exercise in August 1950 (Anthony Pavia).

The Commander-in-Chief's saluting base and flagstaff above Lascaris Bastion. Big hospital lies across the water (Malta Tourist Organisation).

The American radar picket destroyer *Thomas J Gray* passing St Angelo in September 1969. The Maltese Cross on the fort was removed in 1972 (Anthony Pavia).

e guided missile destroyer *Fife* passing the Lower Barracca Gardens during the
0s (Admiralty Constabulary, Vittoriosa).

ding craft in Dockyard Creek, about 1975 (Admiralty Constabulary, Vittoriosa).

Ark Royal leaving Grand Harbour for the very last time, November 16 1978 (Admiralty Constabulary, Vittoriosa).

The Soviet aircraft carrier *Minsk* (43,000 tons) at anchor off Libya in March 1979, under the watchful eye of the British frigate *Antelope* from Malta (Ministry of Defence (Navy)).

Cruising in 1937 was largely limited to ships not needed on the Spanish patrols, and that was an anxious time for the families waiting in Malta. Admiral Cunningham had left Malta a year or two before for another post, but to his great delight he was appointed Commander-in-Chief of the Mediterranean Fleet in May 1937. He hurried overland to Marseilles where the cruiser *Penelope* was waiting to speed him to his ships and men; both Admiral and cruiser were about to start their greatest service for Malta.

Some cruises were carried out. The cruiser *Delhi* went to Varna in Bulgaria and impressed the citizens by coming alongside the jetty smartly – the citizens compared her performance with that of the German cruiser *Emden*, which had been there just before her, and reportedly had not done so well. When *Delhi* sailed, 2,000 people including the leading citizens came down to watch her go; the cruiser left harbour stern first and at high speed, to the resounding cheers of the watching crowds. The flotilla leader *Grenville* went to Salonika, and went through a swing bridge rather fast; a large and appreciative crowd cheered wildly as her stern narrowly missed the wall, and later her Captain found that the current through the bridge was deemed too dangerous for ships to survive it without tugs.

Two uneasy years passed, with the ships' companies endeavouring to live as normal a life as possible. The French Commander-in-Chief, Admiral Abriel, paid an official visit to Malta in 1937, bringing a squadron led by *Algérie*. Not to be outdone, an Italian squadron came to Grand Harbour in mid-summer of the following year; Admiral Riccardi arrived with two battleships and four destroyers, and the records of the visit speak of great entertaining. The Italian influence on the islands was fast waning, however; the policemen wore British uniforms, and the telephone boxes were identical with those in

London. The Italian street names were fast disappearing, too — the main street of Valletta was changed from Strada Reale to Kingsway.

Then came 1939, and the last of the pre-war cruising activities. The fleet at Malta was being built up to its war-time strength, and Admiral Sir Andrew Cunningham was flying his flag in the modernised battleship *Warspite*. The fleet was already using both Malta and Alexandria, in order to become used to the Egyptian port in case of war; but Malta with its great dockyard, drydocks and repair facilities was still its main base with the families ashore, and Valletta and Sliema were the homes and recreation centres for both officers and men.

Apart from *Warspite* the fleet included the battleships *Barham*, *Malaya* and *Ramillies*, and the aircraft carrier *Glorious*. Five of the new 8-inch gun *County* Class cruisers had arrived, but when war came they were withdrawn to chase German commerce raiders on the high seas, and ships of this class played no part in the defence of Malta. More significantly still, eight of the big new fleet destroyers of the *Tribal* Class had joined the fleet, and some of them were to play a glorious part in the defence and sustenance of Malta only two years later.

Another arrival early in 1939 was the trawler *Beryl*, which had been bought in from commercial fishing service. This ship was to play a major role in the tiny Malta minesweeping force in the coming war. The cruising programme in that last year of peace was much curtailed. There were once again no visits to Italian ports, nor to the Black Sea; but Cyprus welcomed many calling ships. The new *Tribals* were shown off there, and the first ships of the *J* and *K* Classes as well, as they arrived from the shipyards of Britain — *Kelly*, flotilla leader of Lord Louis Mountbatten, and resplendent in immaculate paintwork, was a popular newcomer.

The French Commander-in-Chief now Admiral Ollive, paid a further visit to Malta at this time, to confer with Admiral Cunningham on their joint plans in the event of war. Arriving in the battleship *Provence* with four destroyers, his visit was formal and the two days of talks were taken seriously. When the French squadron left, Cunningham took *Warspite* with him, and four of the new *Tribals,* and they sailed in company for Turkish waters, where the British squadron went on to visit Istanbul.

This visit was a great success; the Turkish Navy had for long been Anglophile, and the population showed great interest. The social side of the visit was especially hectic, there were well-attended sporting events, and a ball for 350 guests was held aboard *Warspite.* When the ships were thrown open to visitors, the response of the people was embarrassing; every boat in the harbour had to be pressed into service to carry them, and at one time *Warspite* was overrun by several thousand people. The press gave great coverage to the visit, and the officers and men left feeling well satisfied with the impression they had made.

The warclouds were clearly gathering over Malta, and the Italian-Abyssinian crisis in May built up further tension. The cruiser *Dorsetshire* and the troopship *Neuralia* arrived at the island to evacuate 300 wives and children back to England, and when the fleet was mobilised in August, the reservists for Malta were brought overland from England through France to Marseilles, where the great four-funnelled Cunard liner *Aquitania,* already far from her peacetime Atlantic run, was waiting to rush them through to Malta.

Everyone in the island felt sure that war could not be long delayed. On August 28 the Lieutenant Governor sent this message to the people, through *The Times of Malta:* 'His Excellency the Governor has asked me to say that it gives him great pride and satisfaction, to see how stoutly

CHAPTER 8

The Greater Siege opens, 1940-41

As the war opened in western Europe, the Royal Navy found itself in a complex position at Malta. On the face of it, with France as Britain's ally, the western Mediterranean was safely held by the large French Fleet; and with Italy still neutral, the British Mediterranean Fleet comfortably dominated the eastern half of the sea. In the years before 1939, however, Malta had been written off as indefensible by the British air force and army − against the protests of the navy − and continuing cuts in defence budgets in Britain had left the island at the end of the queue of unsatisfied defence needs.

Malta's fighter force had been authorised as four squadrons of Hawker Hurricanes, but in early 1940 there was not one fighter on the island. There were four airfields in existence, Hal Far near the south coast, to be operated by the Fleet Air Arm during the coming war; Ta'Qali inland near Mdina, and Luqa, a big but unfinished field behind Valletta; and Kalafrana, the flying boat base on the south-east coast.

The island's garrison consisted of just five battalions of infantry. The ancient fortifications of the Knights ringed the harbour, and the Victoria Lines lay on the high ground to the north-west; but there was little enough with which to repel an invasion aimed at what was arguably the best harbour in the Mediterranean. Malta lay to all effects and purposes defenceless and abandoned. The Royal Navy was not at all happy with this situation. It had always regarded the island as the keystone of victory in the Mediterranean, but in 1939 there was not the same close inter-service liaison which was to emerge under the pressures of war. In May 1940 the British and French Fleets made a show of force in an attempt to impress the Italians, who were showing every sign of joining in the war with the Germans. A squadron made a sortie east from Gibraltar, with one British and three French battleships, four French cruisers and ten destroyers, of which eight were British. The battle cruiser *Hood* spent 92 days in Malta dockyard hands at this time − her last visit to the island.

On June 10 1940 Mussolini declared war on the side of Hitler at midnight and the first air raid on Malta by Italian bombers took place at 0655 hours the next morning; Admiral Cunningham had withdrawn the heavy units of the fleet to Alexandria some time before, and there were few guns to resist the invaders, who bombed at will. The old monitor *Terror* was moored in the harbour at this time, to lend her few guns to the thin barrage.

Two weeks later France surrendered to Germany, and the whole balance of naval power in the Mediterranean was changed. The western half of the sea, previously covered by the French, was laid wide open and a Royal Navy squadron, later to be named the famous Force H, was rushed to Gibraltar to cover it. The battleships of the British Mediterranean Fleet could not operate from Malta without fighter cover, and serious consideration was given in London to abandoning the eastern half of the sea, and Malta with it.

As so often before in British history, the real need was seen just in time. Winston Churchill ruled that Malta must be held, or the way to the East would be open. So began the great story of the struggle to keep Malta supplied and to build it up as a striking base − a story which was to run for three harrowing years, and to demand major fleet operations and heavy losses, to ensure the island's safety and effectiveness. The demands on the Maltese people were to be equally heavy.

Admiral Cunningham, in one of his first conflicts with the Admiralty on policy, pointed out that the morale of the Maltese was supremely high even after the fall of France, but if the fleet left the eastern Mediterranean, then it could only be a matter of time before that morale collapsed. The Mediterranean Fleet was quickly strengthened, and the reinforcements passed through included the new fleet carrier *Illustrious* (the Royal Navy's first armoured-deck carrier), to support her ancient sister *Eagle*. Convoys were passed in and out of Malta under cover of the fleet, and with no losses at this time. Admiral Cunningham estimated that he needed to deliver at least two convoys each month to the island, each carrying 40,000 tons of stores, if it was to be kept secure — and that was a formidable target.

The fighter position was still precarious. With traditional British 'make-do' methods, eight crated fighters were found in a hangar at Kalafrana, the naval air station in Marsaxlokk bay. They were outdated Gloster Gladiators, left behind by the fleet carrier *Glorious* when she left Malta for the Norwegian campaign, and now earmarked for *Eagle* next time she visited Malta. Four were quickly turned over to the RAF, just as quickly assembled, and were up fighting the Italian bombers against fantastic odds.

For months their pilots fought valiantly, and brought down many of the raiders for the loss of only one fighter. The other three were nicknamed *Faith*, *Hope* and *Charity* and they became a symbol of the island's growing resistance. Each time these old aircraft went up, they were followed by a wave of prayer for their safety from the Maltese people. Still the authorities in Britain did not appreciate what the island's defenders were going through; soon after the Gladiators were in active service, a signal was received in Malta from the Admiralty department in London, asking why Fleet Air Arm property had been turned over to the Royal Air Force.

The lack of fighters was critical, and in August in Operation Hurry the old carrier *Argus* covered by Force H flew in 12 Hurricanes from a position south of Sardinia, and at last Malta had some up to date fighters. They were still too few, and in November in Operation White *Argus* flew off 12 more, though tragically, due to a navigational error, only four arrived safely on the island. These fighters were but a trickle, compared with the flood of new machines which was to be flown in over the next two years; the failure to supply adequate air defences to Malta while the going was good was already costing Britain dearly.

Convoys were passed into Malta whenever the fleet was able to cover them. In October the first of the combined convoy operations in the eastern half of the sea was mounted. A convoy was run from Alexandria to Malta, and a convoy of empty ships returned east with the escort; and this was quite an escort − four battleships, two aircraft carriers, eight cruisers and 16 destroyers. The threatening proximity of the Italian Fleet with its modern ships was already determining the pattern of the Malta convoys.

In November a convoy of four fast merchantmen came through from Alexandria; from that point on it was to be the relatively small number of fast modern ships with a speed of 16 knots or more which was to sustain Malta. So few were there in service that fast ships of Britain's allies, especially the Americans and the Dutch, were often included in these hazardous convoys.

Malta was not as yet having any great effect as a striking base. True there were submarines based there, but the larger boats were vulnerable in the clear waters of the Mediterranean, and it was not until later in the year that the first of the smaller *U* Class arrived. So it was that in the last half of the year the Italians were able to build up their forces in Libya with little hindrance; of 700,000 tons of shipping despatched from the north, only two per cent was sunk on the way — a situation which needed to be drastically reversed.

As the year closed, the successful Fleet Air Arm attack on Taranto, reducing the Italian battleship and cruiser strength, and demands on the Italian Air Force on several fronts gave a breathing space to the Maltese people and to the British ships' companies, and this was more than welcome.

Germany was not going to allow her Italian partner to suffer losses in this way. In December Fliegerkorps X was moved from Norway to Sicily, and this was to have a marked effect on the war in the Mediterranean; for this veteran air group had been specially trained to attack ships, and had distinguished itself in the Norwegian campaign. Its aircraft included the famous Stuka Ju 87 dive-bombers, Ju 88 bombers and Me 109 fighters. Its new mission was to attack the British Mediterranean Fleet, above all its aircraft carriers, and to neutralise Malta.

During 1941 with the combined German and Italian air attacks on Malta increasing, the strategic importance of the island was debated back and forth between Admiral Cunningham in Alexandria and Winston Churchill and the First Sea Lord, Admiral Sir Dudley Pound in London. A similar debate was carried on between Hitler and Mussolini, and the naval high command in Germany and Italy, with General Rommel in Libya.

It is interesting to contrast the steadfast resolve of Churchill and Cunningham that the island must be defended at all costs (though they did not always see eye to eye on detail), with the refusal of the two Axis dictators to accept that Malta needed to be invaded and captured, in order that their supply convoys could pass from Italy to North Africa without heavy losses being inflicted by the Malta-based forces.

Churchill set the scene on January 21 with a message to the Governor for the people of Malta: 'The eyes of all Britain and indeed the whole British Empire are watching Malta in her struggle day by day, and we are sure that success as well as glory will crown your efforts.'

A few weeks later Cunningham was pressing Pound hard to send more Hurricanes through to Malta from the west, and the First Sea Lord was sending him some dusty replies. What about the risk to the carriers involved, argued the Admiralty? If *Illustrious* with her armoured deck had nearly been sunk, *Ark Royal* would certainly have succumbed to the German Stukas. 'I am not sure,' Pound cabled, 'that you entirely appreciate what is going on outside the Mediterranean,' and he went on to emphasise the Battle of the Atlantic, 'which transcends all other things.'

At the same time the Vice-Admiral (Malta) Wilbraham Ford, said that one of the reasons for Malta's troubles was that the British aircraft were inferior to those of the Germans, and expressed a hope that some Spitfires might soon arrive. This brought a quick retort in London from the Chief of the Air Staff to Winston Churchill: 'I do not regard this officer as competent to express an opinion, or as having any right to do so'. Pound added fuel to the fire by telling Churchill that he was a little critical of the constant pushing by Cunningham.

So other methods were tried. In March the cargo steamer *Parracombe* was loaded with 21 Hurricanes and other stores, including RAF ground staff, and sailed independently eastward from Gibraltar. No more was heard of her until May 2, when the American consul in Tunis reported that she had been mined and sunk, and 18 survivors were in Bizerta. This brought a sharp note from Churchill to Pound: 'This is surely a pretty humble role for the Admiralty to play. I should like to know the reason why 'Potato Jones' (the master of the ship) and his merchant seamen in a poor little tramp steamer carry out Hurricanes, vitally needed by Malta, while the Royal Navy has to be kept far from these dangers. I never thought we should come to this'. A.V. Alexander, the First Lord (Civil) of the Admiralty hastened to reassure him, but Churchill's only reply was: 'I was never an enthusiast for this project. I trust 'Potato Jones' is saved.'

On May 10 Churchill made an important public statement about the island, which again left no doubt of his resolve: 'Malta with Egypt and Gibraltar will be defended with the full strength of the Empire.'

At the same time Cunningham was fighting another of his skirmishes with the Admiralty. He had run another small convoy through to Malta, and had commented that it had only got through because the Luftwaffe was elsewhere. The cause, he said, was lack of adequate air support, as there was no equivalent of the Coastal Command which existed in Britain, and the air force in Egypt had insufficient aircraft with which to protect the sea operations.

The Admiralty suggested in return that he should base a battleship at Malta, to lend more weight to the attacks on the Axis convoys. Cunningham, complaining about constant interfering advice from home, pointed out that a battleship would mean a higher consumption of fuel, and therefore more convoys with that fuel to be run through from Alexandria, and he could not spare a battleship in any case.

Churchill weighed in with the directive that the prime responsibility of the Mediterranean Fleet was to sever communications between Italy and North Africa. Cunningham recorded that he did not reply, as he was too busy with other commitments. He did relent and say that Malta was undoubtedly the correct strategic base for the fleet, but lack of anti-aircraft guns and fighter squadrons made it too dangerous. Churchill commented that the primary duty of the RAF in Malta was to defend the navy against air attack, but with this also Cunningham was unable to agree – in his view, the RAF was there to be on the offensive as well, and to support Force K, the striking force of cruisers and destroyers which was to be based there.

Cunningham continued to press his case for greater air support, sending his Rear-Admiral (Air), R.A. Boyd, to London to argue the case; and by the autumn the RAF had set up 201 Naval Co-operation Group in Alexandria. Air Chief Marshal Tedder visited Malta, and saw for himself the need for further fighter squadrons to be sent there. From this time on, fighters and bombers from the desert were able to support Malta more strongly, even flying to the island's bases as need arose, and in return as Malta's fighter force grew, it flew to join in the desert offensive from time to time.

In June 1941 the Americans were also involved in the debate. By that time some of the larger Royal Navy submarines were playing a vital role in carrying supplies to Malta, and London suggested to Washington that some United States Navy submarines should be converted for this purpose. But Admiral Stark, the Chief of Naval Operations, did not receive this suggestion favourably, though he did agree that a feasibility study be carried out. Unless he was in possession of an accurate knowledge of the needs of Malta, he replied, he could not judge what importance should be attached to this, compared with other strategic requirements. All American long-range submarines were required in the Pacific, as they were the only real American striking force against the Japanese sea command. When asked if US personnel could be detached to serve as volunteers in such a service to Malta, he saw great difficulty in it. He suggested that the Royal Navy convert more of its large submarines first.

Meanwhile the German Admirals were not able to persuade Hitler and Mussolini. Admiral Raeder in Germany was pressing Hitler for an invasion of Malta, as an essential prerequisite for the capture of Egypt. Hitler was sceptical, and said he distrusted Italian inefficiency in such an operation. In April Hitler designated the Russian and western fronts as having first call on German forces, and he said that the victory in Crete had been too expensive in men and materials. Field Marshal Kesselring in command in Sicily was ready to launch the invasion, but had to remain there in frustration.

So the arguments went on, with neither Cunningham nor Kesselring in the Mediterranean given the forces with which to do the task which each saw as vital. History clearly shows the reason for their concern. When the striking forces based at Malta were strong, Rommel's army was usually in retreat, or at least short of petrol and supplies; and when Malta was neutralised in 1942 by German aircraft, Rommel was able to build up his stocks and mount his big offensive against Egypt.

In the first week of January 1941 a large convoy left Gibraltar, with two merchant ships bound for Malta and four more for Greece. Named Operation Excess, the convoy had a strong escort; from Gibraltar came Force H including *Ark Royal*, while from Alexandria came *Warspite, Valiant* and *Illustrious;* both forces were accompanied by cruisers and destroyers. The German dive bombers had been waiting for just this target. On January 10 the Stukas found the convoy west of Malta, and in precision attacks they hit *Illustrious* six times, sank a cruiser and damaged another.

With great difficulty *Illustrious* was nursed into Grand Harbour, and there she was berthed at Parlatorio Wharf in French Creek. Her 12 Fulmar fighters flew off to Malta when she was damaged, refuelled, and were back over the

carrier in a very short time. The ship was badly damaged
and her engines needed heavy repairs, as did her steering
gear, before she would be able to limp eastwards to safety.
Unbelievably the Germans did not attack her for six days,
and good progress was made in the repairs. This respite was
too good to last, and on January 16 a raid of 60 Stukas
concentrated their fury on the damaged carrier; she disappeared amid the smoke of bursting bombs, and received
a further direct hit, while a cruiser lying nearby was
damaged.

On January 18 *Illustrious* was hit again in another heavy
raid, and this time the damage was underwater. To repair
the ship under almost continuous dive-bombing attacks
was a horrifying task, and to encourage the naval divers,
Chief Constructor Joughin sat in a diving boat beside the
carrier, as the bombs rained down.

Mr Joseph Caruana lived through those days of terror:
'The aircraft carrier was across the creek from Senglea (a
mere 1,000 feet or so) and my town was therefore well
within the target area. The noise and commotion was fantastic and my memories are a kaleidoscope of terror. The
whining warcry of the diving Stukas (so different from the
normal steady drone of the Italian high-level bombers); the
loud and incessant firing of the AA guns (especially those
of *Illustrious* across the creek); the terrifying shaking of the
ground and house with each bomb explosion; the alarming
rumble of collapsing houses, followed by choking clouds of
dust which settled as a white powder over everything; all
these things were mixed in mind-numbing confusion. After
the raid I remember people staring, dazed and awed, at the
destruction while others worked with frantic haste to
rescue people buried under the demolished houses. Many
of Senglea's narrow streets were blocked by the remains of
ruined houses while that area of the town abreast the
mooring of *Illustrious* was pulverised into a carpet of

rubble. *Illustrious* was still afloat and apparently un-harmed.'

The carrier was nearly in a fit state to leave, and four destroyers had arrived to escort her. Under cover of darkness and with the repair stages still slung over her side, the great ship sailed in the evening of January 23, quickly worked up speed to 20 knots and ran for Alexandria. She went on to the United States for repairs, and returned to Malta in 1943 for the invasion of Sicily. For both the British and the Americans, the ability of this early armoured-deck carrier to stand up to such heavy punishment was of particular interest.

Cruisers and destroyers of the passing convoy had been coming into Grand Harbour to refuel. The destroyer *Gallant* was mined and badly damaged on her way in; she was never to leave Malta, as she would be destroyed in the raids of 1942.

The month of January had seen the British optimism fade a little. There were 58 air raids during the month, and with the bombers concentrating on the warships, the dock-yard suffered heavy damage. A large bomb exploded in No 2 drydock, which was saved by being half full of water at the time, though luckily with no ships in it; but in No 3 the destroyer *Imperial* was damaged when a bomb exploded on the quay alongside her forecastle. Unexploded bombs were widespread, and had to be dealt with; stores were damaged everywhere, the famous old naval bakery in French Creek was straddled, and − disaster − the fleet latrines were demolished by a direct hit.

Vice-Admiral Ford continued his great work of leader-ship in keeping the dockyard going under these near-impossible conditions. In March he was awarded the British honour of the KCMG, but he commented in character that he would rather have been given three squadrons of Hurricanes. One of his achievements was a repair to the cruiser *Carlisle,* which arrived in Grand Harbour with a damaged propeller shaft. Admiral Ford promptly arranged for a replacement shaft to be shipped into Malta, lashed to the outer casing of a submarine on passage to the island.

February turned out to be a mixture. The German Afrika Korps, under General Rommel, was formed in North Africa, and half of Fliegerkorps X was transferred there to support them; but the number of air raids on Malta doubled compared with January, and damage continued to mount. The night raiders started to drop mines by parachute into the harbours, and the little minesweeping force was kept hard at work. In the first such raid in bright moonlight on February 15, both Grand Harbour and Marsamxett had to be closed temporarily as there were so many mines, and three of them exploded on shore, doing widespread damage. The magnetic and acoustic mines which were being dropped were slow to respond to treatment. On February 19 the drifter *Ploughboy,* towing her magnetic skid sweep and firing bursts into the water from her one Lewis machine-gun to neutralise any acoustics, lifted one ground mine just outside the breakwater; a further four in the harbour entrances exploded themselves in rough weather on the following day. Twice more during that month the harbours were closed due to the mines, and many others were found round the coast.

The island's submarine striking force was by this time hitting out effectively at the Axis convoys. An average of three or four submarines were out on patrol at any one time, and seven successful attacks were made during the months, together with three by the ancient Swordfish of 830 Squadron of the Fleet Air Arm. As a result, the escorts of the Axis convoys were greatly strengthened.

In March the air raids continued at the same frequency, with many of the night raids concentrating on minelaying.

Ships were often hit, but the War Diary faithfully records that three bombs exploded round the Surgeon Rear-Admiral's house at the famous Bighi hospital, while an unexploded bomb was recovered from No 20 latrine. The minesweepers worked hard to keep the channels clear, though the growing shortage of coal threatened to restrict their operations. The submarine *Regent* returned from patrol, and the drifter *Ploughboy* swept her in with her magnetic sweep streamed astern and her acoustic hammer lowered over her bow, and she lifted three mines right in the entrance to Grand Harbour; one near-missed her, and caused such damage that she had to be beached.

A few days later the drifter *Justified*, also towing a magnetic sweep, lifted two mines in the mouth of Marsamxett harbour, and another sweeper operating her acoustic hammer right inside Grand Harbour exploded a mine almost alongside the floating dock.

In April the tempo of the battle speeded up yet again. Force K arrived to strengthen the island's striking power, and the German air attacks increased in proportion, though in severity rather than in numbers, as so many aircraft were occupied in North Africa.

The arrival of Force K at this time demonstrated the renewed British resolve to hold Malta, and to increase the attacks launched from the island against the Axis convoys, as the build-up of the Afrika Korps was going ahead fast, and the menace to Egypt was growing. The force at this time consisted of the 14th Destroyer Flotilla, led by Captain Philip Mack in *Jervis*, with *Janus*, *Mohawk*, and *Nubian*. On April 24 the cruiser *Gloucester* arrived to operate in support of the destroyers. The force refuelled on its arrival and immediately sailed to attack a southbound convoy, which had been spotted by a reconnaissance aircraft from Malta. But the convoy's speed had been over-estimated by the spotter, and they failed to intercept it and

returned to Grand Harbour. Another southbound convoy
was located on the following day, but again the destroyers
could not find it, and this time they were bombed in the
Comino Channel, between Malta and Gozo, on their
return to the islands. Their dashing tactics were, however,
to be rewarded. After another convoy had been located on
April 15 they sailed in the evening under cover of low cloud
and rain, and that night they caught the convoy off its guard
near the Tunisian coast. Five heavily-laden transports were
sunk, and with them their escort of three Italian destroyers.
The only British loss was the valuable destroyer *Mohawk*,
hit by two torpedoes from an Italian destroyer. The
remaining units of Force K returned to harbour at dawn,
the low cloud still covering them from any attacking aircraft. Captain Mack put in an action report which described
this achievement merely as 'the skirmish off Sfax'.

In a further sortie on the night of April 21/22 these
destroyers intercepted a northbound convoy, and sank a
transport of 4,000 tons; but the noise of the attack warned a
valuable southbound convoy nearby, and it escaped.

Only one convoy came to Malta during the month, but
Breconshire arrived on April 21 with aviation spirit, oil fuel
and general supplies, under cover of a fleet movement to
bombard the harbour at Tripoli. This fast naval supply ship
was beginning a remarkable series of runs to Malta, mainly
from Alexandria, and she was to have a significant effect on
Malta's ability to survive. The submarine *Truant* acted as a
lighthouse for her, lying four miles off the breakwater with
a light showing to seaward. Safely unloaded, the supply
ship sailed eastwards again on April 28, this time escorted
by the 14th Destroyer Flotilla, which was leaving for the
eastern end of the Mediterranean after a brief but brilliant
innings as Force K.

That same day the cruiser *Dido* and the fast minelayer
Abdiel came in with stores, unloaded them and left the

same day. They were escorted in by the 5th Destroyer Flotilla, led by Captain the Earl Mountbatten in *Kelly*, with *Jackal*, *Kipling*, *Kashmir* and *Jersey*, and they assumed the role of Force K.

Meanwhile reinforcements of fighters were at last beginning to arrive; for the weakest link in Malta's defences was still her tiny fighter force of only a handful of Hurricanes with the three surviving Gloster Gladiators. Now started the remarkable series of operations by which some 600 new fighters were delivered to Malta in less than two years. In each operation the aeroplanes were ferried out from the United Kingdom to Gibraltar by aircraft carrier, then taken on in other carriers escorted by Force H to a point west of Malta within the fighters' range of the island, and from there they were flown off the carriers' decks and escorted by a larger aircraft to Malta's airfields.

On April 3 in Operation Winch *Ark Royal* supported by the old carrier *Argus* delivered 12 Hurricanes in this way; on April 27 the same two carriers delivered another 23. *Ark Royal* had been well known in Malta in the two years before the war, and it was fitting that she should play so large a part in the ferrying of 327 fighters to Malta until her loss in November 1941, when she was torpedoed by a German U-boat east of Gibraltar on return from one of these ferry trips.

The air raids continued to increase in severity, with an average of 60-70 aircraft bombing the close-packed dockyard cities each night. The Governor, General Dobbie, signalled to the Secretary of State for the Colonies in London that extensive damage had been caused to the city founded immediately after the Great Siege of 1565, and which had stood unchanged since the time of the Knights. This was a profound shock to Maltese sentiment, and the damage to several churches including the cathedral had given deep offence. The Maltese were hardened in their anger towards the enemy. One Maltese, boarding up his shop window shattered in a raid during the night, put it more bluntly: 'We will endure anything except the rule of these barbarous savages (the Italians)'.

The fleet sweeper *Fermoy* in No 5 drydock received a direct hit on her bridge, and the bomb went right through the hull. The destroyer *Encounter* in No 2 was first damaged by splinters from a near-miss, and then hit by a bomb which penetrated her forecastle, burst inside the ship, and blew a hole in her bottom, starting an oil fire in the bottom of the drydock.

There was more damage in the dockyard. The inflammable stores at the Oil Wharf received a direct hit, starting a fire which blazed for two days, and big craters were blown in the quays at Parlatorio Wharf. The War Diary solemnly recorded the number of direct hits on the tennis courts. By the end of the month, 37 unexploded bombs had been dealt with.

May was to be a month of mixed fortunes culminating in the operations round Crete, which were to be so costly to the Royal Navy. During the fighting there at Suda Bay, the minesweeper *Lanner* which was manned entirely by a Maltese crew did excellent work; Petty Officer Anthony Debattista in command received a well-earned Distinguished Service Medal.

The 5th Destroyer Flotilla sailed on May 1, supported by the cruiser *Gloucester*, to intercept a southbound convoy, but the weather was so bad that contact could not be made. When they returned to Grand Harbour disaster befell them. *Kelly*, *Jackal* and *Kelvin* had entered when *Jersey* following astern of them was mined right beside the breakwater and sank quickly, blocking the entrance channel completely. *Gloucester*, *Kipling* and *Kashmir* were still outside, and they had to sail for Gibraltar, so splitting Force K.

Intense and successful efforts were made by Admiral Ford and his team to clear the wreck of *Jersey,* and on May 9 the reduced Force K was able to sail, and they returned three days later after bombarding Benghazi. They sailed for the last time from Malta on May 21 to join the operations off Crete, from which so many of them would not return. The Malta Striking Force did not return until the following October. The Malta-based submarines continued their run of successes against the Axis convoys, though five of them were lost in the middle months of the year. One of the most successful of them was *Upholder.* Her Captain, Lieutenant Commander David Wanklyn, was awarded the Victoria Cross for an action off Sicily on May 24 in which his ship sank four enemy ships and damaged another. One of these ships was the liner *Conte Rosso* of 18,000 tons, which was crowded with troops on their way to North Africa. By the time that Wanklyn and his crew were themselves sunk off Tripoli a year later, they had destroyed three large liners, two other merchant ships, two U-boats and a destroyer. Wanklyn was an inspiration to the officers and men of the 10th Submarine Flotilla.

These pressures on the Axis supply convoys were having their effect. In this month General Rommel and his Panzer army were brought to a halt close to the Egyptian frontier, through shortage of fuel and general supplies.

In Operation Splice on May 21 *Ark Royal* and *Furious* flew in a total of 47 Hurricanes plus some Fleet Arm Fulmars; and on May 15 the minelaying submarine *Cachalot* arrived direct from Britain carrying 76 tons of special stores – the first of a long series of submarine cargo runs which were to contribute significantly to Malta's survival. The German minelaying offensive continued without a break. The submarine *Union* arrived on May 4 to join the flotilla but was greeted by an acoustic mine which gave her a near miss, happily without damage. Grand Harbour was closed for several days during May due to mines, and they were exploding spontaneously near the breakwaters and in the approach channel.

Some relief came during June from the massive air attacks. After the fall of Crete it looked as if Malta itself must come under heavier assault, while Admiral Cunningham was without an aircraft carrier, and was hampered by the damage his ships had suffered off Crete. Gibraltar and Alexandria, each about 1,000 miles away, looked more distant than ever before to the defenders of Malta. Hitler was about to begin his assault on Russia, however, and some of the aircraft of Fliegerkorps X were called away to that front, while another German air group in Italy was withdrawn. The number of air raids on Malta fell by a third, and many of these were carried out by Italian aircraft. The opportunity was taken to fly in two more big groups of Hurricane fighters; in Operation Rocket on June 7 *Ark Royal* with *Furious*, flew in 43, and in Operation Style on June 15 the new fleet carrier *Victorious*, again with *Furious* delivered 44 more.

The Malta submarines threw all their effort into fiercer attacks – five successful ones, but one frustration. On June 24 all available submarines sailed for a point south of Messina, to intercept an important convoy; but at dusk Maryland and Swordfish aircraft from Malta attacked it, and the convoy turned away to safety in Taranto. The waiting submarines saw the attack, but were unable to join in.

July was marked by two major events – the arrival of a big convoy, and a courageous attack on Grand Harbour by Italian surface forces. Early in the month there was little activity, though three cargo submarines arrived. It was decided that a further supply convoy must be run through quickly, if Malta was to survive, and in Operation Substance six large and fast merchant ships assembled at Gibraltar.

Force H would screen the convoy as far as the narrows, and Force X, which formed the escort to Malta, included the cruisers *Edinburgh* (flagship of the 18th Cruiser Squadron), *Manchester* and *Arethusa,* the fast minelayer *Manxman* and 11 destroyers. Eight submarines sailed from Malta to watch for Italian fleet movements. This convoy got through, with some light naval losses, though an Italian motor-torpedo boat managed to torpedo the merchantman *Sydney Star* one night. She reached Malta with the rest of the convoy, but as she entered she was drawing 40 feet of water forward, instead of her normal 20 feet. The convoy brought in 65,000 tons of stores (including submarine torpedoes, Hurricane engines, anti-aircraft guns, 10,000 tons of ammunition, and a good stock of edible oils, sugar, coffee and tea). It was a major landmark in Malta's survival.

Just after the ships had arrived, a brave attempt was made to raid Grand Harbour by craft of the Italian 10th Light Flotilla. The despatch boat *Diana* was loaded with nine explosive motor boats and sailed from Augusta in Sicily on July 25, towing a special motor boat in which were piloted torpedoes. The objective of the raid was to blow a way into the harbour through the bridge on the St Elmo arm of the breakwater, attack the ships recently arrived, and plant underwater charges on the submarines. The Italians planned the raid with daring, but their plans did not work out too well. They sent a ship to within 14 miles of the island during the previous night to test the defences, but it was detected by the island's radar, and an alert went out against a possible attack.

Three air raids had been planned by the Italian Air Force, a light raid on Valletta at 0145 hours to give the attackers their direction, and two heavier raids later to distract the defenders. The first raid never took place, and the other two were late.

The leading piloted torpedoes were to blow up the foot bridge, but after launching they were never seen again; so two of the explosive motor boats charged the bridge instead. The pilots bravely blew themselves up on the bridge supports, but instead of blowing a gap they brought the bridge down, and there was still no clear way through. Then the shore guns opened on the remaining motor boats, and all were sunk. *Diana* escaped as she had not approached the island too closely, but at dawn Hurricanes found two escorting motor boats and shot them up. Italian Macchi fighters jumped on the Hurricanes, but three Italians were shot down for the loss of one Hurricane.

The last day of July brought further troop reinforcements for Malta; *Hermione, Arethusa* and *Manxman* arrived from Gibraltar with 5,000 men. In August the submarines emphasised their ascendancy over the Axis supply convoys. They carried out 12 patrols and sank 50,000 tons of shipping. The Swordfish, not to be outdone, carried out 16 sorties, and claimed a further 43,000 tons of shipping.

It was significant that even at this hour of reduced enemy activity, Admiral Cunningham was foreseeing the crisis which was to come during the next few months. His ideas on how to repel a German invasion of Malta were also gaining credence. On August 1 he signalled to the Admiralty that during the coming months Malta would pass through its period of greatest danger, for not only was the island inflicting serious losses on the enemy, which might force action on him, but in his view, with the known thoroughness of the German, it was doubtful if they would undertake a Libyan offensive whilst this menace to their communications remained in being. In the case of an invasion of Malta, Cunningham thought it might be necessary to take the fleet to the rescue of the island, in whatever strength of ships he might have at the time. He thought it necessary also to study how Force H from Gibraltar might assist, to take the weight of the attack off Malta. The Admiral expressed his concern about the effect on British prestige if Malta was heavily assaulted and perhaps captured, without the fleet going to its assistance. The effect might be incalculable, and might even shake the British Government, let alone the effect it would have in America and elsewhere. The waning Italian interest in the war would receive a great fillip, and the navy's reputation for control of the sea, which had allowed them to do so much with a relatively weak force, would be jeopardised.

In September a second convoy was passed through from Gibraltar, Operation Halberd followed the pattern set in Substance, and nine merchant ships took part. In the escort were three battleships (including the new *Prince of Wales*), *Ark Royal*, five cruisers and 19 destroyers, with nine submarines on watch. The through escort to Malta, again called Force X, consisted of three cruisers and nine destroyers.

An Italian aircraft provided the only incident on the way, by torpedoing the merchantman *Imperial Star*. The through escort increased speed and arrived in Grand Harbour ahead of the convoy, to refuel. They entered on September 27 with flags flying, bands playing and guards paraded fore and aft, and they received a great welcome from crowds on the ramparts. 81,000 tons of stores were safely unloaded from the merchant ships, with 2,600 more troops, and Malta's supplies were safe until the following spring. Empty merchant ships were sailed westwards from the island as the convoy approached, and the through escort sailed quickly from Malta after re-fuelling and caught them up. It was noteworthy that, on this occasion, the escort's orders said clearly that the safe return of the escorting forces to Gibraltar was more important than the safe arrival of the empty ships.

In October the striking forces increased their pressure on the Axis supply routes; the submarines put in 14 patrols, with some of the larger boats completing seven more. A new Fleet Air Arm squadron arrived at Hal Far, and its Albacore aircraft joined the Swordfish in making 17 sorties. No enemy sea traffic from Sicily to Tripoli was detected after October 18, but, to underline the point, Force K returned to Malta after five months' absence – the cruisers *Aurora* (Captain W.G. Agnew), and *Penelope*, and the big destroyers *Lance* and *Lively*.

Three cargo submarines arrived, to keep the supplies trickling in. On each trip one of these boats could carry enough aviation fuel to keep the aircraft then based on Malta in the air for just three days of operations. No convoys came in during October, but on the 16th day of the month *Ark Royal* delivered ten replacement Swordfish for the Fleet Air Arm. The air raids remained at a relatively low level – 56 during the month, including 24 at night.

The following month brought victories for Malta's striking forces, enough to make the British feel that the island could be held after all. The battles to come in 1942 could not be imagined. The Axis supply convoys had actually stopped sailing, due to their losses, but Rommel's forces badly needed reinforcements and supplies, if they were to step up their attacks on Egypt, and so a convoy of seven supply ships sailed on November 8 from Sicily for Tripoli. The German and Italian forces gave this convoy strong protection. Submarines were on patrol in the approaches to Grand Harbour, to detect the sailing of Force K, and the convoy had an escort of six Italian destroyers, with a covering force of two cruisers and four more destroyers.

A reconnaissance aircraft from Malta discovered the convoy on its first day at sea, and sent a sighting report to Valletta in late afternoon. Force K took off to sea at very short notice, and in the dusk the watching submarines missed them. That night in a brilliant moonlight action, Force K attacked the convoy and sank all of the supply ships plus two of the destroyers, while two other destroyers were damaged. The British force had the advantage of using radar, but their attack not only destroyed this convoy, it reduced still further the Axis willingness to risk forces in supplying the Afrika Korps in Libya. The British force suffered neither damage nor casualties, and returned in triumph to Grand Harbour at dawn.

On November 18 the ships at Malta carried out a surprising and unique diversion, to draw the enemy's attention away from Operation Chieftain, a bombardment of the North African coast carried out by the main fleet from Alexandria. From Malta a convoy sailed southwards, to simulate an assault force heading for the Libyan coast near Tripoli. Code-named Operation Landmark, this convoy included *Breconshire* and four merchantmen, and was escorted by Force K. They returned at dawn on November 22, and it was never known if they were detected by the enemy — certainly they were not attacked.

Force K sailed again the following day, and intercepted and sank two fast tankers which were trying to slip through. Returning to Grand Harbour at dawn on November 25, they sailed yet again that evening but, finding nothing during the night, they returned bleary-eyed to harbour in the following dawn.

So effective was Force K in disrupting these vital supply convoys that a further striking force arrived on November 29 to join them. Called Force B this included two cruisers, *Ajax* (with Rear-Admiral Rawlings) and *Neptune* and the fleet destroyers *Kingston* and *Kimberley*. They entered harbour in company with Force K, and the two forces sailed together in the evening light of the following day to seek further targets that night.

This ended a remarkable month for Malta's striking

forces. The submarines had carried out 16 patrols, and Force K had made seven sorties. The Fleet Air Arm planes added a further 17, with a mixture of bombing, minelaying and torpedo strikes. These intensive sorties brought their own problems in supplies; the submarines had only 55 torpedoes left between them in the middle of that month, including 20 which were under repair; they had fired 53 during their October operations alone.

The last month of the year started well, but it was to end in tragedy. The two surface striking forces returned to Malta two days later; Force B had drawn a blank, but Force K sank a merchant vessel, a tanker and a destroyer. After that the ships of the two forces sailed from Grand Harbour independently, as opportunity offered. *Breconshire* sailed for Alexandria on December 5 escorted by *Kingston* and *Kimberley*, while *Ajax, Neptune* and *Lively* made a foray. The supply ship returned escorted by *Jaguar* and *Kandahar*, and the next day a force of three cruisers and two destroyers sailed, but the convoy they were after turned back, and the force returned without firing its guns.

A notable arrival took place on December 13; four destroyers called in, on their way from Gibraltar to Alexandria. More notably still, they had sunk two Italian cruisers on their way. They sailed again three days later, to join the fleet at Alexandria. *The Times of Malta* said next morning: 'The spectacle as the victorious destroyers entered Grand Harbour, amid the cheers of the populace, which were returned by the bluejackets lining their ships, was one that will not easily be effaced from memory. The ships were welcomed by cheering crowds lining the Lower and Upper Barraccas, St Angelo and every vantage point. The cheering conveyed a simple message of pride and gratitude, of sympathy and shared resolve, and of appreciation for the heavy blows they are dealing the enemy in the waters around Malta.'

These sentiments, by no means exaggerated at the time, brought forth this letter to the paper from the Senior Officer of the destroyers, before they sailed: 'The Senior Officer of the destroyers which entered Grand Harbour last Saturday morning, after their successful night engagement, wishes to express his, and all his ships' companies, thanks for the warm and moving welcome accorded them by the people of Malta, when the destroyers steamed into the harbour'. The letter was signed, quite simply: '*Sikh, Legion, Maori,* and *Isaac Sweers*'.

Breconshire continued her impressive series of supply runs by yet another arrival on December 18, escorted by both forces. That evening the three cruisers with four destroyers sailed to make a sweep off the North African coast, and this was to end in disaster. They ran into a moored minefield 30 miles off the coast, and in a short time *Neptune* had sunk with very heavy loss of life, and *Penelope* and *Aurora* had been damaged. These two returned to Malta – at 16 knots, which must have been a remarkable passage – escorted by *Havock* and *Lance;* but *Kandahar* sought survivors from *Neptune,* struck a mine herself and had to be sunk. This unhappy episode finished when *Jaguar* arrived back in Malta on December 20 with the survivors from *Kandahar*.

The year finished with air attacks on the island sharply on the increase – 175 raids and 100 of them by night. Daylight raids were a common sight, and some of the attacks on the airfields met with considerable success. Ships in the harbour were still at risk, and the submarine base at Manoel Island was hit by two land mines, causing great damage to installations. Ammunition was in good supply for once, and whenever the bombers appeared over the cities, the anti-aircraft guns fired a box barrage which was said to be the most formidable in the world – and that was saying something in those days.

At the end of the year there was an important change in the Malta naval command. Vice-Admiral Wilbraham Ford was relieved by Vice-Admiral Ralph Leatham as Vice-Admiral (Malta). Ford had completed five years in that important post, covering the build-up of Malta's capability as a striking base, and the maintenance of the dockyard and base facilities in the face of heavy air attacks; he had performed magnificently for Malta. Admiral Cunningham wrote that it was no exaggeration to say that Ford was one of the mainstays of the defence of the island through one of the most grievous periods of its eventful history.

CHAPTER 9

Malta's finest hour, January-June 1942

This year was to be the greatest test of all, for the brave people of Malta and for their defenders. The assault of the Germans, and especially of the expert bombing force brought specially from Russia, had one objective only – to subdue the island by breaking the will of its people, and by starving them of supplies; supplies of food and ammunition to keep the fortress in being, and for its striking force of submarines and bombers.

Despite all the gloomy predictions of the British Army and Air Force, Malta had been proved to be just that vital island for which the Royal Navy had always argued. The only real threat to the Axis convoys running from Italy to North Africa bearing the arms and men to conquer Egypt, lay in this little island and its striking forces. The Mediterranean Fleet was starved of aircraft carriers and could not strike at long distance from Alexandria in face of the German dive bombers; but that unsinkable aircraft carrier, Malta, could and did. In a neat reversal of their pre-war policy, the combined chiefs of staff in London expressed their view to Churchill that Malta was so important as a staging post for aircraft being ferried east, and as a striking base, that the most drastic steps were justifiable to sustain it.

The Germans knew that they had to subdue Malta, if they were to win in North Africa; as *The Times of Malta* put it so aptly at the end of this epic year: 'El Alamein delivered Malta, but Malta delivered Egypt'.

The German dive-bombers which had so heavily attacked *Illustrious* in the dockyard in December stepped up their attacks, concentrating on the crowded cities around Grand Harbour and on the airfields. The table of air raids tells the story — 262 in January, 236 in February, and about a third of them were at night, so that the exhausted people had only eight raid-free nights in January, and five in February. In the harbour strangely enough things were not yet critical. In January seven warships were damaged; the cruiser *Penelope* and the fleet destroyers *Zulu* and *Havock*, all under repair in the dockyard, received near misses and two submarines were damaged by splinters, but the damage to the ships did not reach the levels that were to come in the spring. There was an omen, however, when the submarine *Una* was attacked by Me 109s on her way into harbour, and the fleet minesweeper *Abingdon* was machine-gunned while she had her sweeps out.

January was the last month before the big storm in which convoys could be run into Malta without too much trouble; RAF fighters based in North Africa were still able to cover the fleet — but not for long. Force K was still able to operate; the cruiser *Penelope* and four fleet destroyers were active from Malta in supporting the convoys.

MW 8 arrived safely from Alexandria on January 19, with three merchant ships out of four completing the journey, covered by the anti-aircraft cruiser *Carlisle* and eight destroyers, with Force K meeting them at sea. At the end of the month a second convoy came in, with *Breconshire* leading two merchantmen, and two empty ships were passed out to their waiting escort outside.

The fast naval supply ships continued to prove their worth on this run; *Glengyle* came in escorted by four destroyers, and *Breconshire*, safely unloaded, left to join the fleet at sea. Two weeks later the same two ships sailed in the reverse directions, with Force K covering them.

The Royal Navy's target of four merchant ships a month into Malta was amply met in January, but next month

Admiral Cunningham was expressing grave concern at the navy's ability to continue to supply the island at this rate. By the end of February merchant ships could only arrive at Malta or sail from there in safety by night. Hard-hitting strikes were being kept up by the striking forces. The 10th Submarine Flotilla carried out 16 patrols in February, and its boats of the short-range *U* Class were ideal for this work — boats with fiery names such as *Upholder, Utmost, Unbeaten, Unique, Upright, Unbroken, United, Uproar* and *Unruffled*, they were the new legend of Malta. The Swordfish of 830 Squadron of the Fleet Air Arm carried out 13 sorties in the same month, but an Italian troop convoy was successfully passed into Tripoli in spite of their efforts.

The convoy MW 9 from Alexandria ran into trouble, and none of its three merchant ships reached Malta. *Breconshire* and three other empty ships were run from the island covered by Force K, but their safe departure was no consolation for the failure to bring any full ships into the harbour during the month.

The dockyard was still receiving damaged ships, in spite of increasing damage to its drydocks and repair shops; the cruiser *Cleopatra* arrived from Gibraltar after taking a direct hit on her forecastle from a large bomb, which passed right through the ship and out through the bottom without exploding. The destoyer *Fortune* arrived with her, with a sad tale to tell. She had sailed for Malta with a heavy deck cargo, but while turning at full speed under an air attack she had rolled heavily, and most of her precious cargo slid over the side, together with her boats.

The first serious warship loss in the harbour occurred in mid-February. The valuable *Tribal* Class destroyer *Maori*, secured to a buoy in the middle of Grand Harbour, received a direct hit in her engine room during a night raid. She caught fire and burning oil fuel spread on the water, threatening all the ships moored in French Creek; it was put out with some difficulty. The raids were causing increasing damage in the naval bases as well; the submarine base in Lazaretto Creek took a direct hit.

Submarine crews of the 10th Flotilla, inspiringly led by Captain G.W.G. Simpson, continued to achieve good results on their patrols, which by now were attracting world-wide attention. The Italians were, however, still able to pass a big convoy across to North Africa with battleship and cruiser cover, and the Malta-based aircraft could scarcely reach it with their limited endurance, and were unable to damage it to any degree. In the bad weather prevailing Force K was unable to leave harbour. Malta's chances of survival suffered yet one more setback when the Mediterranean Fleet had to pass some of its vital ships through the Suez Canal to reinforce the hard-pressed Eastern Fleet. This especially affected the destroyer force at Alexandria, which was reduced to just three flotillas, totalling 24 ships. This reduction, allied to the reduced ability of the RAF fighters in North Africa to be of help, made it no longer practicable for the fleet to attack the Axis convoys without an unacceptable risk from the air, and so General Rommel was enabled to advance towards Egypt. This made it all the more important to Axis forces that Malta's striking forces be neutralised, and equally, the British were determined that the island be defended.

The Germans planned an invasion of Malta, under the code-name Herkules. The landings would take place in two phases; first the paratroopers who had captured Crete would land in the south of Malta away from Grand Harbour, and they would spread out and capture the three airfields, to allow gliders full of troops to land. Then a strong Italian force would make a landing in Marsaxlokk Bay, using 52-ton tanks captured from the Russians on the eastern front.

The preliminaries for the invasion actually took place −

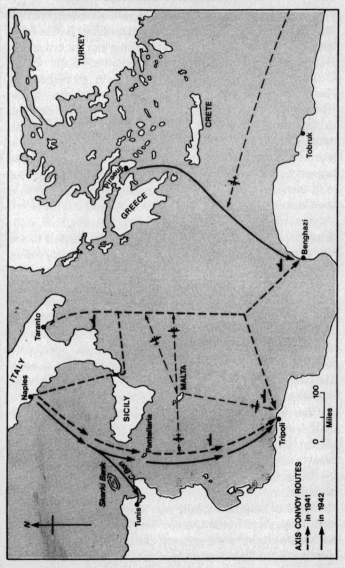

two German beach reconnaissance parties landed, but one was captured and the other achieved nothing. Italian frogmen landed on the coast from submarines to assess the beach defences, but they too achieved little.

Then Hitler's doubts about the invasion intervened; the German paratroopers had suffered heavily against the British in Crete, and the stone walls around the fields in Malta would create an additional hazard. The defences were strong, and then Axis forces had few landing craft at their disposal. Rommel was continuing his successful advance, and so the projected invasion was first postponed and then cancelled. Mussolini proclaimed that the advance on Cairo and Suez was the first priority, and left for North Africa to make a triumphal entry. His chief of staff, Cavallero, with the German Kesselring, continued to see the main necessity as the safeguarding of the supply routes from Italy, and they were proved to be right.

Now came the climax of this fantastic battle – the assault on the cities and harbours of Malta, an assault surely never equalled in Britain, even at the height of the Battle of Britain, or of the Blitz. In a period of just six weeks the towns in the small area round Grand Harbour received a total of 6,700 tons of bombs – the great Blitz on Coventry did not exceed 250 tons. In the same period 21 Royal Navy warships were sunk in the harbour or its approaches, and a further 13 were damaged; nothing like this occurred in the harbours on south-east England. 275 air raids in March, 283 in May, and there were only 11 raid-free nights in three months. No wonder that a message was flashed from Malta to London: 'The two island fortresses are holding out together!'

While the damage ashore was terrible, it was the severe toll of warships in the harbour itself and in its approaches which was to have the greatest effect on Malta's ability to survive. Four fleet destroyers in dock were bombed beyond repair — *Kingston, Lance,* and *Legion* of the big new fleet classes, and the prewar *Gallant,* together with four of the vital submarines of the striking force. The hull of *Kingston* was later used to block the channel between St Paul's Island and the mainland — a sad end for such a fine ship.

During the raids the submarines submerged and lay on the harbour bottom beside their bases, to minimise the risk of damage. *P 36* and *Unbeaten* were sunk while under water in this way, and the crews made remarkable escapes through the conning towers. *P 39* had a yet more dramatic end; she was near-missed by a 2,000 lb bomb which made a direct hit on an oil lighter only 30 feet away. Badly damaged, with the warheads knocked off her torpedoes, she was towed round to the dockyard but there, two weeks later, another bomb exploded underneath her and split her in two. Towed away once again, she was beached in Marsa Creek and her fittings and stores removed for use in other boats. But the bombers were not finished with her yet; during the raids in April she was hit again and again, and finally sank in shallow water.

The shore staff of the flotilla did not fare much better. Captain Simpson recorded that he could not keep abreast of his reports, as his office had been removed to a deep cavern next to the Manoel Island oil fuel tanks, and here they worked by the light of hurricane lamps, with thick dust from the rock roof showering down during the raids.

The oiler *Plumleaf* was sunk alongside Parlatorio Wharf, and came to rest on the bottom with her upper decks just awash; but her tanks were intact, and were kept in use. Eight ships of the vital minesweeping force were sunk, including the last fleet sweeper, *Abingdon,* which capsized from bomb damage at the foot of the naval hospital. The tug *Ancient* was sunk, but raised to enter service again with a boiler salvaged from a sunken trawler. *Ancient* was 29 years old, and was one of the two nursemaid tugs of Malta right through the seige; true to her name, she was only outdone by her workmate *Robust*, which was 34 years old. Both were paddle-wheel dockyard tugs manned by an English master with a Maltese crew, and they greeted every merchantman, every large warship which fought its way through to Malta; later they helped to move the invasion fleet for the assault on Sicily.

There were just as many ships damaged. The cruiser *Penelope* commanded by Captain A.D. Nicholl was repeatedly near-missed in April, and earned herself the nickname of 'Pepperpot' from the hundreds of splinter holes in her hull, which were repaired with wooden plugs. Nearly 1,000 bombers tried hard to destroy her in drydock, and in a period of two weeks she fired 6,500 rounds from her twin 4-inch guns, and brought down three bombers and damaged five more. She proved herself to be a worthy successor to the ship of the same name which had been among Captain Alexander Ball's blockading force off Valletta in 1799.

Damage to the naval base itself continued to mount. By now only the underground workshops were in full operation. The submarine base was hit twice more, as was the naval hospital. The big floating crane was sunk, and many valuable boats were lost in a direct hit on the boat yard. Admiralty House in Valletta was badly damaged, and there were ten heavy direct raids on the dockyard area in April alone.

The long-distance minelaying submarines were playing their part in full. They could each carry about 100 tons of valuable cargo, and while this was but a fraction of the cargo of one full merchantman, it was better than nothing. Six of these boats arrived in a short period; they came in at dawn, discharged their cargo during the day, and left again the same night. *Pandora* was sunk in an air raid, and *Clyde*, sailing in the evening, was attacked by Me 109s just outside the harbour entrance, and had to return. The next big convoy, MW 10, sailed from Alexandria on March 22. It was covered by the 15th Cruiser Squadron with a strong destroyer force, and had a close escort of the anti-aircraft cruiser *Carlisle* with four *Hunt* Class destroyers. The convoy fought its way through with some success, but our spotlight on Malta does not allow room for a description of the action; suffice it to say that two destroyers struggled through to Malta for repairs, after receiving hits from 15-inch shells in that battle. Three ships, the fast supply ship *Breconshire,* and the merchantman *Pampas* and *Talabot* arrived in triumph at the island; but that was not to be the end of this brave but sad story. *Breconshire* had been heavily attacked from the air and badly damaged; after an inspiring fight to save her, led by her commanding officer, Captain C.A.G. Hutchison, she was towed into Marsaxlokk bay by the tugs *Ancient* and *Robust,* though one of the escorting destroyers, *Southwold* sank after hitting a mine just outside the entrance to the bay. The German bombers were not going to allow this valuable ship to escape them; in two further very heavy air attacks *Breconshire* was hit again, turned slowly over, and sank. Her wreck was to remain a feature of this harbour for the rest of the war, and valiant efforts were made to salve as much as possible of her vital cargo. Small ships — including one superbly named *King of England* — came round the coast from Grand Harbour, and her oil cargo was pumped out barrel by barrel and brought back to Grand Harbour in triumph.

Even more seriously, the two merchant ships which had arrived safely were to have fought their way through in vain. The remarkable unloading arrangements which were to mark the arrival of the later convoys had not yet been organised, and for some 12 hours after the ships arrived, not much unloading was done. Then came heavy and accurate air raids, and in spite of the best that Malta's fighters and anti-aircraft gunners could do, both ships were sunk at their moorings. *Talabot* blazed furiously, and had to be flooded to prevent her cargo of ammunition from exploding; *Pampas* grounded on the bottom, but two of her holds were intact, and much of her cargo was salved.

The bombing was the most accurate that the German dive bombers were to achieve, and many of the small craft in the harbour had been sunk or damaged, making unloading that much more difficult. So many of the minesweepers in particular had been sunk, that it was hardly possible to keep the harbours open in face of the constant minelaying from the air. At this time Admiral Cunningham decided to evacuate any ships which could still steam, to save them from destruction in harbour. The cruiser *Aurora* and the destroyer *Avon Vale*, both under repair after heavy damage at sea, were patched up hastily and sailed by night on March 29 for Gibraltar; they were preceded by the convoy's close escort, which returned quickly to Alexandria after delivering its charges. At this sad point in the defence of Malta, Admiral Cunningham was relieved as Commander-in-Chief; he had put in four hard years of fighting, and now he was needed elsewhere. He was relieved by Admiral Sir Henry Harwood of the Battle of the River Plate.

At last new fighters were arriving in Malta from Europe – the modern fighters without which Malta would certainly not have been able to resist much longer the German raids which were destroying her life blood. Hurricanes had been flown in previously, but only the Spitfires could successfully combat the German fighters and dive bombers. The first Spitfires to arrive in Malta were flown in from the carriers *Eagle* and *Argus* in late February. Then came the two large batches flown in from the American carrier *Wasp*, which brought them out direct from England. *Wasp* delivered 47 Spitfires in March, and a further 61 with *Eagle* in April. The arrival in Malta of the first group of Spitfires from *Wasp* was watched by the Germans on radar in Sicily, and they reacted fast. Just 90 minutes after the fighters had landed, a raid by German bombers dropped 40 tons of bombs on Ta'Qali field, and 12 tons on Luqa. Every serviceable Spitfire was put into the air, but nine of them were destroyed on the ground, and a further 29 damaged by rock splinters. The Ju 87 bombers were diving on each individual plane on the ground, and only the pens built of sand-filled petrol cans and rocks prevented much heavier losses. Both fighter fields were turned into a complete shambles, in spite of soldiers working day and night to fill the bomb holes. The larger holes needed 100 tons of material to fill them; but the Germans did not give any peace from their attacks. In that one day they dropped 985 tons of bombs on Ta'Qali and 485 on Luqa; over the next two days nearly half of that total was added again.

Argus and *Eagle* were to fly in 225 more Spitfires in the next four vital months, while *Furious* added a further 100 in the three months to October. Some mystery surrounds the loan of *Wasp* to the British for these two trips. The British records appear to be incomplete, while it is understood that the American records show Admiral King, the US Chief of Naval Operations, was opposed to the deal, and of the opinion that the British had asked for the loan of the carrier for other duties. An Admiralty strategy paper in December 1941 said that the reason for stationing an American carrier with the British Home Fleet was that only in the Atlantic area were the vital interests of the two allies identical. But on March 28 1942 Lord Gort sent an urgent message to the Air Ministry saying that the fighter situation in Malta was extremely serious, and must at all costs be remedied (this was at the time when *Pampas* and *Talabot* were sunk).

Winston Churchill sent a swift cable to President

Roosevelt on April 1, saying that Malta had only 20 serviceable fighters, and asking if *Wasp* could be released for a ferry trip. *Eagle* was in dock for a month, the lifts in *Victorious* were too small to take Spitfires, and *Argus* was too small and too slow. Roosevelt pointed out (clearly briefed by King) on April 3 that *Furious* was scheduled to leave America after a refit that very day, and her lifts could take Spitfires, but Churchill (also well advised) rejoined that *Furious* only carried three fifths of her normal crew, and there would be an unacceptable delay of three weeks. Pound cabled King much to the same effect on April 20, going into more detail on the British carrier dispositions; and on that very day *Wasp* flew in her first batch of 47 Spitfires. Churchill cabled his thanks to Roosevelt on April 23 for the loan of *Wasp,* and said, 'We cordially accept the proposals which Admiral King has made to the First Sea Lord, about disposal of the American heavy ships in the Atlantic'. But there is no British record available to show what those proposals were, and Roosevelt's reply on April 25 included agreement for *Wasp's* second trip on May 9. Two American destroyers escorted her on each trip, and units of Force H came out to join them as they passed eastwards through the Straits of Gibraltar.

On that same day Admiral Stark, the Commander of American Naval Forces in Europe, wrote to Pound that the situation in the Pacific required *Wasp* to be sent there on completion of that mission. Pound cabled King on May 18 with his thanks for the loan of *Wasp;* the British files include a pleasant reply from Stark: 'It is a source of great satisfaction to all of us in our naval service to feel that the *Wasp,* even in a small way, has been able to render assistance in the gallant defense put up by the little island of Malta'.

The episode was rounded off by Winston Churchill's triumphant message of May 11 to *Wasp*: 'Many thanks to you all for your timely help. Who said a *Wasp* couldn't sting twice?'

Some of the fighters were inevitably shot down by the raiders, and the people reacted actively. When one Spitfire hit the sea not far from shore, a small boat went out to rescue the pilot, a crowd of 1,000 on shore watched the proceedings with satisfaction; the local bar was opened, a large whisky brought down to the water's edge for the pilot, a broken door from a bombed building produced as a stretcher, and he was escorted up the beach in triumph to the waiting ambulance.

The striking forces were not sitting idle. Submarines of the 10th Flotilla carried out 25 patrols in two months, though the famous *Upholder,* whose Captain, Commander David Wanklyn had won the Victoria Cross operating from Malta, was lost in April. The gallant old naval Swordfish were still making strikes, but these days they found German intruder fighters waiting for them as they took off from their much-cratered field near the cliffs at Hal Far. Force K was also out frequently – the cruisers *Cleopatra* and *Penelope* with the destroyer *Kingston* attacked an enemy convoy in mid March.

By now the eyes of the world were upon this great struggle by the Axis air forces to subdue Malta, and the unequalled fight back by the island's defences and people. Time was running out for them, however; on April 1 the Governor estimated that the island could only hold out until the end of June, if no further food supplies could be fought through; the oil position was precarious, and anti-aircraft ammunition would only last until mid-May.

The people were driven to take shelter during the raids, and the damage was so widespread that many had to be evacuated from the cities. Valletta's population fell from 21,000 to 6,000 and 35,000 houses were destroyed or damaged in the crowded cities around the harbour. The city was placed on air raid alert 3,340 times during the two years that the air raids lasted; this amounted to 2,357 hours in the shelters, of which 2,031 hours came in 1942, and 372 hours in March of that year alone − the month in which the 2,000th air raid on Malta took place. The damage was tremendous − much of the city of Senglea had been demolished during the attacks on *Illustrious* the previous December; now Vittoriosa, Valletta and Floriana were largely destroyed in their turn. The German bombers were very accurate, but with the ships moored right alongside the city ramparts, the buildings were bound to suffer heavily. There were some remarkable escapes, however. Alexander Ball's little Greek temple in the Lower Barracca Gardens was not hit, nor was the Grand Master's Palace; and the Pro-cathedral, with the colourful gravestones of the Knights of St John forming its floor, was also spared. Only the chapel of the German Knights was damaged, and that twice − the religious people of Valletta were not slow to see the significance of that.

The people themselves were saved by the rock forma-tions of the island, and by the great fortress of the Cottonera Lines behind the Three Cities. Ancient tunnels and galleries were enlarged and housed many thousands of people, caves were dug in the sides of the rock where families built sheds for shelter, and in Floriana the long disused railway tunnel, 1,000 yards long and deep under the ancient bastions, saved many lives.

HMS *St Angelo*, the 11th century fort standing proudly across the harbour from Valletta, with the White Ensign and Admiral's flag flying from its high flagstaff every day, symbolised the people's resistance. The enormously thick stone walls built so many hundreds of years before stood up remarkably well against the destructive power of modern high explosive. The great bastions and cavaliers received as many as 69 direct bomb hits during this period, but still they stood. Damage on the upper levels was inevitably extensive. The naval operations room moved over to the equally massive Lascaris Bastion in the walls of Valletta, and the old slave quarters tunnelled deep into the rock of the fortress during the war against the Turks in the 16th century, now housed the officers and men. Conditions down there were dismal. It was so damp that clothes were covered in green mould in just one day, and the rock roofs of the tunnels had a habit of disintegrating without warning. Some parts were bomb-proof – but by no means rainproof – and the first concert party to arrive were entertained in the wardroom while wearing raincoats and sea-boots, and it seemed doubtful if it were drier inside than out.

The fort started the siege with a grand armament of four Lewis machine-guns and two peacetime saluting guns – compare this with 1761, when it boasted 36 guns of the 24-pounder class, and a further 13 of smaller size. Even in 1942 the old fort was defended by just three Bofors guns.

The air raids seemed to become a continuous tempest of bombs, and even if the supplies held out until a further convoy could get through, there was a grave danger that the people of Malta would not be able to withstand the onslaught. But they are a great race, and although they had only joined in with the British in 1800, they stood firm magnificently, their morale could not be broken, and so they made a remarkable personal contribution to the turning of the tide in 1942. *The Times of Malta* reflected this many times in that fateful year. Leaders spoke of loyalty, steadfastness, and defiance by the people, and a leader reminded them: 'In 1940 the Maltese people gladly and freely chose to be Britain's only ally in Europe'. It was therefore with delight and pride that on April 16 the island fortress received from King George VI the award of the George Cross; and when the new Governor, Lord Gort, brought it to Malta with him, there was a great presentation ceremony in Valletta, outside the Grand Master's Palace.

Malta's links with the Royal Navy also helped to sustain the people. When the Pedestal convoy arrived in August, the *Times* said: 'If the feelings of the people could be expressed in simple action, Malta's George Cross would be nailed to the mast of every ship in harbour'.

Many Maltese men served as stewards in ships of the Royal Navy; most had their contingent – when the battle-ship *Barham* was torpedoed in the Mediterranean in this year, 20 Maltese went down with her. It was typical of some of the close ties of friendship that the ship's company of a fleet destroyer far away at Scapa Flow sent £50 – quite a sum in those days – to the hard-hit dghaisamen, whose ferries ply Grand Harbour.

The air raids continued in May at their very heavy level; 248 raids, and only two raid-free nights. Though the heavy damage continued, the raids showed a slowing-down from June onwards – the crack German bombing group had been withdrawn to the Russian front, though the Italian Air Force continued its efforts. The number of raids fell in June to 173, stayed in July at that level, and in that month there were even 15 blessed raid-free nights. The with-drawal of the Germans had given a respite, and the Axis never again had the chance to remount the same scale of heavy attacks; for by the time they returned in the last quarter of the year, swarms of new Spitfires were waiting for them.

In early May *Welshman* made another successful fast run through to Malta. She arrived at 0530 hours but the bombers were after her, and by the time the unloading had been completed under great pressure at midday, she had already been near-missed six times. The chemical smoke-screen around the harbour was used for the first time to screen her, and she left in the evening, swept out of harbour by Malta's proud but dwindling little group of mine-sweepers. Throughout her stay — a sign of the changing times — strong patrols of Spitfires kept watch over her and fought for her.

A veteran from the Battle of Britain, Air Vice Marshal Sir Hugh Lloyd arrived in Malta in May, to take on the air command. He found that the ground crews had made remarkable progress in extending the airfields, and protecting the aircraft on the ground. The taxiing strips and dispersal points were gradually linked together, until a fighter could move on the ground from one field to another, to find the most serviceable runway. This was achieved in the face of some remarkable odds — there were no tractors available, no concrete and no pneumatic drills. By the end of April there were 358 protective pens for aircraft, some carved out of the solid rock face, and every raid was countered by swarms of fighters. The fighter pilots themselves were liable to be carried shoulder high in the streets after the raids, old ladies curtsied to them, and men raised their hats.

However, no convoys sailed in May to replenish Malta's supplies, and the situation looked bleak. The 10th Submarine Flotilla were forced to withdraw to Alexandria — their boats were being sunk in harbour, and their crews could get no proper rest between their patrols. For the time being, Malta was losing its sting as a striking base, and the Axis air forces were some way towards achieving their objective of neutralising the island. Italian convoys at this time were able to pass within 50 miles of Malta in safety, escorted only by one or two torpedo aircraft.

In April 1942 when the bombing was at its height, pre-war plans were revived to build bomb-proof underground pens for both submarines and motor-torpedo boats. This was too late in the day, and the funds for this work had been denied before the war; had these pens been available in

1942, the submarines would not have withdrawn from Malta. This failure to take such an obvious step, at a low cost and in rock which was easily excavated, may be compared with the successful construction by the Germans of bomb-proof pens for their U-boats in the later years of the war. The proposals to build such pens at Malta were now progressed quickly, and some construction was commenced. Those for the submarines were to be built at Hay Wharf, under the Msida Bastion, and so would be safe under many feet of rock and masonry. The work would take some two years to complete, and would have provided berths for ten submarines at the remarkably low cost of £298,000 − the going price of one new submarine.

The motor-torpedo boat base would probably have been excavated next door to the submarine pens, with the same rock cover overhead. Initial excavation would provide space for one flotilla of eight boats, and further digging would add berths for an additional eight of the larger D type design. The overall cost of the MTB base would have been £150,000, and the berths would have been completed for use progressively. The tunnel space for the MTBs was to be 32 feet wide, with a height of 36 feet, so giving an internal height of 24 feet clear above water level. An alternative site for the MTB base was at the head of Pieta Creek, just below the Floriana fortifications. There the berths would have been inside a free-standing concrete structure (similar to the German U-boat pens), but it was thought that this would not give adequate protection against the swell set up by the strong *gregale* winds, and the water in that position would also need dredging, so the site next to the underground submarine base was preferred.

Early in May plots of enemy surface craft were seen on Malta's radar by night; the coastal defence guns, manned by Maltese, were eager to engage them, but the early type of radar then in use on the island was not accurate enough to control the guns, and surface anti-E-boat patrols were established at night outside the harbour. On May 7 *ML 130* was on guard outside Grand Harbour and in the early hours of the morning she was seen from shore to be in hot action with E-boats for about 20 minutes, before a loud explosion was heard, and a ship was seen burning for hours. At dawn an RAF rescue launch dashed out, but no survivors of that ML were ever found.

The E-boats had been laying mines, and a further tragedy came next day when the big submarine *Olympus* sailed, having discharged her cargo and with many valuable passengers on board. The first anyone knew of the sinking was when a survivor struggled ashore − *Olympus* had been mined in the approach channel, and there were only 12 survivors.

E-boat minelaying continued on most nights that month around the island's shores. Two days after the submarine disaster, the small sweepers *Beryl* and *Trusty Star* were operating their sweeps at night just outside the breakwater, and were near-missed by three torpedoes. During the following night E-boats were heard off the north coast, the searchlights caught them and the shore batteries engaged them at 10,000 yards. The E-boats retired behind a smoke-screen, then returned and one was hit by a shore gun. At dawn a damaged E-boat was seen out at sea, and a flight of Hurricanes took off to attack it, but they were beaten to it by some Me 109s, which sank the E-boat without more ado.

This minelaying kept the few sweepers busy. Any remotely suitable small craft were pressed into service, even dockyard lighters. *Beryl*, *Trusty Star* and *St Angelo* (the last was a tug) did most of the sweeping in Grand Harbour, with *Eddy* and *Swona* marking the swept channel with danbuoys. The lighter *C 308* was sunk while sweeping, followed by *Eddy,* and then by the gallant little *St Angelo* just outside the breakwater.

Though the air raids decreased a little, they were still serious enough to stop any shipping movements. The big submarines *Porpoise* and *Clyde* arrived at Marsaxlokk early in May with cargo; they were swept in through the minefields by *Beryl* and *ML 126* to a berth where they could lie on the bottom by day, and surface at night to unload at the seaplane base.

Welshman made yet another dash into Grand Harbour, and the sweepers cut some mines just ahead of her in the approach channel. *ML 126* was attacked by Me 109s as she cut some, and shot one of her attackers down and damaged another. *Trusty Star* was, however, lost to a mine then, and even the old paddle tug *Robust* was pressed into service as a sweeper.

It was decided at highest level that Malta must be maintained — the Spitfires were arriving in greater numbers and could help to control the bombers within their fuel range from the island, but only merchantmen fought through with supplies could really hold the situation. Winston Churchill wrote to the Chiefs of Staff: 'We are absolutely bound to save Malta'.

In June two convoys were planned, to be passed through simultaneously — Vigorous from Alexandria with 11 cargo ships escorted by three cruisers and 11 destroyers, and given distant cover by Admiral Sir Philip Vian and his cruiser force, and Harpoon from Gibraltar with a heavy covering force of a battleship, two carriers, cruisers and destroyers, and a through escort to Malta of the anti-aircraft cruiser *Cairo* with 13 destroyers. Four fleet minesweepers were to pass through, to reinforce the hardpressed sweepers at Malta, and six minesweeping MLs went with them. *Welshman* would make another of her fast runs through from the west, under cover of the convoy's heavy escort.

In spite of the greatest gallantry by the British warships

from Alexandria, Vigorous was beset by Italian surface opposition and by heavy air attacks, and in the end the convoy had to turn back to Egypt. Harpoon had some success. Two merchant ships were fought through to Grand Harbour, under strong Spitfire cover in the closing stages, and the ships unloaded 43,000 tons of stores. This eased the pressure on Malta for a little while, but did not lift the blockade. A sad incident marked the arrival in triumph of the ships from Harpoon. There were still mines in the approach channel, and four ships were damaged by mines on their way in — the valuable merchantman *Orari*, the destroyers *Matchless* and *Badsworth*, and the Polish destroyer *Kujawiak*, and only the latter sank.

The ships entered harbour during the night of June 16/17, *Orari* and *Troilus* to their unloading berths, and *Cairo* and *Welshman* the destroyers and minesweepers to the naval base. The two cargo ships were safely unloaded in four days, *Troilus* by Maltese labour and *Orari* by service personnel. Work went on by day and night, while the escorting warships refuelled and left without delay.

The little Malta minesweeping force, such as was left, had worked flat out to clear the approach channel before the convoy arrived; but they were sweeping on average a dozen mines a day, including magnetic and acoustic types, and the casualties on arrival were a great blow to the sweepers. Me 109s attacked them as they swept, mines dropped around them by parachute — it was like the great minesweeping days of the previous year in the Thames Estuary, but with far fewer sweepers.

The reinforcements went to work as soon as they arrived. Dubbed the 17th Minesweeping Flotilla, the four fleet sweepers had cleared the approach channel by the end of the month to a point three miles out from shore, and had accounted for 60 mines, with *Hebe* receiving some damage from colliding with one of them.

CHAPTER 10

Survival, July–December 1942

As the second half of this grim year came, the people of Malta were hard put to it to maintain their morale. In this month of July, the island came nearest to being starved into surrender; the Governor kept a running estimate of the number of days during which the fortress could still hold out, related directly to the stocks of food and fuel. When the Pedestal convoy came through in August, only ten days were left before surrender would have been unavoidable. It was that close.

Much of the cargo received from the Harpoon convoy had inevitably been fuel and ammunition, and torpedoes for the submarines. Food supplies were at a very low ebb indeed — rations in Britain at the height of the Battle of the Atlantic look generous when compared with Malta's weekly rations in mid-1942: 73 oz bread, 3 oz fats, 1¾ oz cheese, 1¼ oz coffee, 3 pints goats' milk, 3 lb tomatoes, 1½ lb potatoes, plus 8 gallons of water per day. There just was no sugar, rice, tea, oil, butter, soap or meat, and when coal ran out, there was no electricity either. For a long time, the staple daily diet consisted of soup and bread.

The air raids continued during July — 188 during the month; but the growing number of Spitfires was beginning to make itself felt — over 100 were operational — and in this month at last there were even 15 raid-free nights for the tired people of Valletta and the Three Cities. Enemy aircraft losses were mounting — 1,237 definitely destroyed during the past two years, with the high figure of 153 in July alone. The anti-aircraft guns, largely manned by Maltese, played a significant part in this growing toll.

The only supplies that could be fought through came from the fast minelayer *Welshman,* making yet another fast dash through, and from two cargo submarines.

The increasingly effective air defences allowed the 10th Submarine Flotilla to return to the island. Captain Simpson led them back early in July, the first boat to enter Lazaretto Creek suitably being the famous *Unbroken.* She was joined by *Ultimatum, United* and *P 42,* and soon there were nine boats on offensive patrol again. The Flotilla Diary solemnly records that on return to Malta after their short absence, they found that the English families had grown noticeably thinner, while the Maltese families had not, due to the type of rations available. So the Flotilla started its own pig farm, to help things along, and in August the same Diary noted that both sows had farrowed that month, one producing nine piglets, while the other, which was very victory-minded, gave birth to a grand total of 20.

The air striking force was also reinforced. Beaufort torpedo bombers were making successful sorties against the Axis convoys, escorted by Beaufighters, striking at longer range than had been possible before. The morale of the defenders was raised when a somewhat astonished Italian flying boat crew landed their machine in St Julian's Bay and surrendered. The crew of one of the Beauforts had been shot down while attacking a convoy during the night, were picked up by the Italians, and were being taken to Italy when the Beaufort crew overpowered the Italians and forced them to fly to Malta.

The RAF Spitfires were also suffering some losses. One pilot was shot down 15 miles from the island, baled out and boarded his dinghy. The weather was hazy and the rescue planes could not find him, so he paddled by hand towards the shore, first by eye, then at night by the stars, and he arrived safely 16 hours later. The striking forces were really making their mark; the submarines sank 36 enemy ships totalling 100,000 tons, and the torpedo bombers added another 12 ships.

August was the month of the greatest convoy of them all; but right up to its arrival in Grand Harbour the situation was really critical. The air raids remained at a high level, and the people together with the forces who protected them were becoming progressively more and more hungry and exhausted. The cargo submarines continued their mercy runs; they made five trips in August, and they were swept in and out by the newly-arrived fleet sweepers. The 10th Submarine Flotilla continued its patrols with great success, sinking 17,000 tons of enemy shipping in the month, and carrying out an average of 27 torpedo attacks in each month during the summer. The fleet carrier *Furious* flew in a further 27 Spitfires early in August, to swell the fighters crowding the airfields behind Grand Harbour.

It was, however, abundantly clear that only another successful convoy run to Malta could save the gallant island from surrender. The Governor calculated that if help were not speedily forthcoming, then the island would be starved into surrender by the middle of August. Churchill and the Admiralty reacted strongly, and a very large convoy operation was quickly put together. It was not reasonably possible to prevent news of the build-up for this convoy reaching the Germans and Italians; and as the merchant ships and warships assembled, so the opposing forces in Sicily and Sardinia were heavily reinforced to defeat them, once they reached the Mediterranean. Extra bomber squadrons assembled on the airfields, the flotillas of E-boats were brought up to greater strength, and German and Italian submarines deployed for maximum effect.

The convoy itself was indeed a remarkable one, and reflected the importance which Britain still placed on the survival of Malta. The naval escort, designated Force Z, consisted of two sister battleships, *Nelson* and *Rodney* with

Vice-Admiral Sir Neville Syfret, a South African, flying his flag in *Nelson*. With him was an aircraft carrier squadron under Rear-Admiral A.L.St.G. Lyster, flying his flag in *Indomitable*, with *Victorious* and *Eagle;* even the names of the capital ships seemed to reflect the mood of the moment. The carrier squadron itself was a new departure, as it was the first time in the Royal Navy that three such ships had worked together, and they carried between them a large force of fighters for the defence of the convoy. There were three cruisers with the main escort, *Phoebe, Sirius* and *Charybdis,* each modern and with a strong anti-aircraft gun armament; and the destroyer force was of 14 ships, under Captain R.M.J. Hutton in *Laforey,* leader of the 19th Flotilla. In addition there was a close escort to the merchantmen, designated Force X, which would go through with them all the way to Malta, while Force Z with the valuable heavy ships would have to turn back for Gibraltar, once the Skerki Narrows were reached. Rear-Admiral H.M. Burrough of the 10th Cruiser Squadron commanded the close escort, with his flag in the cruiser *Nigeria.* With him were the cruisers *Kenya, Manchester* and *Cairo,* and 11 destroyers of the 6th Flotilla, led by Captain R. Onslow in *Ashanti.*

There was another small force, consisting of the fleet carrier *Furious* and a destroyer escort. She was to carry a further 38 Spitfires for Malta, and would operate with the fleet until she flew them off, some 500 miles from the island. Last but not least, two fleet oilers, *Brown Ranger* and *Dingledale* would operate independently of the fleet, with their own close escort of destroyers and corvettes under Captain J.E. Broome. A rescue tug, *Jaunty,* would sail with the convoy, and eight submarines from Malta would be on patrol off the Italian naval bases, to attack any units emerging to intercept the convoy.

The merchant ships themselves represented the best

peacetime practice in fast ships, built just before the war: *Wairangi, Waimarama* and *Empire Hope* from the Shaw Savill Line; *Brisbane Star* and *Melbourne Star* from the Blue Star Line; *Dorset* from the Federal Steam Navigation Company; *Port Chalmers* from the Port Line; *Rochester Castle* from the Union Castle Line; *Deucalion* from the Blue Funnel Line; *Clan Ferguson* from the Clan Line; *Glenorchy* from the Glen Line.

With them proudly came three American merchantmen of the same high class; *Santa Elisa* from the Grace Line and *Almeria Lykes* from Lykes Brothers, and last but impressively, the tanker *Ohio* from the Texaco Oil Company. She was taken over by a British crew for this run, and was specially fitted out on the Clyde; her sister ship *Kentucky* had been sunk in one of the previous convoys, and extra seatings were fitted to cushion her main machinery against explosions. So the United States with these three ships made a significant contribution to this great enterprise.

Code-named Pedestal, the convoy assembled in sections, and sailed from the Clyde and from Scapa Flow on August 2. Exercises in operating as a fleet at speed were carried out on the way down to Gibraltar, and the remaining units of the naval escort joined from there and from Freetown as the ships approached the Straits of Gibraltar, and passed into the Mediterranean during the night of August 10. Early next day an Italian submarine sighted the convoy south of Ibiza, and the battle was on. There were 18 Italian submarines on patrol awaiting the convoy, while three German U-boats were also there, with special orders to penetrate the destroyer screens and attack the carriers. *U 73* was in position north of Algiers when the Captain heard propeller noises, came up to periscope depth and sighted the big ships. Although there were seven destroyers between him and his quarry, he managed to attack the carrier *Eagle,* and his full salvo of four torpedoes hit her on her port side. She turned quickly over on to her side, still steaming fast, and slid beneath the waves in under eight minutes. *Eagle* had played a big part in the defence of Malta, and her loss was a sad one, though most of her company were saved.

Later in the morning an Italian submarine made an abortive attack, and shadowing aircraft confirmed that the convoy had been reported. Then a high-level bombing attack was made, but no damage; the anti-aircraft guns of the larger ships fired an impressive barrage overhead. *Furious* flew her Spitfires off to Malta just then, and turned back for Gibraltar with her destroyer escort. In the evening a further attack developed, with 36 Ju 88s, and Heinkel 111s, diving out of the approaching darkness with torpedoes and bombs. Once again the convoy and its escort beat off the attack with gunfire, and escaped damage. It seemed too good to be true. Next morning, August 12, shadowing aircraft circled the convoy early, and an attack by *U 205* was beaten off by the destroyers *Pathfinder* and *Zetland.* Now torpedo and bombing attacks came in at regular intervals, and the fleet was twisting and turning to avoid them, and the anti-aircraft guns were firing almost continuously. Ju 87 dive-bombers attacked *Nelson, Rodney* and *Cairo,* but near-misses were the sum of their efforts. The merchantman *Deucalion* was badly damaged by near-misses, and she dropped out of the convoy, steaming towards the African coast; in more air attacks a torpedo hit her, and she caught fire and blew up.

There were more submarine attacks in late afternoon; *Pathfinder* and *Ithuriel* sank the Italian *Cobalto*, but *Ithuriel* rammed her in the last stages of the action and had to limp back to Gibraltar with damaged bows. Two other submarines were driven off by *Lookout* and *Tartar.* As night drew on, the convoy approached the Skerki Narrows, with surprisingly little loss to that point. The anti-aircraft crews in the ships were exhausted, and the carrier fighters had been almost constantly in the air, while the anti-submarine teams in the destroyers had been ever watchful; their efforts had been well rewarded.

The Germans had, however, planned one more big raid before the nightfall; over 100 bombers approached from Sicily, and they had a strong fighter escort. Italian torpedo bombers came in from a different angle, and the fleet's barrage was quickly in full voice again. First the destroyer *Foresight* was torpedoed in the stern, and had to be sunk by her consort *Tartar*. Then 40 Stuka dive-bombers attacked the fleet carrier *Indomitable;* she disappeared amid great columns of water as the bombs fell, and her guns could be seen firing defiantly amid them, but three bombs struck the flight deck, and blazing petrol was swilling over the deck. The carrier turned away downwind to fight the flames, shepherded by the cruiser *Charybdis* and some destroyers; it was a heart-breaking moment, for she had been fighting against the special ship-striking wing of the Luftwaffe, and although the enemy fighters outnumbered the carriers' planes by two to one, nine German planes were shot down. In the late evening Admiral Syfret had to turn back with the heavy escort, and Force X and the convoy pressed on into the night. Even then, however, only one merchantman had been lost.

Their good fortune was not to last, and the night was to be made hideous by destruction. The Italian and German E-boats were lying in wait north of Cape Bon, but before the convoy reached them, a further bombing and torpedo attack came in from Sicily, and this one struck home. The cruiser flagship *Nigeria* was hit by a torpedo under her bridge, and the cruiser *Cairo* was hit in the stern. Another torpedo hit the vital tanker *Ohio*. The convoy was in trouble. *Nigeria's* steering gear had jammed, and she was circling out of control. Admiral Burrough transferred his flag reluctantly to the destroyer *Ashanti*, and after emergency repairs, *Nigeria* steamed back towards Gibraltar at 14 knots, escorted by three destroyers. *Cairo* was in a worse state, her crew was taken off, and she was sunk by gunfire. As Admiral Burrough was out of touch for the moment, *Kenya* took over command of the convoy, and some emergency turns were ordered; but this was not easy in the darkness, and with the remaining ten destroyers largely busy tending the damaged ships, for a while the merchantmen lost their tight formation.

Then yet another formation of Ju 88s came in for a low-level attack, with 20 aircraft. One torpedo hit *Brisbane Star* forward, and she lurched out of control across the path of the convoy. *Empire Hope* stopped to avoid ramming her, and in this state she was attacked and hit by three dive-bombers. Her petrol cargo caught alight, and she was soon burning fiercely. *Clan Ferguson* was hit by a stick of bombs, and blew up. Now the battle was really on. Two of the close escort cruisers had gone, and three merchantmen, while two others, including the valuable *Ohio,* lay stopped and badly damaged. Ten destroyers remained of the original 14. Admiral Syfret, on his way back to Gibraltar, sent back the cruiser *Charybdis* and two destroyers, but they would not arrive before dawn. Then the cruiser *Kenya* had a scare. A torpedo from the Italian submarine *Alagi* hit her in the bows, though by skilful handling the cruiser missed two more. The damage was not bad, and she soon rejoined her cruiser consort *Manchester* at the head of the convoy. The crew of the tanker *Ohio* made desperate efforts to get her under way again; late that evening they succeeded, and the destroyer *Ledbury* came to guide her back to the convoy. The latter, however, was running into more trouble.

The ships had reached the area north of Cape Bon and

three destroyers now led the convoy with high-speed mine-sweeping gear streamed, as it was thought — and correctly — that the Italians could have laid a special minefield there for them. Many mines were cut by the sweeps, and some of the ships missed these cut mines narrowly as they floated past. At this time, the convoy consisted of the two cruisers, *Ashanti* and two merchant ships; the others were out of visual touch, after the events of the evening.

The E-boats struck next, and the night was soon filled with parachute flares and lines of tracer from the British ships. 19 E-boats in all were waiting in the area, and they made their attacks very effectively, coming in from both sides of the convoy. The cruiser *Manchester* was struck by a torpedo under her forward guns soon after one o'clock, both engine rooms were flooded, and she stopped helpless in the water. The American *Santa Elisa*, which had lost touch with the main body, was also torpedoed, and her petrol cargo went up with a roar. Her consort *Almeria Lykes* was also hit and sank shortly afterwards, as were *Wairangi* and *Rochester Castle;* but although the latter was heavily damaged forward, her crew managed to get her under way again, and worked her back up to 13 knots. Of the E-boat force, eight Italian and two German boats had inflicted all this damage on the convoy, without any of their own boats being lost.

As dawn came, Admiral Burrough had with him two cruisers, as *Charybdis* joined, and seven destroyers, with five of the precious merchant ships. The Italian Fleet was expected to come out on this day, and the outlook was hardly a good one. Two Italian cruiser divisions did in fact put to sea, but some skilful double bluff on the radio by Wellington bomber crews from Malta during the night persuaded them to put back to port. The British submarine *Unbroken* intercepted them, and hit two of the cruisers, which strugged into port.

Ohio and *Ledbury* regained visual touch with the convoy
early in the morning, and long-range Spitfires and Beaufighters from Malta arrived over the convoy; but this good
news was offset by the fact that *Nigeria* and *Cairo* had been
fitted as the fighter direction ships, and in their absence,
contact with the fighters from Malta could not be made.
Nearly 200 miles still remained between the convoy and
Malta, but they had just passed the island of Pantellaria.
Air attacks soon resumed from the Sicilian airfields, now so
close by, and in the first one *Waimarama* was hit, her petrol
cargo caught fire, and a gigantic pyre of smoke and flame
erupted from her. The destroyer *Ledbury* dashed in to
carry out a daring rescue of some of her crew, and the rest
of the convoy steamed on by, with the merchantmen
formed up in two columns.

At half past nine a heavy attack by 60 Stuka dive-
bombers developed, and they concentrated on hitting
Ohio. A very near miss forward was followed by a damaged
Stuka crashing into the ship forward of the bridge, though a
bomb still on board the aircraft luckily did not explode. She
steamed on, but her luck was too good to last. The bombers
were dropping torpedoes, another kind which circled, and
parachute mines; and soon *Ohio* received a very near miss
from a bomb, which stopped her. More and more bombs
rained down around her, until it seemed impossible that
she could survive, but her crew fought back valiantly.
Ohio, however, stopped, and lay dead in the water. *Dorset*
too had been stopped by a stick of bombs, and lay helpless
not far away.

An Italian torpedo bomber attack came in, and *Kenya*
was almost hit again, but she extinguished an engine room
fire, and was soon back in station. The merchantman *Port
Chalmers* picked up a torpedo in her paravane wires; she
went slowly astern, and the torpedo exploded as the wire
was cut. She had been very lucky. The fight to save *Ohio*

went on. Her own gunners were aided by those of *Ledbury*, who stood by as the tanker's crew fought to get their ship under way yet again. *Penn* arrived, and *Ledbury* was sent off to look for survivors from the damaged cruiser *Manchester*, which had in fact sunk during the night. Efforts were made to have *Penn* tow the tanker, but steel plates hanging down from her hull made towing next to impossible, and then in a further close air attack, a bomb hit *Ohio* amidships, just below the waterline. *Penn* came alongside and took off her crew, but stood by the abandoned tanker.

At mid-day the main part of the convoy came at last under the protection of the close-range Spitfires from Malta, and the German and Italian planes shied away. During the afternoon, the Malta minesweepers *Rye* and *Speedy* came out with motor launches to assist, and Admiral Burrough withdrew his escorting warships to the westwards late in the day, leaving the survivors of the convoy to cover the last leg of their journey with the local escort. In the evening they passed into Grand Harbour, *Melbourne Star, Port Chalmers,* and *Rochester Castle;* only *Ohio* with her escort remained outside, as the struggle desperately went on to get her into harbour. The tanker was still resisting efforts to tow her in. The destroyers *Penn, Bramham* and *Ledbury* were doing their utmost, with the minesweeper *Rye,* but just as the other merchantmen entered Grand Harbour, yet another German air attack fell on the little convoy, still out to the south of the island. The tanker was hit yet again, over the engine room, and she had to be abandoned. Astern of her, *Dorset* had also been struggling to get in, but she too was hit, by three bombs, and sunk so close to her destination.

During the night *Penn* tried again to tow *Ohio,* but without success; but in the morning further efforts by the exhausted crews were more successful. The Germans had still not given up, however, and during the morning there was a further heavy attack by dive-bombers; but this time the shore-based Spitfires, still operating at a disadvantage as the ships could not communicate with them, beat off the attack. In spite of their best efforts, a bomb fell in the wake of the tanker, shaking her up badly yet again. Still the tanker's crew kept her going, with less than 50 miles to go. In the evening the coast of Malta was clearly in sight, from the decks of the little group of ships, and the towing went on steadily throughout the night, in spite of a scare that E-boats might be attacking yet again. They even had to edge the tanker clear of a friendly minefield, but at dawn more tugs came out from Grand Harbour, and slowly but surely *Ohio* was nursed along the approach channel, and through the harbour entrance. The Maltese people had been waiting with bated breath, hearing on the radio of the great battles taking place to the westward. As the first three merchantmen passed into Grand Harbour, they were greeted by scenes of unrestrained joy. The entire population seemed to be lining the ramparts and every vantage point, as the deeply laden ships passed inwards through the breakwater, and as the ships passed below the two Barracca Gardens, great cheers rang across the water, and bands were playing and flags waving everywhere. Even Lord Gort, the Governor, was down on the ramparts with the people, sharing in the relief and gladness.

When *Ohio* came slowly into the harbour, with her faithful three destroyers and the minesweepers, there was a further great demonstration of gladness by the people. As the escorts passed by, their guns were still pointing up into the sky, their crews still beside them stripped to the waist, and surrounded by piles of empty shellcases. They cheered the people back in their turn, and this must have been one of the most moving moments of the war. As *Ohio* was nursed gently up the harbour, her decks were almost awash, but her cargo was largely intact. She was secured alongside the sunken *Plumleaf* at Parlatorio Wharf, and she came gently to rest on the bottom as she was berthed. Her oil cargo was then pumped out quickly to oiltanks beneath the rock, where the bombers could not reach it.

So Pedestal came to Malta, and the island's people with the defending forces lost no time in unloading the precious stores. The same remarkable organisation that had been tested with Harpoon went into action — day and night unloading without rest, an endless chain of trucks to take the stores away inland, and roads lined with shaded lights at night to speed them on their way. 12,000 tons of oil fuel, 3,600 tons of diesel fuel, and 32,000 tons of general cargo — that was the prize for which the gallant men of the convoy had fought and died.

There was one more incident to close the story of this great convoy. The merchantman *Brisbane Star* had been damaged earlier in the battle, but her crew had carried on by themselves, once they managed to restart her main engines. Now, after a string of adventures along the French coast, which included outwitting a German U-boat, she approached Malta proudly on her own, but with a personal escort of Spitfires. Triumphantly she came up Grand Harbour soon after *Ohio* had been brought in; she was down by the head with damage, and some of her holds were flooded, but she delivered most of her vital cargo intact to Malta.

Operation Pedestal
The merchantmen

Deucalion	Sunk
Empire Hope	Sunk
Clan Ferguson	Sunk
Santa Elisa	Sunk
Glenorchy	Sunk
Almeria Lykes	Sunk

Wairangi	Sunk
Waimarama	Sunk
Dorset	Sunk
Ohio	Damaged – Arrived
Brisbane Star	Damaged – Arrived
Melbourne Star	Damaged – Arrived
Port Chalmers	Damaged – Arrived
Rochester Castle	Damaged – Arrived

Warship losses during the convoy

Sunk

Eagle	Fleet aircraft carrier	Force Z
Manchester	Cruiser	Force X
Cairo	Cruiser	Force X
Foresight	Destroyer	Force Z

Damaged

Indomitable	Fleet aircraft carrier	Force Z
Kenya	Cruiser	Force X
Nigeria	Cruiser	Force X
Ithuriel	Destroyer	Force Z

The supplies fought through with Pedestal did not themselves raise the siege, but they did allow an increase in the people's rations, and they brought fresh hope for the future. The convoy had included much of the desperately needed food, to relieve the siege conditions, and it had also delivered fuel for the fighters, the strike bombers and the submarines, and ammunition – torpedoes, cannon shells, and large supplies for the heavy anti-aircraft guns.

The Rome correspondent of the *Tribune de Genève* carried this report a few days later: 'No further attempts to neutralise Malta will be made for the present – the Axis Command considers that the supplies which got through with the last great convoy have assured an effective resistance by the island for some time to come. The German and Italian Air Forces in the Mediterranean are now being diverted to the defending of convoys from Italy and Sicily to Libya and Egypt, against increasing Allied attacks'.

So Malta's defenders and people survived. The Royal Navy sympathised with them, all the way through their ordeal. On September 4 the Commander-in-Chief in Alexandria sent a telegram to the Governor, expressing the congratulations of the whole Mediterranean Fleet to the people of the island, on the occasion of yet another anniversary of the Great Siege of Malta in the 16th century.

It was to be three months more before the siege was to be finally lifted by the November convoy. In the meantime the great force of Spitfires now based on the island had the Axis air raids under control, the anti-aircraft box barrage was no longer rationed on ammunition and was in full voice again, and no serious damage was being inflicted on the cities.

Now that some fuel was available, it was even possible to use some for sending in trucks to start clearing the narrow streets of rubble, and to untangle the demolished cranes and workshops in the dockyard. A start was made on clearing some of the wrecks, but it would be the following spring before the specialised equipment could be shipped in to tackle this immense task in earnest. Among the ships dealt with at this time was the little old harbour tug *Ancient,* twice sunk by bombing and now raised yet again, and taken in hand for her third complete refit in two years.

There was an average of no more than 50 raids a month in this period, except for the brief German offensive in October; and perhaps most wonderful of all, there were 20 raid-free nights in September, and even 26 a month by the end of the year.

Away from the island's fighter range however, the Axis Air Forces still flew in control of the seas, and so it was the long-range submarines which kept the supplies still trickling in − *Proteus, Rorqual, Parthian, Porpoise, Clyde, Traveller* and *Thrasher* all made trips to Malta in the closing months of the year.

The 10th Submarine Flotilla continued its successful strikes against the convoys, making 27 attacks in October. In retaliation, on a few nights E-boats were active in laying mines in the approaches to Grand Harbour. They were engaged by the shore batteries, and the Malta sweepers were kept busy clearing the swept channels, but mining casualties were by this time a rare occurrence. In September the sweepers' bag topped the 300 mark, and while ground mines laid by parachute became rarer as the raids were reduced, moored contact mines continued to be found right through to the end of the year. On October 29 the 3rd Flotilla of motor launches swept their 100th mine, crowning a remarkable sweeping effort.

As the time of the great land battle of El Alamein in October approached, the Axis Air Forces stepped up their attacks on Malta, hoping to neutralise the striking forces, as the Axis convoys in their turn struggled to get through. In that month alone they lost 40 per cent of their supplies en route, and this was a critical factor in the desert battle.

Ju 88 bombers and Me 109 fighters fought fierce battles every day over the island with the Spitfires and the anti-aircraft guns; 1,400 sorties were flown against Malta in the first week of October, and 114 Axis aircraft were shot down, for the loss of 27 Spitfires. The number of raids during the month climbed again to 152, though these were mostly by day, and fought at a great height. By the third week of the month, as they were making no impression on the strongly-defended island, the bombers were removed to land operations farther north, and the raids were carried out by fast fighter-bombers, though with no great success. The air offensive was called off, and to this point Malta had cost the Axis some 1,500 planes definitely shot down, and a further 500 damaged. Even then the defenders could not relax. On December 18 a raid of 30 German bombers attacked the airfield at Luqa, and destroyed nine Wellington bombers and four Spitfires on the ground.

Then it came — the final convoy which really did raise the siege. Called Operation Stoneage, or more prosaically MW 13, it sailed from Alexandria on November 19 with four merchantmen, the 15th Cruiser Squadron and 16 destroyers. All four of the cargo ships, *Robin Locksley*, *Denbighshire*, *Mormacmoon* and *Bantam*, arrived safely though one old friend of Malta, the cruiser *Penelope*, was badly damaged on the way and had to be towed back to Alexandria in a full gale. The cruiser *Euryalus* and ten *Hunt* Class destroyers entered Grand Harbour with the merchantmen, and this sight again gave to the people of Malta a chance to greet the navy and the relieving supply ships; the bastions and every vantage point were crowded with cheering people. As *Euryalus* entered harbour, with her Royal Marine band playing on the quarterdeck, she saluted HMS *St Angelo* as in pre-war days and then, as she drew abreast the famous old Custom House, her ship's company stood to attention, and the band played the Maltese Hymn — a very moving moment for all who saw it, and the Royal Navy's tribute to an heroic and friendly people.

The unloading of these ships followed the pattern of Pedestal; the precious cargo was not to be lost again. At the unloading berths lighters and plentiful willing hands were ready; queues of trucks waited to carry the food inland to distribution centres, and the navy staff controlling the operation slept no more than two hours in every 24 over a period of five days.

The convoy was still supplemented by further fast supply runs; *Welshman* came in from Gibraltar, and her sister ship *Manxman* arrived from Port Said escorted by six destroyers. The cruiser-minelayer *Adventure* brought supplies out from England to Gibraltar, for *Welshman* to pick up for a second fast dash through. This was a fitting climax to *Welshman's* contribution to Malta, as sadly she was to be torpedoed and sunk three months later on her way from Malta to Alexandria.

In North Africa, British forces captured Bardia and Tobruk, and the convoy situation from the east at last looked secure. On October 26 the great victory at El Alemain was won by General Montgomery and his armies, and the British forces quickly advanced westwards.

The Allies now built up their offensive in the Mediterranean, and Operation Torch, the invasion of North Africa was launched; in this Malta was able to turn eagerly to her first real offensive role. No wonder was it that the Italian naval staff were to record that the island was the rock on which their hopes in the Mediterranean foundered.

The 10th Submarine Flotilla was joined at Malta by two others, and a total of 20 submarines were operating out of the island. Five of the boats based there were lost in this landing operation; their role was to prevent the Italian Navy from interfering in the landings.

The Fleet Air Arm planes from Hal Far continued their sorties, and they also manned Hurricanes which carried out intruder operations over Sicily.

Now with the siege ended, the main effort was in building stocks up in Malta, and the rations of the Maltese people were at last restored to a reasonable level. Lord Gort wrote at this time to Lord Cranborne, the Secretary of State for the Colonies, and his thoughts were already turning to the future. In particular he pointed out the need for a big emigration programme after the war, as it was clear to him that the islands could not possibly support the ever-increasing population. It was a problem which was exercising the minds of many of the more far-seeing Maltese. Almost as an afterthought, Gort reassured Cranborne that the recent increase in the air attacks had if anything increased the people's morale, by taking their minds off their continual hunger and weakness. More food stocks were still urgently needed to increase the rations and restore the people's strength.

The next convoy to be run through was named Portcullis, arriving in December from Alexandria with no trouble. The five merchantmen including a tanker were escorted by four cruisers and 14 destroyers – still a fleet-size operation. It was a sign of the times that Grand Harbour was too congested to receive all these ships without first sailing nine empty ships in ballast, escorted by a cruiser and 11 destroyers. The *Hunt* Class ships, with their good anti-aircraft armament, were as always prominent in these movements. Then a series of four convoys, called Quadrangle, was carried through. Each convoy included two merchantmen, with a somewhat smaller escort, and the last two arrived over the Christmas holiday. These December convoys brought to the island their welcome Christmas present of 77,000 tons of cargo. An American merchant ship which was in Grand Harbour over the holiday brought the spirit of goodwill with her. The crew asked that their turkey dinners be given to the children of Maltese ratings in *St Angelo* and in the harbour tugs, and 70 children sat down to a bumper Christmas dinner that year.

A force of 27 submarines was by this time making strikes from Malta, and they carried out 26 attacks in December. Better still, Force K was back and working in full strength, sailing to protect arriving and departing convoys, and carrying out strikes against Axis shipping. Two comments in the Italian war diary show how successful the Malta striking forces had become. The Chief of the Italian General Staff, Marshall Cavallero, wrote that it was a problem of life and death — if Malta was not neutralised, they would lose everything. Count Ciano in the government recorded that Italian shipping had been reduced by the attacks to one million tons; at that rate the African problem would automatically end in six months, since they would have no more ships with which to supply Libya.

What a year that had been for Malta! What a change from the early months of the year! From very heavy air raids, frequent sinkings of warships in the harbour, then the evacuation of all shipping, to siege conditions, near starvation and almost to surrender; then heroic convoys arriving, the building up of the Spitfire force, and the year ending with ample food supplies and Malta on the offensive.

Captain Simpson, who had led the 10th Submarine Flotilla so brilliantly for two long, hard years, left Malta at the turn of the year, and was able to record that in that short period submarines of his flotilla had sunk over half a million tons of enemy shipping, including five cruisers, eight destroyers, eight submarines, eight liners, eight tankers, 65 merchant ships, and 27 other ships and craft, ranging from armed merchant cruisers to schooners and a floating dock. Another 250,000 tons, including two battleships and four more cruisers, had been damaged; and the achievements of Force K and the bombers were in addition to this formidable list. Lord Gort also 'recorded triumphantly at this time the real weight of the attack which the Maltese people and their defences had withstood. 13,750 tons of bombs had rained down in less than a year, and mainly on the crowded cities around Grand Harbour. 1,104 Maltese had been killed (one in 70 of the population) and 75 per cent of the houses in Valletta had been destroyed or damaged. There was an estimated one and a half million tons of debris from the raids lying in the streets of Valletta and Floriana alone, and the people were largely living in underground shelters, of which there were nearly 1,500 in operation — giving four square feet of space to each person. Here was the triumphant justification for the great battle to keep Malta in British hands, for the great fleet actions fought with heavy losses to get the convoys through, and for the great privations which the people and garrison of Malta had been asked to bear. Whatever the lack of preparations before the war, the Allied forces amply made up for it by their valiant efforts during the battles of 1941 and 1942. No wonder that at Christmas 1942 the great churches of Malta were full of thanksgiving worshippers, and no wonder that 1943 seemed a bright prospect.

CHAPTER 11

Malta turns to the offensive, January-June 1943

Rarely in history can there have been so rapid a turn-round in the fortunes of a fortress. In less than a year the situation had moved from the desperate convoy battles, to the island becoming the springboard for the invasion of Sicily. Even in Britain there had been a longer build-up period between the turning of the tide and the assault on Normandy. The year opened with the pressure on the Italian supply route to North Africa building up to its climax. Force K and Force B continued their strikes from Malta, with the cruisers *Cleopatra*, *Euryalus* and *Orion* (forming the 15th Cruiser Squadron) supported by big fleet destroyers, usually including *Jervis*, *Javelin* and *Kelvin*. The Fleet Air Arm squadrons and the RAF bombers also stepped up their attacks still further, and the United States 12th Air Force, newly arrived in North Africa, added the weight of their Flying Fortresses to the attacks on the Italian naval bases. The submarines kept up their effective strikes, and the ten boats of the *U* Class, forming the now famous 10th Submarine Flotilla, were joined by some bigger boats of the *S* and *T* Classes.

The result of this co-ordinated campaign was that of the 51 ships sailed from Italian ports in January, less than half arrived in North Africa; and of the 24 ships sunk, the submarines claimed 11 and the surface forces four. A third surface force, dubbed Force Q, of cruisers and destroyers joined in from their newly-captured base at Bone, and they worked in close co-operation with all the forces working from Malta. A new initiative in Malta was the establishment of a motor-torpedo boat base; the previous one had been destroyed in the bombing, but a new one, fittingly named HMS *Gregale*, after the strong wind that blows up suddenly at Malta, was opened at the end of February, and MTBs operating from it joined in the attacks on the Axis shipping.

The Italians were still attempting to get supply convoys through to North Africa, where the German and Italian Armies were under great pressure from the Allied forces advancing from both east and west. Every available ship was pressed into service, including many merchant ships from Vichy-controlled France, but the losses continued to mount, and in February and March out of 78 ships sailed for Tunisia, only 41 arrived, and some of them in a damaged condition.

While all this was going on, and showing all too clearly the reversal in the fortunes of Malta, convoys were passed through regularly to the island from Alexandria. Still strongly supported by destroyers in case the Italian Fleet sought to intervene, the convoys all arrived in safety, to build up the supplies on the islands to adequate levels. The convoy MH 8 left Alexandria on March 1 with three store-ships and two tankers, while MW 21 followed, to land 28,000 tons of stores, MW 22 with 20,500 tons of general cargo, and MW 23 with 18,000 tons, mostly of fuel. The destroyer escorts were drawn from the 12th Flotilla of the war-built *P* Class, and also from the hard-working little ships of the *Hunt* Class.

In February Admiral Sir Andrew Cunningham returned from his shore post in Washington to take up command again of the Mediterranean Fleet, and later of the naval assault forces for the invasion of Sicily. Admiral Harwood had been in poor health, and returned home while Vice-Admiral Sir Ralph Leatham, who was already acting as Governor in Lord Gort's absence, also stood in for Cunningham until he could arrive. His return was welcomed by the ships' companies, and his dashing style was soon in evidence. He travelled about his command in a Beaufighter which was specially allocated to him, and his pilot became well-known – especially for a landing at Luqa which turned out to be much too fast. The preparations for the invasion started in earnest; Vice-Admiral H. Kent Hewitt, US Navy, commanded all American naval forces in the Mediterranean, and Vice-Admiral Stuart Bonham-Carter was the energetic Vice-Admiral (Malta). The harbour at Valletta was already thronged with ships, compared with just a few months before; ships of the two surface forces, submarines and smaller craft were constantly on the move, and the cruiser-minelayer *Abdiel,* a sister-ship of Malta's old friend *Welshman,* was working from Grand Harbour laying mines in the Sicilian Channel; in this some of the MTBs joined her. *Abdiel* laid her mines in the dark and at high speed; on one occasion she steamed at 35 knots into a heavy swell, accompanied by the destroyers *Lightning* and *Loyal.*

In April the attacks on the Axis convoys reached their peak; in that month the casualty rate ran at 60 per cent of the ships sailed, with others damaged by air raids in harbour. Supplies were not getting through to the Axis Armies in North Africa, which were steadily falling back under the Allied assault, and General Rommel was re-called to Germany.

With astonishing courage and perseverance, some Axis ships still made the attempt. Not only merchant ships but destroyers too tried desperately to get supplies through; and the forces from Malta and Bone continued to take a heavy toll of them. This could not go on, and the last surface action of its kind took place during the dark hours of May 3, when part of Force K, the destroyers *Nubian, Paladin* and *Petard* sank a supply ship of 8,000 tons off Cape Bon. Three more supply ships did try to get through a few days later, but although they succeeded in reaching the North African coast, they found that all the ports had been captured by the Allies, and they had nowhere to go; as they steamed up the coast trying to find a refuge, they were attacked and destroyed by Allied aircraft.

Now the stage was set for the final drama in North Africa. Cut off from all their supplies, the Axis Armies were hemmed in on the Cape Bon peninsula, and the Royal Navy was determined that there should be no evacuation to Sicily. In the aptly-named Operation Retribution all available destroyers – even those escorting the convoys from Alexandria to Malta – were called to the Sicilian Channel to intercept any Axis craft trying to escape. In a triumphant signal, Admiral Cunningham ordered: 'Sink, burn, and destroy. Let nothing pass'. The Axis forces were in no position to contest this hard-fought stretch of sea any longer. Small craft, motor boats, sailing and rowing boats and rubber dinghies did set out from the shores of Cape Bon, and from them some 1,000 prisoners were taken, while none got through to Sicily. The British destroyer crews enjoyed this operation, which they in their turn dubbed the Kelibiah Regatta. A German hospital ship carrying 240 patients was captured, and brought safely into Grand Harbour. It was all over; on May 12 the Axis Armies surrendered in North Africa, and prisoners taken totalled a quarter of a million. The church bells in Malta rang out for the first time since Italy declared war in 1940, to celebrate the final triumph of the Allied forces. Now another happy event took place – the first through convoy from Gibraltar to Alexandria since the early days of the war.

As soon as the Axis Armies had surrendered, a large minesweeping force was assembled at Malta, to clear a channel through the Sicilian Narrows where Axis mines had long made the passage of convoys hazardous. The minesweepers were British; Captain J.W. Boutwood in a brilliant operation led the 12th and 13th fleet sweeping flotillas, two flotillas of motor minesweepers and three groups of minesweeping trawlers. Together they cleared a channel two miles wide and 200 miles long, from the Galita Channel through to Sousse, and on to Tripoli. They swept 190 moored contact mines, and in the course of their clearance *MMS 89* was sunk by striking a mine, and the fleet sweeper *Fantome* lost her stern to another.

The first through convoy, KMS 14X, sailed from Gibraltar on May 17, and arrived at the other end safely nine days later. In the meantime, just to show that they were still in business, the Italians laid a small field of contact mines just outside Grand Harbour. Malta's minesweeping force still consisted of the same hard-working ships, and three of the motor launches of the 3rd Flotilla carried out a shallow skim sweep ahead of the four fleet sweepers, as they tackled the field four miles off St Elmo on May 15. They cut and sank three moored mines quickly, but a fourth got through and was struck by the flotilla leader *Speedy;* she was badly damaged, and suffered some casualties, but was towed safely in.

Axis air raids on Malta also continued on a regular basis. The growing fighter force based there was able to keep the raiders away from Grand Harbour, and usually no damage was done; but in a raid on May 21 by 36 Fw 190 fighter bombers, escorted by Me 109 fighters, three Fleet Air Arm Albacore aircraft were destroyed on the ground at Hal Far. Perhaps the Germans wanted to show their concern at the activities of the navy planes, for they made 30 sorties in the month of May, and sank a 10,000-ton tanker and a 4,000-ton supply ship with their bombs, and their minelaying closed the port of Catania in Sicily.

During the first half of 1943, a separate but very important operation was being carried out in Grand Harbour, in preparation for the invasion of Sicily. Before the harbour could accommodate the invasion fleet, the wreckage of the dockyard had to be cleared away, and the berths and drydocks brought back into full use. As the Director of Plans at the Admiralty noted on January 23: 'Malta remains the key to the Mediterranean, as long as the war continues'.

It was a horrifying salvage problem which had to be tackled. The large salvage team which was assembled did not have time on their side, as the assault date had been set for early July. All five drydocks had been put out of action, with ships destroyed inside or the gates and walls badly damaged by bombs. In March some of the wrecks blocking the approach channel to No 2 drydock were cleared away, so that it could be used by shallow draft ships, and by *Hunt* Class destroyers in fine weather. In No 4, the water was pumped out and the wreck of the fleet destroyer *Kingston*, which had been blown on to its beam ends, was patched up and removed in two sections. Bad cracks were found in many of the dock walls. In spite of the extent of the damage, however, by June four of the five drydocks had been patched and could be used again.

The berths for ships to moor alongside were in no better shape. Every single one was out of action; Hamilton Wharf was blocked by the wrecks of two submarines, and Boiler Wharf by the destroyer *Legion*. The sunken oiler *Plumleaf* at Parlatorio Wharf had platforms built over her decks at water level, to enable ships to berth alongside her. Even when the wrecks had been moved, the quay walls all required a survey to see if they were safe, and as long as the air attacks continued, divers could not be sent down to do this work. The wharves were blocked with the wreckage of bombed sheds and cranes, and motor transport could not get close to them. The dockyard machinery was in a rather better state, as much had been done in excavating underground workshops; by early 1943 a quarter of all the machine tools in operation were underground. Replacement machinery was ordered from Britain, but losses occurred during the passage of convoys, and supplies were piling on the quays at Alexandria awaiting shipment to Malta. Two coastal salvage vessels completing in Britain were sent to Malta, and the South African Navy's salvage vessel *Gamtoos* arrived early in the year, and did great clearance work, not least on the wreck of the destroyer *Maori* in mid-harbour. Ths floating crane had been sunk, so a 60-ton derrick crane was hurried over from the United States. 'Camels' of 80 tons, giant flotation tubes for lifting sunken wrecks, were sent to the island since the time was just not available to disperse many of the wrecks with explosives.

On June 20 King George VI visited Malta. Only a year had passed since its people had been on the point of starvation and surrender, and its harbours had been unsafe for any warships; now it was considered entirely safe for the king to make a visit to the heroic island, a demonstration yet again of the swiftness with which the fortress' fortunes had changed. The king was visiting his forces in North Africa, and asked Admiral Cunningham if he could visit Malta. The Admiral jumped at the opportunity, and an impressive ceremony was quickly arranged. The cruiser *Aurora* which under Captain W.G. Agnew had been so active in the defence of Malta was chosen as the king's ship, and she was escorted by four fleet destroyers of Force K, *Jervis*, *Eskimo*, *Lookout* and *Nubian*. The little squadron steamed overnight from Algiers and arrived at the entrance to Grand Harbour at dawn. As the ships approached a strong umbrella of fighters circled overhead, and the minesweeping force met the ships and swept them in.

For security reasons the visit had been kept a secret until very early in the morning, but by the time that *Aurora* passed through the arms of the breakwater, all the ramparts and quays and the Lower and Upper Barracca Gardens were packed with cheering people, waving British and Maltese flags. *Aurora* was flying an enormous royal standard, and a special platform had been built forward of the bridge, so that the king could stand there in the warm morning sunshine and be seen by all. The church bells were ringing, and the scene was reminiscent of the arrival of the Pedestal convoy. The king was received at the Custom House steps by the Governor, Lord Gort, with Vice-Admiral Arthur Power, previously ashore at Malta during some of the worst of the siege, and now returned as Lieutenant Governor of the islands. Then the king made a detailed tour of the bombed cities, walking informally among the people, and escorted by the Rev. Canon Emmanuel Brincat, Archpriest of Senglea. Everywhere he went, there were great demonstrations of joy and affection, and the day was a moving one for all who were present. He took lunch with the Governor in the Verdala Palace, and in the evening he re-embarked in *Aurora*, and the squadron departed for Tripoli. It had been a great day for the island. Perhaps it was an indication of the changing perception of Malta in Britain that this was the first visit by a British monarch to Malta since Edward VII had landed there in 1903; belatedly, at least, the importance of the island and the heroism of its people had been recognised.

CHAPTER 12

Sicily invaded, and Italy surrenders, July-December 1943

The preparations for the invasion had been started early in the year. The first essential condition was that Malta should be re-established as an operating base for large naval forces, including battleships and aircraft carriers. Work on restoring the dockyard to full efficiency was pushed ahead at full speed, and most of the wrecks had been cleared, and much of the damage to the quays and the dockyard machinery made good, by the time the invasion armada started to assemble. A major base for all types of landing craft had to be established in Grand Harbour, and special repair facilities provided for them including light drydocks. Malta was to be a main base for the landing of casualties too; the army's wounded would be taken in other directions, in 12 hospital ships and six hospital carriers, but all the warships would return their wounded to Malta. The island would also be used as a main fuelling base, especially in the vital period D-3 to D+16. As much as 25,000 tons of oil fuel and 1,000 tons of coal were specially shipped out there for this purpose; two large oil tankers were stationed there, with smaller tankers carrying special blends. Over 650 ships were to refuel at the island in that brief period. All the warships would replenish their stocks of ammunition there. To give an idea of the magnitude of this one item, for the British warships alone the following stock would be needed, and they do not include the main armament needs of the battleships and cruisers:

4.7-inch (destroyers)	50,000 rounds
2-pounder pom pom	350,000 rounds
20 mm Oerlikon	500,000 rounds

0.5-inch machine-guns	230,000 rounds
Torpedoes	330 rounds
Depth charges	3,000 rounds

All damaged warships were to return to Malta for repair, and all landing craft on release from the beaches, and especially the valuable Landing Craft, Tank, would re-assemble there. The big personnel ships of the assault convoys were to land their troops at the beaches, and then return to Malta, where the reserve troops were held. To provide the material for this operation, many convoys arrived in the months before the invasion was launched on July 10. The anchorages around Grand Harbour filled up once again with ships, but now they were of many types.

The battleships and aircraft carriers were to return for the first time since 1941 − famous names, *Nelson, Warspite, Formidable* and *Illustrious* (fresh from her repairs in the United States); cruisers and destroyers in profusion, and landing craft massed in the narrow creeks until it was almost possible to walk from one shore to the other across their decks. More significantly still, the Stars and Stripes of the United States flew proudly in many places among the myriad White Ensigns, and this partnership of the two great navies was to show remarkable standards of friendship and co-operation in this operation.

Admiral Sir Andrew Cunningham shifted his head-quarters from Algiers to Malta on July 3. He arrived in the cruiser *Uganda* with his staff, and took up residence in Admiralty House with the Vice-Admiral (Malta) Arthur Power. He resumed his old office in Lascaris Bastion, overlooking Grand Harbour and *St Angelo,* and his flag once more flew proudly from the saluting base on the ramparts. His operations room was in a tunnel dug deep in the bastion from the soft sandstone, and there was a big wall chart showing the sea and air operations. This head-quarters was in 1978 restored by the Maltese Government, and will remain as one of the memorials on the island. A week later General Eisenhower and General Alexander arrived for the final planning; General Montgomery joined them soon after.

The opening moves in the invasion itself were made by stealth. Submarines of the 10th Flotilla sailed with naval reconnaissance parties, to land them by night in folding canoes on the invasion beaches, to test the soil for the assaulting forces. *United* sailed first in February on such a mission, and *Unrivalled* in March. For the assault, 25 RAF squadrons would be based at Malta, and to handle them, an additional 6,050 ground crew were shipped in, with 750 vehicles, to join the crowded airfields. Many raids were made on Sicily from Malta before the assault, and Luqa, Ta'Qali and Hal Far had never known such busy days.

Three small Italian islands are located in the sea around Malta, and they needed to be captured before the landings; these minor operations were conducted by the Royal Navy with energy and humour, in Operation Corkscrew. First to fall, on June 11, was Pantellaria. For three weeks previously four cruisers and eight destroyers operating from Malta had bombarded this island, as it was the most important of the three. General Eisenhower and Admiral Cunningham embarked in the cruiser *Aurora* at Bone, and went to watch; Winston Churchill wanted to come out to join them, but they advised that it was too risky. On the morning of the assault the weather was calm, and the landing force was swept in by four fleet minesweepers. There was little active opposition, and by 1130 hours white flags were beginning to show ashore. At 1215 hours the Governor sent a message begging to surrender 'through lack of water'. 21,000 people were found on the island, and they had had neither food nor water for three days.

Next to fall was Lampedusa, on the following day. The ships of the 15th Cruiser Squadron were ordered to seize the island with all despatch, and they bombarded it all night. The assault ended in comedy, for the island surrendered quickly – to a Fleet Air Arm Swordfish, which had force-landed there through lack of petrol. A landing craft was sent in with a company of Royal Marines to accept the surrender, and they took 5,000 prisoners. Last of the three to fall was Linosa, where the fleet destroyer *Nubian* landed a small force, who reportedly found the commandant in bed.

An invasion was clearly building up for Sicily, and the Axis forces were alive to it. Motor-torpedo boats from Malta patrolled at night off the Sicilian coast, and on one night had a fierce battle with E-boats based on the island. During this build-up period, air raids were still taking place daily against Malta, but the raiders were often of the light fighter-bomber variety, and the swarms of Allied fighters which now took to the air on every alert ensured that they did little damage.

The minesweepers worked hard to ensure that none of the many warships using the island became casualties. The four faithful fleet sweepers, *Speedy, Hythe, Hebe* and *Rye* were racing each other to be the first to bag 100 mines, and the race was fierce, each ship having a score of over 80 by the end of June.

When the assault was launched, many of the ships came from bases other than Malta – convoys direct from Britain, from North Africa, and from North America. Malta was the vital springboard for the attack, but her harbours could not contain the armada needed for this major leap forward.

First to sail were four submarines of the 10th Flotilla, *Unruffled, Unseen, Unison* and *Unrivalled;* they were to go ahead, submerge off the landing beaches, then as the assault landing craft approached, they were to surface and show beacon lights to guide them in. Soon the complicated series of assault convoy operations was under way. Some convoys steamed directly to the landing beaches, others passed by Malta, to enable their escorts to refuel.

Force H with its battleships, aircraft carriers and destroyers arrived from Gibraltar off the southern Malta swept channel at daylight two days before the assault. Six destroyers from Force K steamed out from the island to relieve the incoming destroyers, which went in fast to Malta to refuel, then dashed out to rejoin. Similar fuelling operations were carried out for several big assault convoys which passed close to Malta, the island's destroyers protecting the big personnel ships, while the smaller ships refuelled. Malta was very congested at this critical time, and it was agreed that the battleships and cruisers would only go in to refuel if they were very short.

Then the warships at Malta took up their invasion stations. Four cruisers sailed on the day before the assault, to protect convoys en route, after which they would bombard enemy positions. Two big convoys of landing craft sailed from Malta on the same day, including 110 Landing Craft, Infantry, heading direct for their landing beaches. As the troops were lifted forward from Malta towards Sicily, the Immediate Reserve Division and a tank brigade arrived at the island direct from Britain. Numbers of fleet minesweepers joined assault convoys as escorts, ready to undertake sweeping operations when they arrived off the beaches.

So the assault went in on July 10; 2,500 ships in all made the journey, and fighters based on Malta destroyed 106 enemy aircraft during this phase. Admiral Cunningham recorded in his despatches that for those who had fought through the Mediterranean campaign from the beginning, it seemed almost magical that great fleets of ships could remain anchored off the enemy's coast, within 40 miles of his airfields, with only slight losses. This was a great time for the Maltese people, as the ships sailed away into the hazy distance to the north. There was much quiet satisfaction in seeing this hard evidence of the turning of the tide. Soon after the assault, many of the attacking warships came streaming back to Malta. The landing craft established a ferry service from the island to the beaches, and later to the captured ports on the mainland. The distance from Malta to the landing beaches was 120 miles there and back, and many of the landing craft made good some remarkable times, like these:

LST	12 hours on passage	10 hours turnround
LCT	18 hours on passage	16 hours turnround
LCI(L)	10 hours on passage	8 hours turnround

Force H sent its First Division of battleships and aircraft carriers back to Malta. Among them was *Warspite,* and this was the first time battleships had been seen in Grand Harbour since December 1940. The fleet carrier *Indomitable* was hit by an aerial torpedo in the assault area on July 15, and the cruiser *Cleopatra* was damaged by a U-boat's torpedo. They were escorted back to Malta for urgent repairs. There was no more heroic story than that of the Royal Marines in *Cleopatra.* The traditional action station for the Marine band was at the transmitting station for the main armament, low down in the ship. When the torpedo hit, the whole band was trapped at its action station, and 11 of them were killed or wounded. The remaining five bandsmen fell in on the quarterdeck as the cruiser limped into Grand Harbour, and they played the ship in as on the calmest peacetime cruise.

The main harbour was becoming crowded again, so the battleships *Valiant* and *Warspite* moved round to Marsaxlokk on July 17, and *Warspite* made a high speed dash from there to bombard Catania, after an urgent call for help.

Two swept channels were established between Malta and Sicily, with one-way traffic north or south. Four big convoys sailed north in the first four days after the initial landings, and General Alexander transferred his headquarters from Malta to Sicily three days afterwards.

As soon as the conquest of Sicily was completed early in September, an assault was quickly launched against Salerno, on the Italian mainland. For this operation many landing craft returned to Malta for quick repairs, and on September 6 the fresh armada sailed for Operation Avalanche. The smaller ships went first, and the big ships of Force H sailed a day later and overtook them. Four battleships and two fleet carriers steered round the south side of Malta and up across the Sicilian channel, keeping out of the way of the massed landing craft.

Admiral Cunningham was concerned that the Admiralty should not withdraw too many warships from his command once Sicily had been taken, since the assault on Salerno was yet to come, and German U-boats were still operating in the area in some numbers. The Americans had withdrawn many of their ships for the urgent Pacific operations, but the Admiralty went along with Cunningham's request for a few months. Four escort carriers were sent through to him, some large troopships were actually returned to him from Britain, and he retained the battleships *Howe* and *King George V*.

However, greater events were already in train. The Italians had started negotiations for an armistice, and this was signed on September 3, though it was not announced until September 8, just as the assault on Salerno was about to go in — and this would seem to have had an effect on the morale of the attacking forces. Included in the armistice terms was the surrender of the Italian Fleet; it was ordered to steam south from its bases, Genoa, Spezia and Taranto, towards Malta. The fleet from the first two ports duly sailed, but the Germans were not prepared to see it go that easily. While the ships were steaming south between

Corsica and Sardinia German aircraft attacked, Ju 88 bombers with radio-controlled glider bombs, and the flagship *Roma* was hit and sank with heavy loss of life, while several other warships were damaged.

The remaining ships steamed towards Malta as they had been instructed, and ships of the Royal Navy hurried to meet them. From Malta came units of Force H; *Warspite* was to bring off a neat double, for she had been present at the surrender of the German Fleet at Scapa Flow in 1918. With them were the fleet carriers, including *Illustrious* (what a sweet moment that was for her ship's company); American warships also came to join in. The Italian naval ports were too distant for RAF fighters to cover the surrendering ships all the way to Malta, but the fighters threw an umbrella over the Italian warships at the limit of their flying range – and that was a strange sight indeed.

On the morning of September 10 Force H sighted the Italian Fleet off Bone. At first the British Fleet steamed parallel with the Italians, 12 miles apart and with all guns trained on them, but when it became clear that the surrender was being carried out as ordered, all guns were trained fore and aft, and the British warships escorted the Italians in silence. There were no messages of greeting, no cheering from the British ships, and it was all rather eerie after the great battles of the past few years. There were six American airmen aboard one of the Italian destroyers; their plane had been shot down off Sardinia, and the Italian ship had picked them up, but they had no idea what they were getting into, and now they watched this historic sight in amazement.

General Eisenhower and Admiral Cunningham embarked at Bizerta in the destroyer *Hambledon* and cruised round the combined fleet, rejoicing in the great moment of triumph, so far from the convoy battles of only a year before. Next day the Italian Fleet anchored off Malta. Only the destroyers wers allowed into Grand Harbour to refuel; all the other ships were kept at anchor outside the break-water and later were dispersed, some led by *Warspite* to St Paul's Bay to the north-west, others to Marsaxlokk on the south-east. Admiral de Zara, the senior Italian officer, landed at the ancient Custom House in Grand Harbour, and was received by a full naval guard of honour. From there he was taken on a somewhat roundabout route so that he could see the destruction caused to Valletta by the bombers, and also so that the Maltese people could see him; then he was conducted to Lascaris Bastion, where Admiral Cunningham was waiting to receive him.

Now Cunningham sent a triumphant signal to the Admiralty, one that will go down in history among the famous moments: 'Be pleased to inform their Lordships that the Italian battle fleet now lies at anchor under the guns of the fortress of Malta'.

As many as 27 Italian ships arrived at Malta that day; they included four battleships, seven cruisers, ten destroyers, four submarines, and some smaller ships. Other Italian warships continued to arrive, but there was one interesting occurrence further to the west.' A cruiser and three destroyers had picked up the survivors from *Roma*, and took them to Port Mahon, in Menorca. There two of the destroyers were scuttled, rather than be interned. The third destroyer gave herself up, and was moored alongside the 18th century British naval base at the head of the bay.

Other Italian contingents continued to arrive from the mainland ports. The destroyer *Hursley* sailed from Malta to escort in those from Taranto, two battleships, two cruisers and a destroyer. As they steered towards Malta, *Hursley* was relieved to see the 12th Cruiser Squadron with the American cruiser *Boise* come up to assist her, and nearer to Malta the battleship *King George V* with a division of destroyers swelled the escort for this powerful Italian squadron. The battleship *Guilio Cesare* made a long voyage from Venice, but arrived safely in Malta with her destroyer escort. A total of 21 submarines had surrendered on the island by late September; the destroyer *Isis* proudly escorted a group of seven of them in all by herself.

Arrangements were soon made to disperse the Italian Fleet to ports where they could be handled with greater ease, but a large Italian Fleet remained in Malta, including three of the battleships. Force H escorted a big squadron to Alexandria, and Admiral Cunningham left on September 22 in the cruiser *Euryalus* for Taranto, to work out the details of the laying up of the Italian ships, though the destroyers would be used on escort duty.

Ashore there were great celebrations to mark the islanders' final deliverance; squares in Valletta and in the villages were named after the date of the surrender, and they retain their names to this day. Finally on September 29 Marshal Badoglio arrived from Taranto in the Italian cruiser *Scipio Africano*. He was received aboard the battleship *Nelson* by General Eisenhower, Admiral Cunningham, General Alexander and Air Chief Marshal Tedder. Lord Gort, the Governor was there, and in this distinguished company the plans for Allied-Italian co-operation were worked out. That evening Marshal Badoglio returned to Taranto in the Italian cruiser, escorted by the British destroyers *Jervis* and *Petard*.

Meanwhile the Allied landing at Salerno had run into strong and unexpected German resistance, and urgent calls went out to the British and American Navies for heavy gun support from the sea. As soon as the Italian Fleet had surrendered, as many units of the Mediterranean Fleet as could be spared were withdrawn to Britain, some to take part in the Normandy landings, others to reinforce the hard-pressed anti-submarine forces, and yet others again to refit before sailing east to join the operations in the Pacific. In mid-September the battleships *Valiant* and *Warspite* with the fleet carrier *Illustrious* and escorting destroyers sailed from Malta for Britain as part of this plan; but the call for help from Salerno saw the two battleships steaming at full speed for the battle area, and they had their big guns in action against the Germans on the following day. German aircraft soon swooped down and after many attacks *Warspite* was hit by two radio-controlled bombs. She was badly damaged and could not steam. Three American fleet salvage tugs, *Hopi, Moreno* and *Narragansett* were close by, and they started to tow the battleship at four knots towards the Straits of Messina, and Malta's dockyard beyond. The Germans knew they had hit her and sent out aircraft that night to finish her off, but although they found *Valiant* they never found *Warspite*. The cruiser *Euryalus* tried towing, and in the straits two British tugs from Malta, *Nimble* and *Oriana* with a salvage ship joined in. But the currents were strong, all the towing wires parted, and *Warspite* went through the straits sideways. She arrived safely in Malta to be patched up, and then was taken in tow for Gibraltar and home in early November, escorted by four big rescue tugs and four destroyers.

Meanwhile the battle of Salerno continued, with the offshore fire support supplied by the warships based on Malta. The ammunition reserves in the island were critical to the operation; on September 16, as an example, the American destroyer *Gleaves* arrived at speed to collect more shells for the bombarding cruisers. This was a long, hot summer, and Malta experienced a new and strange privation — a serious water shortage. By this time, however, all things were possible, and a special distilling ship was sent post haste from Gibraltar.

With the land campaign producing results in Italy, and with some of the warships already being withdrawn for other duties, there were signs of relaxation among the Maltese people. The majority of the dockyard workers came out on strike, claiming that their war bonus did not purchase sufficient food to keep their families reasonably well fed; Lord Gort held firm against their demands, and refused to involve the government in Britain. For a time the flag officer commanding at Gibraltar feared that the strike might spread to the dockyard there, but the Maltese workers agreed to return to their duties, as the maximum war effort was still required.

Early in October the garrison was reduced; the Chiefs of Staff in Britain decided that the danger of an invasion was by that time non-existent, a surface attack could only be made by submarine (and that was unlikely), and whilst bombers from Italy could still attack, they would not be able to sustain their sorties. By the end of October most of the larger British and American warships had left the Mediterranean, together with large numbers of the landing craft. Escorts were again in short supply, and three basic escort groups were formed, each composed of five of the *Flower* Class corvettes. The flag officers were changing as well; on October 16 Admiral Sir John Cunningham succeeded his famous namesake as Commander-in-Chief of the Mediterranean Fleet, and hoisted his flag afloat in the *Hunt* Class destroyer *Hambledon*. Admiral Sir Andrew Cunningham hurried back to London, to succeed the dying Admiral Pound as First Sea Lord.

CHAPTER 13

Victory in the Mediterranean, 1944-45

The operations on the Italian mainland continued well into 1944, but in Malta the emphasis was on operating as a main fleet base without air attack, and on planning for the post-war needs of the fleet. At the turn of the year the Governor proposed that the Union Jack should fly in perpetuity on the tall flagstaff over the Grand Master's Palace, where the air raid warning flags had flown, and the movements of ships were controlled. He argued that this flag would symbolise for ever the partnership in war between the British forces and the Maltese people, and commemorate the valiant defence of the island. Winston Churchill set the new mood by a brief reply: 'I think Malta has had enough recognition for the present'. He did, however, relent and decreed that of all the islands in the Mediterranean, only service on Malta would qualify servicemen for the campaign medal Africa Star. The base played its full part in the assault on Anzio, and while the main force sailed from Naples, large numbers of warships came into Grand Harbour to refuel and restock with ammunition. Apart from the shore bases, which had been much expanded for the Sicily invasion in the previous year, 12 depot and repair ships were moored in Grand Harbour to give support in this operation. The built-up convoys for Anzio were largely concentrated on Malta. There was excellent co-operation between the British and American naval forces during this period; the American escorts coming in with the trans-atlantic troop and supply convoys stayed with them as far as Malta, so releasing the Mediterranean escorts to hunt the U-boats, of which four were still operating on the convoy routes nearby. Seven escort groups of mixed British and American warships hunted the U-boats down, and two were sunk in these combined operations.

Warships of other nations also participated. There were French destroyers and submarines; seven Italian warships were organised into convoy escort groups and two Italian hospital ships switched to the British flag while berthed in Grand Harbour. Three of the big Italian battleships were still lying in St Paul's Bay, but they could not be used, though other Italian warships were in service as ferries. There were 15 Yugoslav warships also operating under Allied control in these waters. The destroyers were especially busy in these months. Among their other duties, the British *T* Class flotilla was based on Malta for offensive forays into the Adriatic, and they and other destroyers returned to Malta on more than one occasion to change the guns in their main mountings, worn out by constant bombardment of shore targets.

The 10th Submarine Flotilla continued their energetic operations, though some of them were now based at Maddalena in Corsica, nearer the Anzio beaches. When the assault was launched, two boats acted as night beach markers, and they were familiar sights taking passage on the surface with convoys from Malta to the Italian mainland. Units of the new *V* Class were joining from the builders' yards in Britain, to support the hard-pressed *U* Class; *Vox* and *Vampire* were the first to arrive in April. *Brittany*, in better days a cross-Channel steamer on the St Malo-Channel Islands run, was kept busy ferrying torpedoes and supplies for the submarines from Malta to Maddalena. The 1st Submarine Flotilla arrived in Malta from Beirut, to swell the striking force still further.

Minesweeping was a major activity. The swept channels from Malta to the Italian mainland needed constant attention, and the sweepers followed fast on the heels of the advancing forces in the Adriatic and Aegean. The numbers of sweepers continued to grow, as mine clearance was started.

A new sight to be seen in Grand Harbour was the procession of impressive new warships passing through Malta on their way to join the fast-growing British Pacific and East Indies Fleets, where the Royal Navy was keen to support the Americans in their Pacific war. Among the strangers seen in Malta for the first time were the light fleet carriers *Vengeance* and *Venerable,* early units of a large new class, fleet destroyers of the *U* and *V* Classes, and many units of the *Hunt* Class and *Black Swan* Class.

In parallel with the operations, much planning was done to equip Malta as the fleet base when hostilities had ended. The Royal Navy had been frustrated before the war, when money had not been made available to build Grand Harbour up to the necessary level of efficiency; but the lessons had been learned in 1942, and now some impressive projects were put in hand. Sadly, post-war economies in Britain were to cut some of them back yet again, but the navy got its planning right. It was expected that the fleet would be of roughly the same size as in 1939, but the types of ships would be different. Even in 1944, it was planned to have two battleships there, but there would be a higher proportion of aircraft carriers – as many as five in Grand Harbour together on many occasions in the years after the war. Minesweepers would remain in some numbers, even after mine clearance had been finished, and the fleet destroyers berthed in Marsamxett harbour would be joined by equal numbers of frigates.

The Admiralty decided that Malta was the only naval base in the Empire where naval air training could be carried out together with general fleet training. The airfields were well laid out to take the disembarked aircraft of a fleet carrier squadron, and eight RAF fighter squadrons for defence could be based there as well. The whole base was surveyed in 1944, to see what improvements were necessary. The largest project was the construction of a very big new drydock, to take the place of Parlatorio Wharf. The dock would be 1,200 feet long and 150 feet wide, to take the new fleet carriers, and the estimated cost was £6 million, including a fitting-out wharf. An argument developed between the Director of Plans at the Admiralty, and the Director of Dockyards. The latter pointed out that the floating dock had been sunk during the war, which had been a major drawback; and there was no dock between Britain and Singapore on the Mediterranean route to the Far East, which could take the large new fleet carriers. The Director of Plans replied that such a drydock would be a white elephant, as there would be no large ships at Malta in any future war, due to the development of the bombers (there seemed to be no mention of guided missiles at that stage). His colleague retorted that floating docks were a wasting asset, and that of the 130 docks of that kind operated by the Germans, 100 had been sunk by bombing.

Honours were even, and the new drydock was approved, but put on a low priority, with no possibility of its being constructed before 1955. The world has changed again since then, and it is ironic to see this new drydock being completed in 1980, but by the Chinese, and to take giant tankers, not warships.

Malta's airfields were reorganised. The fighter field at Ta'Qali was used by the navy from early in 1944, and in January 1945 was commissioned as the Fleet Air Arm base HMS *Goldfinch*. Accommodation was provided for 111 aircraft, and this was evenly split between naval aircraft stationed at Malta, and planes disembarked from passing warships.

Hal Far on the southern cliffs had been used by the Fleet

Air Arm throughout the war, and in 1946 it was turned over formally by the RAF. It was commissioned as HMS *Falcon*, a name borne by ships in the Royal Navy over 700 years; the name also had ancient associations with Malta, for the falcon had been the emblem of Grand Master Jean de la Valette Parisot, who had defeated the Turks in 1565. The falcon is now included in the arms of the city of Valletta.

The RAF retained the big airfield at Luqa, together with the satellite strips at Safi and Krendi, though the Fleet Air Arm also used the latter.

The most ambitious project, however, was a renewed proposal to build underground harbours, which would be safe from air raids in any future war. The previous plan in 1941 had been to drive underground pens for submarines and motor-torpedo boats into the rock under the west side of Valletta; some work had been done on this in 1943, before the preparations for the invasion of Sicily took priority. Now the work was taken up again, but the Vice-Admiral (Malta) reported in March 1944 that the rock was unsound in that area, and the project was abandoned when about ten per cent of the excavation had been completed. Work was then started on a much more ambitious scheme, which would provide an underground harbour running under Valletta, and with two entrances, one in Grand Harbour under the ramparts of Floriana, and the other in Marsamxett harbour, near St Michael's bastion. This tunnel would be 40 feet wide, and would have berths for seven of the new *A* Class fleet submarines, a flotilla of coastal minesweepers, 12 large motor-torpedo boats, and tugs, oil lighters and harbour craft. The latter would be berthed in two shorter tunnels at the Grand Harbour entrance.

As always, there were many debates among the naval staff in the planning stage. The Admiral (Submarines) said that seven submarines was too few, and the Admiral

(Coastal Forces) wanted berths for as many as 48 of the largest type of motor-torpedo boats, including slips for six boats at a time, and extensive workshops, torpedo and fuel stores, and living accommodation. The minesweeping flotilla was agreed to be essential, for keeping the approaches clear for the strike craft.

A further tunnel was planned, to be built under Senglea, with a single entrance into Dockyard Creek. This tunnel would take numbers of diesel-powered harbour launches and lighters, the loss of which in air raids had seriously impeded the unloading of arriving cargo ships. In July 1944 the Admiralty approved the construction of both tunnels, but again post-war financial economies caught up with the planners, and no work on excavation was ever commenced.

The war in western Europe was coming to a close, and by the time VE Day came in May 1945, the people of Malta had largely settled back into their peacetime routine. Food was plentiful once again, the ships of the fleet continued to crowd into the harbours, employment in the dockyard and the naval bases continued at high level, and the throngs of sailors in the streets of the cities around Grand Harbour brought prosperity to the people. Victory had come for the Maltese with the surrender of the Italians in 1943, and the busy fleet base represented to them an economic revival, more than the continuance of operations up to the Italian coasts. The Royal Navy, however, finished the war in the Mediterranean on a highly satisfactory note. The fleet's ascendancy had been firmly re-established, and Malta had been proved once more to be a vital naval base in a unique position.

CHAPTER 14

Peace — with overtones, 1946-64

As the months of 1946 went by, there seemed to be a determined effort to relegate the war to the history books, and to return to the peacetime routine of the fleet. *The Times of Malta* showed in its pages a gradual return to the pre-war reporting of the social round, and of the naval sporting events. '*Ocean* too good for *Arromanches*' ran one football headline — seeming almost to recall the Mulberry Harbour at the Normandy invasion, damaged by a storm. The movements of warships were regularly reported once more, as were the more important naval appointments, and full details of the warship building programmes. A brave new strategy was reported in May: 'The Mediterranean could no longer remain a British lake, and Malta was as obsolete as a bomber of 1940'. Opinions on that were to change a number of times over the next few years.

Grand Harbour was cleared gradually of the remaining and more difficult wrecks. The famous tanker *Ohio* was raised in two sections from its resting place in Rinella Bay, below Fort Ricasoli, and towed out to sea, and sunk by naval gunfire; the merchantman *Pampas* followed in her wake, but her consort *Talabot* proved more difficult to raise, and followed a little later.

The Royal Navy was being reduced rapidly in numbers of ships, and some were being turned over to Allied navies; the *Hunt* Class destroyers *Catterick* and *Lauderdale* were turned over to the Greek Navy on May 21, while they were berthed in Sliema Creek, and other ex-British warships were soon calling in at Grand Harbour with strange ensigns flying from their sterns.

A sense of history was preserved, too. The battleship *Duke of York* arrived on June 14, and with her the new cruiser *Superb;* the latter was presented with a relic, taken from the wall of Sheer Bastion. This was a steel plate from the ship's side of the *Superb* of 1882, showing a shot-hole received during the bombardment of Alexandria in that year. It had been bequeathed to Malta in 1927 by a Miss Hughes-Hallett, a resident of the island, and sister of the Captain of *Superb* in 1882.

The first of the post-war peace-keeping roles appeared as early as this year, 1946. This was a requirement for the Mediterranean Fleet to patrol the sea areas off Palestine, to detect and detain unauthorised ships carrying emigrants for the new state of Israel. This need was covered by the cruiser *Ajax* and a flotilla of destroyers (at first the 14th Flotilla, *Chequers,* Senior Officer) and this force was based at Haifa. It was a distasteful duty for the destroyer crews, but as always, cheerfully and efficiently carried out. Malta was closely involved, as the patrol ships sailed and returned from Grand Harbour; the waterside bars were alive with lurid stories from the returning sailors. Early in the year, the immigrant ships were mostly of the Greek 'caique' type, of 500-1,000 tons gross. Their sea speed was only seven knots, and they were each crowded with up to 1,000 immigrants. In later months, larger and faster ships were used, and instead of attempting to evade the patrols, they openly tried to run the blockade, seeking publicity. These ships were in several cases ex-*Flower* Class corvettes from both the Royal and Royal Canadian Navies, and this made the patrol duty all the more distasteful for the destroyer men. Among these ex-corvettes were *Beauharnois* and *Norsyd* from Canada.

On May 13, for example, the destroyer *Jervis* intercepted the *Smyrni* south west of Jaffa. She had been located by a Warwick aircraft of the RAF, and *Jervis* moved in at 23 knots. The ship was flying the Star of David at the mast-head, but no other national colours, and was clearly head-ing for Tel Aviv. *Jervis* had difficulty in closing her, as she was yawing about up to 30 degrees off her intended course. The destroyer Captain called by loud-hailer: 'Please steer a steady course, or we shall hit one another, and then we shall both sink'. The reply, in gutteral English was not clear, so *Jervis* rather obviously cleared away her B gun for action, whereupon the immigrant ship put her wheel hard over, and lurched across the destroyer's bows. The destroyer *Chequers* joined at this point, and her Captain persuaded *Smyrni* to stop by crossing her bows, and firing bursts from a 20 mm Oerlikon into the water. A boarding party found the ship incredibly crowded, but the people aboard were pleasant.

The following day the destroyers *Charity* and *Chaplet* intercepted two more ships, and sent boarding parties aboard each. Then *Venus* and *Haydon* picked up the *Colon* in the same area; this ship, too, suddenly altered course, and *Venus* had to go astern at 14 knots to avoid a collision.

In July the *Akbel* needed four destroyers, *Saumarez*, *Virago*, *Haydon*, and *Talybont* to make her stop without an accident. In the end *Haydon* dropped a depth charge close ahead of her, *Talybont* one on her port bow, and *Virago*, living up to her name, stopped right across her path. That ship was carrying over 1,000 immigrants, and they were short of food and water.

Another ex-*Flower* Class corvette, renamed *Josiah Wedgewood,* made a dramatic dash for the coast that month, when intercepted by *Venus* and two other destroyers. Taken to Haifa, she was found to have some 1,500 immigrants aboard. *Talybont* and *Brissenden* found another ship the same day, broken down and drifting towards the Lebanese coast.

In the first seven months of 1946, 6,436 immigrants were

stopped at sea, as opposed to 54 by land; and it was estimated that only 50 had got through by sea, against 500 by land. The naval patrols from Grand Harbour had worked with great efficiency.

July 1946 saw the Royal Navy evacuating its Egyptian bases, and the Commander-in-Chief, Mediterranean Fleet, Admiral Sir Algernon U. Willis, set up his head-quarters in Malta; once more the Admiral's flag flew from the saluting platform above Lascaris Bastion, by the Upper Barracca Gardens. The cruiser *Mauritius* arrived, too, as flagship of the 15th Cruiser Squadron, and the harbour was busy with warships calling in on their way to or from the British Pacific and East Indian Fleets.

To underline its return to peacetime routine, the Mediterranean Fleet sailed on September 18 for their first post-war Autumn Cruise. The main reason was to create opportunities for sea and harbour training for the fleet, but the chance was also taken to show the flag in a number of harbours in Cyprus and Greece.

Phoebe (Rear-Admiral, Destroyers) and her flotillas went first to Larnaka, while the carrier *Ocean* and the cruisers *Liverpool, Mauritius, Ajax*, and *Leander* went to Famagusta.

The Commander-in-Chief sailed from Malta in his aptly-named yacht *Surprise* (a converted *Bay* Class frigate) and after transferring his flag to *Liverpool* at Nauplia he paid visits to King George of Greece and King Farouk of Egypt.

On October 22 the destroyers *Saumarez* and *Volage* were mined while passing through the Corfu Channel, while in company with the cruisers *Mauritius* and *Leander*. The fleet abandoned its exercises and laid on a quick rescue opera-tion. The depot ship *Ranpura* and the hospital ship *Maine* quickly arrived in Corfu from Malta, and the two ships were patched up and towed back to Grand Harbour for repairs. Their casualties had been heavy, and were brought swiftly back to the Naval Hospital at Bighi, across Grand Harbour from Valletta.

Another Summer Cruise was carried out in July 1947, with 32 ships. They paid their first visit to Turkey since 1939, but the Palestine Patrol was still a drain on the fleet's resources. The immigrant ships were still coming in, and the patrols were still as energetically intercepting them. The sloop *Mermaid* even shadowed one all the way through the sea from Marseilles.

The dockyard was by now able to fill all the needs of the fleet, though the drydocks were not yet big enough to take the light fleet carriers, and a floating drydock capable of lifting 50,000 tons was towed from Bombay to Grand Harbour, as the East Indies Fleet was reducing in number of ships.

The British mine clearance commitment in the Mediterranean was completed in 1947. From four flotillas of *Algerine* Class fleet sweepers in 1945, the minesweeping force had been reduced to just one large flotilla, and the Royal Navy had cleared 12,670 mines in the Mediterranean, out of a post-war total swept of some 20,000.

In 1949 Princess Elizabeth flew out to Malta for Christmas, to join Prince Philip, who was in command of the frigate *Magpie*, whilst his uncle Earl Mountbatten was Flag Officer of the 1st Cruiser Squadron there. Then with Philip in *Magpie* and Elizabeth in the Commander-in-Chief's yacht *Surprise*, the couple carried the flag to some friendly ports, and received a big welcome in Athens.

However, after a few peaceful years, 1956 brought more sombre events, as the clouds gathered over the Suez Canal. In June British troops withdrew from the Suez Canal Base, under the agreement with Colonel Nasser of Egypt, but on July 26 he announced the nationalisation of the Canal, and the British and French Governments started putting pressure on for the Canal to be kept open as an international waterway. Diplomacy, however intense, did not seem to be able to solve this problem; after all efforts appeared to be failing, the British and French were ready for an assault on Alexandria, to be launched on September 15, under the codename Musketeer. But after the ships had been loaded, there came a postponement, as last efforts were made to find a peaceful settlement. Early in October, Colonel Nasser began to receive Russian military experts as advisers, and the British Mediterranean Fleet was carrying out intensive exercises, in readiness for what seemed an inevitable battle. The light fleet carrier *Albion* carried out over 1,000 jet landings in four weeks of training in this period. Time was running out. On October 29 Israeli forces attacked Egypt and the following day Britain and France told both Egypt and Israel to withdraw their forces ten miles from the Canal, so that an Anglo-French peace-keeping force could occupy the area, and ensure the safe passage of the ships of all nations. But there was no reaction from either of the combatant nations. In New York there was opposition to the use of force by the United States Government, and at the United Nations, by now in constant session, resolutions by America and Russia were vetoed by Britain and France.

That same day Anglo-French bombing of Egyptian air-fields began, by aircraft based on Malta and Cyprus; and the invasion fleet of about 100 ships sailed by squadrons from Malta to attack Port Said. This gave rise to further diplomatic problems, for the smaller landing craft could only make good five knots through the water, and it would take them three and a half days to reach their objective — leaving plenty of time for further political argument, after the decision to attack had been taken. As they sailed steadily east from Malta, we may examine as much of the composition of that force as has so far been released from the closed files.

The Commander-in-Chief of the Joint Expeditionary Force, General Sir Charles Keightley, was based in Cyprus, from where some of the transports sailed. His deputy was the French Vice-Admiral Pierre Barjot, an old friend of Britain. The Commander-in-Chief of the Mediterranean Fleet, Admiral Sir Guy Grantham, remained at the base in Malta, while the Commander of the Naval Task Force was Vice-Admiral L.F. Durnford-Slater, with his flag in the depot ship *Tyne,* and his deputy was the French Rear-Admiral Lancelot. This was an amusing sequel to Nelson chasing Napoleon in the same direction in 1798, and was the reverse of the naval command situation in Malta during the First World War.

The British Cruiser Squadron was composed of *Jamaica* (flag), *Newfoundland, Ceylon* and *Orion;* the Carrier Force included *Eagle* (Flag Officer, Aircraft Carriers, Vice-Admiral M.L. Power), *Bulwark, Albion, Theseus* and *Ocean;* the last two carried the helicopter assault force for an embarked Royal Marine Commando. There were almost certainly one or more French aircraft carriers present also, but firm details are not available.

The fleet destroyers included at least three ships of the big post-war *Duchess* Class, as well as a full flotilla of the *C* Class, and anti-submarine frigates. The assault force was made up of Landing Ships, Tank, of the British post-war design, and of the smaller Landing Craft, Tank. There were fleet replenishment ships, seagoing headquarters ships, and a large salvage fleet, as by that time it was already known that the Egyptians had sunk a number of blockships in the Canal.

The names of the French warships taking part are not available, but it is believed that the battleship *Jean Bart* was there, with cruisers, destroyers, and some submarines. There were newspaper reports of the French sailors' berets, with their red pompoms, mixing happily with the white hats of the British seamen in the streets of Valletta and the Three Cities. There were colourful scenes in the streets around Grand Harbour as the force embarked. Convoys of trucks, full of soldiers, rumbled their way down to the landing craft hards. There were heavier tracked and armoured vehicles as well, many towing field guns. The LSTs and LCTs of the Amphibious Warfare Squadron awaited them, with their bow doors open, and from the parade ground in Floriana columns of combat-clad troops marched down to the attack transports. Crowds of Maltese gathered to watch them pass, recalling the great days of the invasion of Sicily in 1943.

As the ships were loaded, they pulled away from the quays and ramps to anchorages, leaving their berths free for fresh ships. From England came troopships loaded with more army units — *Empire Fowey* had 1,600 men, *Asturias, Dilwara,* and *New Australia* were there too. Civilian passenger liners had not been chartered for this operation, but several of them were caught in the Mediterranean on their way eastwards to pass through the Suez Canal. *Dunnottar Castle* and *Orion* turned back westwards again, but the P&O liner *Strathmore* (24,000 tons) came into Grand Harbour, full of nervous passengers watching the troops embark.

The heavy units of the fleet sailed on October 29, ahead of the landing force. The aircraft carriers, the cruisers, and many destroyers and frigates passed out of Grand Harbour, in the traditional channel below the Barracca Gardens, as their forebears had done over several centuries, watched by the naval families with crowds of Maltese. The assault was under way, with the Anglo-French codename of Musketeer Revise.

In addition to the bombers attacking the Egyptian Air Force bases, British and French carrier-borne aircraft joined in, and French planes attacked and set on fire off

Alexandria an Egyptian destroyer of the Russian *Skoryi* Class. The cruiser *Newfoundland,* on patrol, sank the Egyptian frigate *Domiat;* rather sadly, as she had been the Royal Navy's frigate *Nith* in happier days.

On November 3, as the assault fleet neared its destination, the British Admiralty warned all merchant shipping to keep clear of the eastern Mediterranean — though they can have needed little bidding by then, as the movements of the assault force had been freely reported. Even the names of the task force commanders had been announced. In England, the nation was torn between the hawks and the doves, but the forces based on Malta, as always, carried out their orders without question. A second fleet of transports and landing ships embarked other army units in Cyprus, and sailed to join the assault force as it passed south of the island. Newspaper reports spoke cheerfully of White Ensigns and tricolours flying proudly together among the gathered ships.

The air assault on Egypt went on for days, and over 2,000 sorties were flown by the carrier force. On November 5 at dawn the airborne attack went in, and achieved a complete success, to open the way for the seaborne troops and their heavier equipment. The following dawn saw these too go in, covered by fire support from the destroyers offshore. Just ahead of them went a Royal Marine Commando, in their helicopters from the carriers *Theseus* and *Ocean* — believed to be the first assault of its kind. Valiant and Canberra bombers from the Malta airfields roared overhead, delivering their loads on to the defenders, as the landing craft charged up to the beaches.

The naval task force commander reported that the seaborne landing went just like an exercise, with little serious opposition. The assault force moved quickly along the Canal, and had captured 23 miles of the canal bank by the evening.

Then the order to cease fire was flashed from London and Paris, and the fighting was over. The British and French fleets stood by off Port Said, and Israel agreed to withdraw her troops from Egypt. On December 5 the Anglo-French force started to withdraw, as it was agreed that a United Nations peacekeeping force should take over; they had completed their withdrawal by December 22. The ships started to stream back to Malta; *Eagle* came into Grand Harbour on December 9, and *Theseus* brought in the army's casualties the following day. The Royal Marine Commandos returned in triumph in the troopship *Empire Fowey*, and the LST *Striker* sailed in the reverse direction from Malta, with the first UN observers.

Offshore at Port Said, the destroyer *Chevron* remained with the senior naval officer embarked, while the survey ship *Dalrymple* charted the 20 wrecks in the Canal; and the Anglo-French salvage fleet of 30 ships started work on clearing the waterway. A minesweeping force of coastal sweepers from Malta searched the adjacent areas, but found no mines, and eight LCTs maintained a ferry service between the ships and the shore; these had been in reserve at Malta when the emergency arose, and they had been made ready for sea in two days, while National Service crews were flown out from England. So the active phase of the assault on Alexandria came to an end; and once more Malta had found itself in the focus of world attention, with its great harbour the springboard for a seaborne assault.

Back in Europe, England had been torn between the use of force, and the wish to avoid another war. Two Ministers of State in the Government resigned over the issue, and the Prime Minister, Sir Anthony Eden, resigned in January 1957, in ill health. In the United States there was much opposition to the use of force. General Eisenhower was involved in an election campaign for a further term as President, and the Americans put much pressure on the

British and French to withdraw. Indeed, there were strong rumours at the time that the United States Sixth Fleet, based in the Mediterranean, had been ordered to lay itself across the path of the seaborne assault force, on its way from Malta, but this was officially denied on November 20. Had this been correct, the situation would have been embarrassing. The Sixth Fleet had two large aircraft carriers, *Randolph* and *Coral Sea,* and were reinforced at this time by a third, *Antietam.* Vice-Admiral Brown, in command, also had at his disposal the heavy cruisers *Salem* and *Macon,* and four destroyer squadrons, each of eight ships. Admiral Boone, in overall command of American naval forces in Europe, flew to join Admiral Brown in his flagship, and the situation must have been tense. It must have been all the more difficult, as the ships of the British and American Fleets in the Mediterranean often met, usually in Malta's Grand Harbour, and many of the crews were good friends.

It was notable that at the time the seaborne assault force left Malta, there were other events taking place, of equal importance. The NATO Supreme Allied Commander in Europe, the American General Alfred M. Gruenther, was about to hand over to his successor, the US Air Force General Lauris Norstad. General Gruenther actually paid his farewell visit to Malta on October 8, as the assault force was assembling; he was met at Luqa airfield by the Commander-in-Chief of NATO forces in the Mediterranean, Admiral Sir Guy Grantham, who must have had his hands full at the time, with the needs of the Allied naval forces crowding Grand Harbour. The Admiral's appointment to Malta, too, had its significance. On relinquishing his naval appointment, he became Governor of Malta for the years 1959-62 – the first naval officer to hold this post since Sir Alexander Ball in 1800.

Far away to the north, at the same time, Russia was

throwing its forces into Hungary. Later, after 20 years, Russia would be seen as a possible contender to follow the British in the use of Grand Harbour.

In spite of all the comings and goings in Grand Harbour in relation to the assault on Suez, life in Malta went on much as usual. The emigration movement of Maltese to Australia was in full swing, and among the assembling seaborne force were to be seen the liners *Aurelia* and *Castel Felice*, taking full loads of families to a new life in the southern hemisphere. In the same period, a minesweeping exercise was conducted out of Malta with the Italian Navy. Six Italian minesweepers came to Grand Harbour, to join six Royal Navy sweepers, in Exercise Dragex Medina. The days of warfare between the two nations were firmly in the past, and co-operation was not to be disturbed by the other goings on.

CHAPTER 15

From independence to the republic, 1964-78

Independence was the goal towards which the Maltese people had looked for so long; but when it came, it brought with it not only freedom from the ties of all the preceding centuries, but also the problems of bringing prosperity to the islands in a different way.

The relations with the Royal Navy had gradually been changing since 1945, as successive cuts in defence budgets in Britain continued in each year to reduce the number of warships in commission. Economic problems, the growing independence of the old Empire and general government policies all contributed to this sad situation. In 1945 the Royal Navy had in commission 14 battleships, 52 aircraft carriers, 56 cruisers, and 536 destroyers, sloops and frigates. By 1962 this fleet had been reduced to just one battleship, (appropriately named *Vanguard*) eight carriers, eight cruisers, and 126 destroyers and frigates; and by 1978 that group of ships totalled no more than 75.

Admiral Sir John Hamilton was the last Commander-in-Chief of the Mediterranean Fleet, and when he left in June 1967 the fleet had become a shadow of its former self. The only force based there was one escort squadron of frigates, proudly wearing the red and white Maltese Cross on their funnels, and one squadron of inshore minesweepers, though British warships continued to call in, for working-up exercises of newly-commissioned ships, or for social visits. Even the small force based at Malta was finally phased out in March 1969, ten full years before the final departure. This rundown inevitably affected the naval bases. Gradually the White Ensign came down for the last time at one shore establishment after another, and those farthest from the base at St Angelo were most at risk. Even Admiralty House in Valletta, where so many Commanders-in-Chief of the Mediterranean Fleet had lived, was closed down, and then re-opened by the government as a National Museum of Fine Arts.

From 1967 onwards the Flag Officer, Malta, was in charge of the naval base, and he also held the office of Commander, South East Mediterranean Area within the NATO command. For six more years he flew his flag from the tall staff at the tip of *St Angelo,* and ships of NATO, both American and British together with those of France, Italy and Turkey continued to call at the harbour, until the contretemps of 1971. There was a splendid moment when a Turkish naval commander made his first entrance to the naval headquarters in Valletta: 'Gentlemen', he said, 'I believe I am the first Turk to have penetrated this far!' Whenever the ships were there, the shops and bars of Valletta and the Three Cities were still crowded with sailors, and in the evenings 'The Gut' maintained its reputation as one of the more famous fleshpots of the western world.

Much of the money contributed by the United Kingdom during the period of the rundown (£51 million over a period of ten years) was used to encourage and develop new industries, to replace the British forces as the main employer in the islands. Light industries have sprung up, mainly in the new trading estate at Marsa, and merchant ships of the world continue to use Grand Harbour as one of the important trading posts of the Mediterranean. The yachting industry has grown quickly, too; big marinas now prosper where not so long ago the sleek hulls of the submarines lay alongside the quays, and in the bays of Marsamxett harbour the buoys once occupied by trots of destroyers and frigates are now the lair of pleasure yachts and sightseeing steamers.

The tourist industry has grown to be one of the largest contributors to Malta's economy. The rising standards of living in western Europe since the war, and the search for holidays in the sun, have brought throngs of travellers; new hotels have been built, and sightseeing has become well organised. The Maltese Government has, however, wisely restricted the number of beds available in the islands to tourists, so that the area is never overcrowded.

By 1966 73,000 holidaymakers visited Malta, and of these one quarter arrived in Grand Harbour in cruise ships. By 1979 the numbers arriving had doubled, and it was ironic that as the British forces finally pulled out, six out of every ten tourists were British, and British Airways alone was running 16 flights a week to the islands. In 1978 tourism brought in £70 million, while manufacturing industry contributed about the same amount. Malta drydocks produced some £20 million, and the British bases £17 million.

One of the success stories since independence is the way in which the old naval dockyard has been turned round into a profitable company, Malta Drydocks, in the face of fierce world-wide competition. After 1945 the badly-damaged workshops and repair yards were rebuilt by the Royal Navy. New buildings sprang up everywhere on the quays and around the drydocks, and machinery of modern design was installed in them. The five drydocks, built in the previous century, were also brought up to date with new cranes replacing those destroyed in the bombing. In 1958, five years before independence, the naval dockyard was closed down; with the Mediterranean Fleet so much reduced in size, there was not enough naval repair work to keep these extensive facilities occupied. First one British ship repair company, then another took on the Maltese Government's contract to run the dockyard, and turn it round on a commercial basis; but many difficulties were found. The facilities of the yard were in excellent condition, and there was a workforce with many skills and much experience. The pace of work in the old naval days, however, especially when the fleet was away on cruises, had been less hectic, and far from the competitive atmosphere of commercial ship repair yards. The time taken to complete repairs on a ship turned out to be too long to be commercially profitable, either in costs or in the time that the ship was out of service; and the yard craftsmen were out of balance — there were not enough boilermakers, or expert welders, and there were too many electricians.

It took some long and difficult years for management and workers to come to terms with the new situation; in 1971 the Prime Minister terminated the agreement with the British company then running the yard. Since that time, building not only on the Royal Navy heritage but also on the good work done by the two British companies, great progress has been made. The Malta Drydocks Corporation was formed, with a board half of whose members came from the workforce. The company now prospers under its dynamic General Manager, Mr Joe Calleja, and there have been no strikes since 1971 — so important for shipping companies, which need their expensive ships back on time. The company prides itself on paying the best wages and benefits in Malta, and demands efficiency from its workers.

The result has been a growth in the value of repair work handled, from £3 million in 1959 to £23 million in 1978. The yard has made a real profit in each of the last five years, which is a remarkable result in a period of acute shortage of repair work on a global scale, and a steep rise in the costs of steel and many other materials. In 1977 Malta Drydocks was turning work away despite the recession, and the drydocks were used to 97 per cent of their capacity. At the same time yards in other countries around the Mediterranean were cutting their prices by up to 35 per cent to attract business. To cope with this order book, the Malta workforce has been increased only marginally, to 5,500.

The ships handled represented an interesting mix — 63 nationalities in 1979 and 235 ships. These included very large tankers and bulk carriers, several of over 100,000 tons deadweight each, with a marked increase in ships connected with offshore oil exploration from America, France Germany, Holland, Panama and Liberia. Two tankers, each of 6,038 deadweight tons, were constructed and delivered to China in 1979. Naval work is still being handled, depending on the needs of calling ships, now that no fleet is based on Malta. Perhaps the most startling fact in the turn-round of Malta Drydocks is that in 1958 99 per cent of the work was for warships and 1 per cent for merchant ships; today that balance has just about been reversed.

The drydocks — the backbone of the dockyard — also show some interesting trends. Five drydocks had been built in the 19th century, to service the British Fleet. One of these in Dockyard Creek was used for submarines; two in French Creek were used by destroyers, and later for frigates, while the other two in the same creek were for the battleships and cruisers, and latterly for the aircraft carriers. In addition there was after 1945 a floating dock capable of lifting light fleet carriers. When the dockyards went commercial in 1958, the floating dock was towed away for further Royal Navy work. The two largest drydocks were lengthened, by cutting into the wall at the inner end of the dock, in order to take the tankers and bulk carriers, which were longer than most of the warships. One more, and truly dramatic move was needed. Malta was in danger of being forced out of the lucrative supertanker market as the existing drydocks, even after lengthening, could only take ships of up to 110,000 tons deadweight, while the new generation of ships measured up to 300,000 tons. A sixth and very large new drydock was started, using a plan drawn up before 1939 by the Royal Navy, but never implemented. The contract for construction was awarded to China, with a loan from the Chinese Government attached to it. The public works department of Malta carried out the actual construction, supervised by a Chinese design and technical team. The dock was to be completed in mid-1980 and known as the No 6 Dock. It was constructed on the site of the old Parlatorio Wharf in French Creek — the scene of the great repair under bombing of *Illustrious* in 1941. The whole of the old wharf has disappeared, and the rock side of the hill has been blasted away. This new dock is a remarkable 360 metres long and 62 metres wide, and will be serviced by a 150 ton crane — three times larger than any previously operated within the dockyard.

In June 1971 Mr Dom Mintoff's Labour Party won a general election in Malta; its election platform was built around a new policy of non-alignment with any power, and the revision of the 1964 defence agreement with Britain. Now a new and difficult relationship arose between Mr Mintoff and the government in London. The British refused to negotiate with him on the grounds that the existing agreement was valid until 1974; Mr Mintoff disagreed, and unfortunately one of the points at issue was the visits paid to Grand Harbour by the ships of the United States Sixth Fleet. The Maltese Government discouraged these visits, and the United States Navy stopped sending any of its ships to Malta, saying that they would not call if they were not welcome, no matter what the existing treaty said about their rights. The negotiations between Valletta and London continued for nearly a year, with the Maltese Government demanding up to £30 million a year for the use of the base by the Royal Navy, and finally settling in March 1972 for a package deal of £14 million a year, plus a further and complicated payment of £10½ million, together with some specialist assistance to be provided by the United

States. It had been a long and difficult period and at one point in January 1972 the British Government actually started to withdraw their forces from the island, though they soon returned.

The new agreement was to run for seven and a half years, to March 31 1979 (which was to be the day on which the Royal Navy finally left Malta). The base was only to be used by the Royal Navy, and other NATO powers could not use it unless a separate agreement was made. London agreed to maintain the Maltese work force in the base establishments, and following the Maltese Government's new policy of non-alignment, an undertaking was given that Malta would not be used as a springboard for an attack on any Arab country.

It was also agreed that the warships of the Warsaw Pact countries could not use the base, and a further result was that the United States Sixth Fleet was not able to renew its visits. From reports at the time there seems some doubt as to whether this was the Maltese Government's intention, for the American ships' companies had built up close friendships and spent much money during their visits to Malta. It appears that NATO argued that even courtesy visits by Russian ships would constitute tactical use of Malta, the Maltese Government agreed, and that disbarred the American ships as well. There was one more side effect from this new agreement. During the negotiations the NATO command transferred its Malta headquarters ('Navsouth') to Naples, and it remains there to this day. Two and a half years later on December 13 1974, the Maltese Government declared the islands to be a republic. A new emblem replaced the Maltese Cross, though the symbol of the George Cross remained on the Maltese flag; but the great Maltese Cross which had for years adorned the seaward end of the ancient walls of Fort St Angelo was removed. Although there was by this time no permanent

Royal Navy force based on Malta, British warships continued to make extensive use of the base facilities. Ships working up or passing through the Mediterranean called in regularly, bringing friendship and money to the island in their traditional way. In 1977 a total of 57 British warships paid visits to Malta, and in 1978 the squadrons manoeuvring in Grand Harbour included some of the latest destroyers and frigates in the Royal Navy. It was the sincere hope of the officers and men of the fleet that these visits would continue after the final withdrawal, but with the independent dockyard providing the facilities.

In the final ten years to 1979 no British warship called in at Grand Harbour more regularly than the aircraft carrier *Ark Royal;* and it seemed fitting that this great ship was retired from the service in December 1978, so close to her navy's final withdrawal from the base. Her final sailing from Grand Harbour on November 16 was a sentimental one; the ramparts and the Barracca Gardens were packed with people as she move slowly out towards the breakwater, below Sir Alexander Ball's little Greek temple in the Lower Barracca. The carrier was flying an enormously long white paying-off pendant, her Royal Marine band was drawn up on the flight deck with the entire ship's company, and the band played 'The Last Farewell' as the accompanying tugs sounded their sirens and the people waved. Once clear of the breakwater the ship's company reverted to the relaxed ways of the navy. A battered upright piano was brought up to the flight deck and attached to the steam catapult over the bows; then with the entire ship's company standing rigidly at attention, and the Royal Marine band now playing the funeral march, the Captain gave the signal and the piano was solemnly launched into the deep off Malta.

Over a period of 65 years ships bearing this honoured name have maintained a special place in the hearts of the

Maltese people, and this has been warmly reciprocated by the ships' companies of the three ships concerned. As the fourth *Ark Royal* steams away from the island, we may appropriately pause to review that special relationship, including two other rather special aircraft carriers.

The name of *Ark Royal* goes back in Royal Naval history to the Battle of the Armada in 1588, when the first ship of the name was of only 800 tons, but was the flagship of Lord Howard of Effingham. Not until 1914 was the name used again, when rather surprisingly it was given to a collier of 7,400 tons which was converted to carry seaplanes whilst still on the stocks. This ship was based on Grand Harbour throughout the First World War, and was present at the Dardanelles operations; she was re-named *Pegasus* in 1935 to free the name for the big new fleet carrier of 22,000 tons then under construction.

The third *Ark Royal* was a famous ship. Before 1939 she was a familiar sight in Grand Harbour, and she played a major role in ferrying Hurricane fighters into Malta in the early war years; it was whilst returning from one such sortie that she was torpedoed by a German U-boat within sight of Gibraltar in November 1941, and sank. She was a serious loss. Her role for Malta was taken over by the newer *Illustrious*, the first armoured-deck carrier in the Royal Navy. Her fight against the German dive-bombers while being repaired in Grand Harbour in 1941 is now a part of Maltese history.

Then a very large new aircraft carrier was designed, and three of the class were laid down in 1943. One was to be named HMS *Malta*, and this ship would have been of roughly the same size and capability as the United States Navy's *Midway* Class, then also under construction. *Malta* was however cancelled on December 21 1945, as the European war progressed. What a difference those three big ships would have made to the British Pacific Fleet in

1945! Apart from a tug in Victorian days, this would have been the first ship of the name to serve in the Royal Navy since the captured French *Généreux* was re-named *Malta* in 1800.

While *Malta* was on the stocks, the next *Ark Royal* was being designed. She too was a big carrier, though not as big as *Malta,* and she was completed in 1953. Strangely she did not come out to Malta for the assault on the Suez Canal, but over the next 20 years she was to be the largest British warship to visit, and she became a regular caller.

As this third *Ark Royal* steamed back towards England, the Admiralty announced that two of the new class of 'through-deck' cruisers or mini-carriers of 20,000 tons to be built for the Royal Navy would be named *Illustrious* and *Ark Royal.* So were Malta and the great battles of 1941 and 1942 to be remembered, even as the Royal Navy pulled out for the last time. So too, many officers and men, and surely many Maltese as well, must be hoping that these new ships, with their names so hallowed in the history of the islands, will be regular and welcome callers to Grand Harbour in the years to come.

	Completed	Standard displacement	Overall length	Number of aircraft
Ark Royal(2)	1914	7,400	366	12
Ark Royal(3)	1938	22,000	700	72
Illustrious(4)	1940	23,000	753	36
Malta(3)	—	46,900	916	81
USS *Midway*	1945	45,000	986	137

(Standard displacement in tons; overall length in feet; number after ship's name is the number of times used.)

As 1978 drew to a close, the Royal Navy's bases and many of its historical treasures were being offered to the Maltese Government. Fort St Angelo especially is rich in memories, and its chapel of St Anne, restored after the

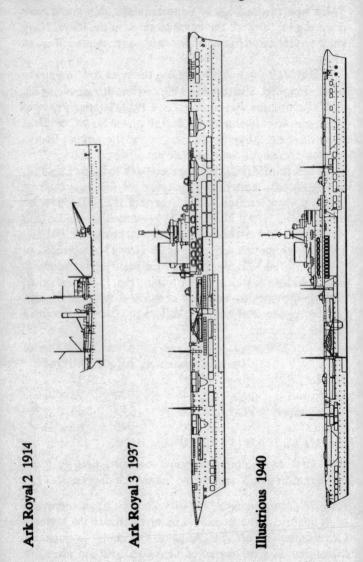

Ark Royal 2 1914

Ark Royal 3 1937

Illustrious 1940

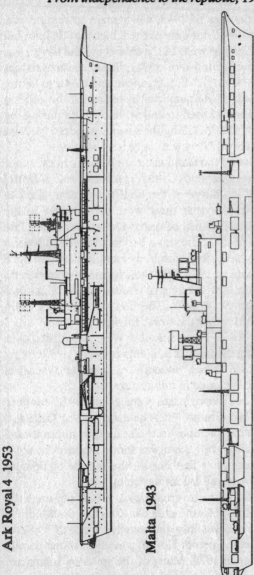

Ark Royal 4 1953

Malta 1943

Drawings by Ian Sturton

The drawings of *Ark Royal* (3) and *Illustrious* (4) have been adapted from the general arrangement drawings in the National Maritime Museum collection, and that of *Malta* (3) from drawings first published in *Warship International* in 1971.

heavy bomb damage of 1942, will remain to remind succeeding generations not only of the Knights of St John but of the Royal Navy as well. In the chapel are the navy's war memorial of the Second World War, listing all the warships which were sunk in the Mediterranean and closer to home, the Malta Book of Remembrance, listing all the officers and men who were killed in and around Malta during the Greater Siege, and including the several hundred Maltese ratings of the Royal Navy who were lost in action.

There are over a thousand ancient plans still in existence of the fortresses around Grand Harbour, and Admiral Oswald Cecil, in charge of the final evacuation, went to great trouble to see that these were turned over to the Maltese Government in good order. One trophy whose fate lay undecided at that time was a bed in which Lord Nelson is supposed to have slept with Lady Hamilton. It had been brought to Malta in 1943 after the capture of Naples, and since that time had become a feature of the Captain's House in HMS *St Angelo*. The bed was a rather plain wooden one and rather the worse for wear.

The former Royal Naval hospitals were also turned over intact, including the famous buildings at Bighi, overlooking Grand Harbour. Much modern medical and surgical equipment was included in this gesture.

The Royal Air Force bases were given to the Maltese people as the last aircraft left. The main base at Luqa had on transfer all the facilities to maintain it to international aviation standards, but there was some criticism from Mr Mintoff's government that not all the mobile equipment such as bulldozers and trucks was being left.

Across the harbour the great Lascaris Bastion, once the headquarters of the Commander-in-Chief of the Mediterranean Fleet, and set into the massive walls of Valletta above the ancient Custom House, was given to the people of Malta earlier in 1978. Many of the spacious rooms are now used by the national education department, but later that year the government decided to restore the famous War Room to its state during the war. Situated deep down in the bastion, it held the naval operations room in 1941 and 1942, when bombs drove its occupants from their previous room in *St Angelo,* and in 1943 it was from this same room that the invasion of Sicily was both planned and launched. Captain A.J. Pack, the retiring director of the Royal Naval Museum in Portsmouth, and a noted historian in his own right, made a special visit to advise on the restoration of the War Room, and from the spring of 1979 it has been open to the many tourists now visiting Malta.

A fine national war museum has been installed in the old Fort St Elmo at the seaward tip of Valletta's peninsula, and this will combine with the War Room in recalling the days of the Greater Siege, while Fort St Angelo will recall several centuries more of naval history.

CHAPTER 16

The Royal Navy withdraws, January–March 1979

As the New Year opened the British withdrawal from Malta gathered momentum, with March 31 as the date set for the final departure. Just as Nelson's blockade of Valletta had been a dramatic interlude, and just as the following 178 years of British association with Malta gave rise to exciting and even desperate times, so the farewell was an emotional period both for the remaining British forces, and for many of the Maltese people. As an integral part of this naval history, the final scenes should be recorded.

The Commander British Forces in Malta was Rear-Admiral Oswald Cecil; a popular and attractive figure, he showed a splendid sense of history during these months, and it was under his leadership that the British forces withdrew in friendship and in sadness, and entirely removed from the politics of the situation. On January 26 Admiral Cecil initiated the final moves by transferring from his official residence, the Villa Portelli on Kalkara Creek, to the Hotel Phoenicia outside the main gates of Valletta. Later that week the Royal Naval Port Division was disbanded, and the last 111 sailors completed their duties. That day the Admiral was joined by Commander J.L. Duffett, the last Commanding Officer of HMS *St Angelo* in a final mass in the ancient chapel of St Anne in the fortress. History repeated itself on February 22, when Admiral Cecil held the final meeting of his staff at the Palazzo d' Aurel, by permission of its owners, the Baron and Baroness Trapani Galea Feriol. This splendid building had been the headquarters in 1800 of General Graham, who had commanded the British and Maltese forces in the final siege of the French in Valletta, and even then the same family had owned the palace. Now the Union Jack and Maltese flag flew side by side in the garden.

Two weeks later the guided missile destroyer *London* arrived in Grand Harbour. She was to be Admiral Cecil's flagship during the final phase, and on March 12 he struck his flag in *St Angelo* and hoisted it in *London*. Three Royal Fleet Auxiliary ships, *Olna, Sir Lancelot* and *Tarbatness*, also arrived to lift the departing British forces. Now a series of nostalgic events followed fast on each other. On March 22 the last of the Royal Marine commandos, Salerno company of 130 men, marched symbolically unarmed from the RAF base at Luqa to Vittoriosa, where they embarked in *Sir Lancelot*. They were led by ten Marine drummers. Next day the Royal Marine Band and the Band of the Armed Forces Malta marched together down Valletta's Republic Street. There, before the Grand Master's Palace, they beat retreat at sunset, and the President of the Republic took the salute from the balcony. This was a most moving occasion, and many red and white flowers were thrown on the ground at the bandsmen's feet.

Yet another colourful event took place in the old Manoel Theatre on the evening of March 25. The two bands gave a concert, first one and then the other playing, and they finished together with a spirited rendering of Tchaikovsky's 1812 Overture, the applause for which shook the old theatre.

Then came one of the most extraordinary of the farewell events. Admiral Cecil came on stage with the President of the Republic, Dr Anton Buttigieg; they received a standing ovation as they embraced, and red and white flowers showered on to the stage from the audience. Then a choir joined them, and sang the 'Parting Song', the words for which had been specially composed by the President, and the music by Admiral Cecil himself. An emotional singing of 'Auld Lang Syne' followed, and cheering crowds surrounded the cars of the President and the Admiral, as they tried to drive away after the evening was finally brought to a close.

The British Forces Broadcasting Service closed down next day, with a farewell broadcast which included contributions from Admiral of the Fleet Lord Louis Mountbatten, Nicholas Monsarrat the author, and Miss Mabel Strickland, all good friends of Malta. Admiral Cecil broadcast his own farewell message from *London* to the people of Malta. In it he recalled that they and the British had been through a very great deal together. The Royal Navy had been asked to come by the Maltese in 1798, and they were leaving in the same spirit of friendship in which they came. His broadcast was heard throughout the islands, and not least in the waterfront bars of Valletta with the well-loved names — the Manchester Bar, the British Bar, and many others on the 'Barbary Coast', and up 'The Gut'. They were quieter now, these bars; gone were the cheerful, free-spending British sailors. Admiral Cecil's last words were: 'Thank you for a very happy memory, and good luck, Malta!'

Now the farewell moved inexorably into its final phase. On March 30 Fort St Angelo was turned over by the Royal Navy to the Maltese people; in all its history, this fort had seen no more significant day. The Royal Marines mounted their last parade there, then sailed in *Sir Lancelot,* lining the decks as she left harbour. *Tarbatness* and *Olna* followed her out, filled with other British servicemen. On March 31 an impressive ceremony was held before a great crowd in Vittoriosa, outside the gates of St Angelo. A great monument had been erected (designed by Mr Mintoff himself) and one minute before midnight a young sailor from *London* lowered the Union Jack, and a dockyard worker hoisted the Maltese flag in its place. Church bells were rung, and a great display of fireworks was let off. The President made a speech, during which he was visibly moved; then he laid red and white flowers on the monument, and Mr Dom Mintoff, the Prime Minister, together with Mr George Agius, General Secretary of the General Workers' Union, climbed the rocks to the summit and, carrying two torches, lit a flame which was to be kept forever burning. Mr Mintoff had invited foreign heads of state to the ceremonial, but the only one to come was his friend Colonel Gaddafi of Libya. He was greeted at Luqa airport by large numbers of Libyan students, and Maltese helicopters manned by Libyan pilots flew low over the airport. Down in Grand Harbour lay the cruise liner *Toletela*, in which many more Libyans arrived for the festivities; near her lay *London*, preparing to leave. Ten countries were represented at ministerial level and others sent their ambassadors.

On the morning of Sunday April 1 the destroyer *London* made her final departure, bearing Admiral Cecil and his staff. The weather had broken overnight, and high *gregale* winds swept the harbour; but the bastions and the quays and the Barracca Gardens were thronged to overflowing by great crowds of Maltese, waving flags, and with many in tears. From Luqa airport there now appeared a lone RAF Nimrod aircraft, piloted by Air Commodore H.D. Hall, the last Air Commander Malta. He flew low over Grand Harbour and the crowds, dipped his wings in salute, then made a last circuit of the islands' shores before setting his course towards Gibraltar. As the destroyer moved slowly down the harbour, Admiral Cecil on the bridge returned the waves of the crowds, and the ship's company of *London* lined her decks, while her Royal Marine band played on the quarterdeck. They too were feeling the emotion and the historical importance of this last farewell.

One of the largest crowds was gathered in the Lower Barracca Gardens, where stands the little Greek temple erected to the memory of Rear-Admiral Sir Alexander Ball, who had done so much to free Malta from the French occupation of 1798, and who had been the first and well-loved Governor of the islands under British rule. It seemed fitting that Rear-Admiral Cecil should pass below this temple, and near it the burial place of Admiral Ball in Fort St Elmo, as he passed down Grand Harbour. The first and the last of the British Admirals, they had both been good friends of the Maltese. At Fort St Elmo at the mouth of the harbour, the President of the Republic waited to salute the Admiral as he passed slowly by. A distinguished retinue of officials accompanied him as he stood on the high bastion in the cold wind. As the destroyer turned north away from the fort and between the arms of the breakwater, she fired a 21 gun salute, and a Maltese gun battery in the fort acknowledged with another. Then *London* disappeared into the mists of the grey sea, leaving only her wake behind her for the silent crowds on the ramparts to see.

CHAPTER 17

Who next for Malta? 1979-2000

The final departure of the British forces raised some intriguing questions about the future of the islands. During the previous year there was some increasing friction between the British and the Maltese, as the run-down of British forces in the islands progressed. It took a good deal of tolerance on the part of the British High Commissioner and Admiral Cecil to ensure that the situation was kept cool. Mr Mintoff barred British journalists from Malta for a time, in retaliation for their method of reporting; he closed down the British Forces Broadcasting Service in Floriana for the same reason. Britain, urged on by the EEC, felt obliged to place some restrictions on the import of Maltese textiles; in return Mr Mintoff barred the import of British cars. A sense of humour was needed to get through those months, and a well-known firm of trumpet manufacturers provided it. Flooded by competition from other countries, the firm closed down its factory in Malta, and a British newspaper predictably came out with a banner headline: 'Last Trumpet for Malta'.

Mr Mintoff followed a policy in that year of re-naming those streets which evoked memories of the British period. Churchill Square in Zurrieq became Republic Square; Prince of Wales Road in Sliema, so well known to the destroyer crews, became Balluta Street, and Duke of York Avenue leading out of Valletta, and Britannia Street in Cospicua were re-named after a Maltese painter and sculptor.

At the midnight ceremony on March 31 the President, Dr Buttigieg, said in his speech that apart from rejoicing in their 'Freedom Day', they had gathered to swear never again to have a foreign military base on their soil, and that Malta would remain for evermore a free republic run by the Maltese for the Maltese. It had freed itself from the foreign military base not out of hate or vengeance, but out of a strong act of faith, because it wanted to fulfil a new mission of peace in the Mediterranean in the interests of world peace. The removal of the military base was considered a big step forward towards this goal. Mr Mintoff saw Malta as a bridge of peace between Europe and Africa. The world of Islam was making big strides at this time, stretching from Morocco round to Turkey, and Malta could perhaps be a frontier post between the Christian and Islamic worlds, as the island had been in the centuries before 1800. He made great efforts, and with success, to persuade the other 34 nations of the European Security Conference to neutralise the Mediterranean, and to guarantee Malta's independence, with financial aid. At the review conference in 1978 it was agreed to review this at the Madrid meeting in 1980. In February 1979 a further conference was convened in Malta; an objective of this meeting was to set up a direct dialogue between those nations and the non-European countries bordering the sea, but only three of the eight in this last category attended. The conference discussed cultural, economic and scientific relations between the countries, but kept out of political debate.

The British withdrawal has meant the loss of the annual £35 million paid to Malta for the use of the bases, and this deficit more than the peace initiative dominated the scene in Malta in 1979. Mr Mintoff had some difficulty, however, in finding alternative sources of financial backing. France and Italy made it clear that his demands would be difficult to meet, and Italy was reported to be offended when a 40-man military mission to Malta was sent home by Mr Mintoff, as the Italian Government had not indicated the extent of their financial aid before the British withdrew. Soft loans seemed to be on offer from France and West Germany, but Malta's main backer seemed to be Libya. Colonel Gaddafi had for some time offered Malta financial and economic aid. He confirmed this in a speech while he was attending the 'Freedom Day' celebrations, and promised to set up joint industrial projects in Malta, to sell oil to the Maltese below the market price, and to offer financial assistance over a five-year period. It was, however, a disappointment that the nations to the north were not joining more quickly in offering aid, leaving Libya at that time as possibly the sole benefactor. One of Libya's aims was reported in newspapers to be to persuade Malta to remain outside NATO. Mr Mintoff had turned the Americans away a few years earlier, Russian ships were not allowed in Grand Harbour, and with the British ships also withdrawing the policy of neutrality would ensure that Malta remained independent. It was of timely significance that in the very same week in which the British forces finally departed from Malta, the peace treaty between Egypt and Israel was signed in Washington.

Mr Mintoff's ability to keep his islands out of the political arena depended quite heavily on the developments between the major powers, and the strategic scene has changed several times in the Mediterranean since 1945. The manoeuvring between the United States and Russia has been the dominant theme. The American Sixth Fleet was the most powerful naval force in the Mediterranean since 1945, with the Royal Navy's fleet declining rapidly in size as Britain's economic problems grew. Malta, with its large dockyard and naval facilities, had provided a convenient central base for the American ships, and their friendship with the British in Grand Harbour was a source of strength to NATO. Ships of other friendly nations also frequently called in, and there was no need to question too closely the strategic importance of the island in those first decades of the guided missiles.

When the Sixth Fleet no longer felt welcome in Malta in 1971, it became more dependent on its excellent fleet train support, with its tankers, supply and repair ships, and by rotating the warships regularly back to the United States it avoided the need to have a main fleet base in the Mediterranean itself. The fleet remained as strong as ever, and in 1979 included the world's largest warship, the nuclear-powered carrier *Nimitz* of 91,400 tons.

Subsequent events, however, brought fresh thoughts on the strategic problems in what Winston Churchill called the 'soft under-belly of NATO'. Turkey closed down some of the American bases in its country, and as an economy measure the RAF withdrew from Malta the Shackleton and Canberra aircraft which had filled an important surveillance role in shadowing Russian submarines. The security of the oil tanker route from the Arab states to the west remained as vital as ever; indeed, the revolution in Iran in 1979 showed just how dependent the western world, including the United States, still was upon that route.

A major concern was the rapid growth in size of the Russian Fleet, with most of the increase coming in new warships of impressive design, and including aircraft carriers for the first time. After Mr Mintoff barred Russian warships from visiting Malta, they found a base in Egypt, where for some years Russian advisers and arms had been flooding in. The Egyptians requested the Russians to leave their country in 1975, and the Russian Fleet lost its naval base in the Mediterranean. Its ships have managed rather uncomfortably since then, anchoring in shallow waters off the North African coast and to the east of Crete to carry out their essential maintenance and to get some rest. The Russian sailors must have badly missed their runs ashore in Alexandria, and if their fleet could have used Grand Harbour they would have enjoyed excellent shore facilities in an island where their officers would feel secure.

The Russian Fleet also lacked shore-based air cover, since it lost the use of the former RAF base at Cairo West. The new aircraft carriers were no doubt in part an answer to that, but as the Americans and British would probably agree, carriers are no substitute in the long run for good shore bases for reconnaissance planes. The excellent former RAF and naval air bases in Malta would have provided an ideal base for Russian aircraft. The Russian Government started making overtures to Mr Mintoff. Delegations came to Malta, and significant numbers of Russian merchant ships started to come to Malta Dockyards, too, to use the excellent repair facilities. Through these changing influences, the NATO view on the importance of Malta also changed. The Americans were worried when the British agreed with Mr Mintoff to pull out of Malta, and the French Government, outside NATO, recognised the changes by transferring most of its major warships to the Mediterranean, to counter the growth of the Russian fleet in that area.

NATO views on the conduct of a future war appeared to be changing as well. In spite of the dominance of the ever more sophisticated intercontinental ballistic missiles, the view was growing that in any future war convoys would still have to be run, especially to guard the passage of the vital oil tankers. The escort destroyers and frigates of today are larger and more independent than their predecessors of 1945, but they would still need convenient bases from which to operate close to the convoy routes.

Even the Chinese have appeared upon the Maltese scene, with their loans and technical help in the construction of the gigantic new drydock in Malta, and so as the British withdrew in March 1979 all the major powers had an interest in the island and its future. The latest possible contender for a place in the sun in Malta is the Order of the Knights of St John. While the present headquarters of the Order is in Rome, an office has always been maintained in Valletta; their Grand Master, Fra Angelo de Mojana, paid a visit to Mr Mintoff in 1978, and inspected the old quarters of the Knights in Fort St Angelo. The Knights are still a major organisation with some 10,000 members, and they run hospitals in many parts of the world. When the Pope was buried in Rome in 1978, the representatives of the Knights of St John were accorded the status of a head of state.

Mr Mintoff will no doubt make every effort to maintain his policy of neutrality in the future, despite any growing pressures from the major powers around him. In a way it would seem fitting and also appropriate to that policy, if after 181 years and more after the French ousted them from the island, the Knights of St John could return in peace, and re-occupy St Angelo to carry on their good works. Whatever happens, the islands of Malta will remain of great interest to the rest of the world, and the 178 years of association with the Royal Navy will remain one of the most glorious periods in the colourful history of the islands.

Appendices

1 Ships in the blockade of Malta, 1798-1800

French

Escaped to Malta from the Battle of the Nile

Ship of the line	*Guillaume Tell*	80 guns	Vice-Admiral Decrès
Frigates	*Diane*	40 guns	
	Justice	40 guns	

Captured from the Knights of St John

Ships of the line	*Athenien*	64 guns	Rear-Admiral
	Dego	64 guns	Villeneuve
Frigate	*Carthagenaise*	36 guns	

Blockade Runners

Ship of the line	*Généreux*	74 guns
Frigate	*Boudeuse*	36 guns

British
The first blockading squadron, September 1798

Portuguese

Ships of the line	Four ships		
		74 guns	Rear-Admiral the Marquess de Niza

British

Ship of the line	*Lion*	74 guns	Captain Manley Dixon
Fireship	*Incendiary*		
Brig	*Menorca*		Captain George Miller

Captain Ball took over the blockade, October 1798

Ships of the line			
	Alexander	74 guns	Captain Alexander Ball
	Culloden	74 guns	Captain Thomas Troubridge
	Colossus	74 guns	Captain George Murray

At the battle with the French Généreux, *February 1800*

Ships of the line			
	Queen Charlotte	100 guns	Vice-Admiral of the Red Lord Keith
			Captain Andrew Todd
	Foudroyant	80 guns	Rear-Admiral of the Red Lord Nelson
			Captain Sir Edward Berry
	Audacious	74 guns	Captain Davidge Gould
	Northumberland	74 guns	Captain George Martin
	Alexander	74 guns	Lieutenant William Harrington, Acting
	Lion	64 guns	Captain Manley Dixon
Frigates	*Success*	36 guns	Captain Sheldham Peard
	Sirena	36 guns	(Neapolitan)
Sloops	Three ships		

At the battle with the French Guillaume Tell, *March 1800*

Ships of the line			
	Culloden	74 guns	Captain Thomas Troubridge
	Foudroyant	80 guns	Captain Sir Edward Berry
	Alexander	74 guns	Lieutenant William Harrington, Acting
	Lion	64 guns	Captain Manley Dixon
Frigate	*Penelope*	36 guns	Captain Henry Blackwood
Sloops	*Perseus*		
	La Bonne Citoyenne		
Brig	*Menorca*		Captain George Miller

At the escape of the frigates Diane *and* Justice, *August 1800*

Ships of			
the line *Northumberland*	74 guns	Captain George Martin	
Généreux	74 guns	(under the White Ensign)	
Frigate *Success*	36 guns	Captain Sheldham Peard	

2 British warships at Malta in the First World War

Class	1915	1916	1917	1918
Battleships	0	15	10	3
Cruisers	0	5	5	4
Light Cruisers	2	16	13	11
Seaplane Carriers	0	1	2	2
Monitors	0	16	14	14
Destroyers	15	36	37	42
Torpedo Boats	6	7	8	8
Sloops	0	11	19	31
Submarines	3	16	14	9
Depot ships	1	3	4	5
Repair ships	0	2	1	1
Minesweepers	0	2	3	3
Armed boarding steamers	0	11	6	7
Messenger ships	0	2	3	3

All figures taken in January of the relevent year.

3 Patrols by 10th Submarine Flotilla in 1942

Number of patrols	*By each of these boats*
14	*Una*
11	*P 35*
7	*Utmost, P 34, P 44*
6	*Upholder*
5	*Urge, P 46*
4	*Unbeaten, P 31, P 36, P 42, P 43*
3	*Unique, Upright, P 211*
2	*P 37, P 212, P 247*
1	*P 39, P 45, P 48*

Total patrols from Malta: 58

4 Cargo submarines and minelayers for Malta in 1942

Month	Ship	Minelayers	Submarines
March	*Thunderbolt, Clyde, Olympus, Turbulent, Tempest, Pandora, Welshman*	1	6
April	*Clyde, Welshman*	1	1
May	*Welshman*	1	0
June	*Porpoise, Clyde, Welshman* (2)	2	2
July	*Parthian, Clyde, Welshman*	1	2
August	*Rorqual, Clyde, Otus*	0	3
Sept	*Rorqual* (2), *Proteus, Parthian, Clyde, Thrasher, Porpoise, Traveller*	0	8
Oct	—		
Nov	*Parthian, Clyde, Traveller, Thrasher, Welshman* (2), *Manxman*	3	4
Dec	*Welshman* (2)	2	0
Total cargo trips made		11	16
Total cargo carried, approx tons		3,300	2,600

5 Spitfires ferried to Malta in 1942

Month	Aircraft carriers	Number delivered	Monthly total
March 6	*Eagle* and *Argus*	15	
March 21	*Eagle* and *Argus*	16	
March 29	*Eagle* and *Argus*	16	47
April 20	USS *Wasp*	47	47
May 9	USS *Wasp* and *Eagle*	61	61
June 3	*Eagle* and *Argus*	32	
June 9	*Eagle* and *Argus*	27	59
July 15	*Eagle*	31	
July 21	*Eagle*	28	59
August 11	*Furious*	36	
August 17	*Furious*	29	65
October 3	*Furious*	29	29
Total flown in safely			367

6   Air raids on Malta in 1941 and 1942

1941	Number of raids	Including night raids
January	58	6
February	107	28
March	105	22
April	90	25
May	97	26
June	67	25
July	72	53
August	30	18
September	31	21
October	56	24
November	76	40
December	175	100
Totals	964	388

1942	Number of raids	Including night raids
January	262	73
February	236	109
March	275	90
April	283	96
May	248	62
June	173	60
July	188	57
August	101	37
September	57	17
October	152	41
November	30	13
December	35	8
Totals	2,040	663

Total of air raid alerts in Valletta	3,340
Number of hours under alert	2,357
Number of hours in 1942 alone	2,031
Total tonnage of bombs dropped	16,500
Tonnage dropped in 1942	12,500

7 Naval forces for invasion of Sicily, July 1943

	British	American
Battleships	6	
Fleet aircraft carriers	2	
Cruisers	10	5
Destroyers	71	48
Escort vessels	35	
Minesweepers	34	8
Submarines	23	
Anti-aircraft ships	4	
Fighter direction ships	2	
Monitors	3	
Minelayers	1	3
Headquarters ships	5	4
Landing ships (Infantry)	8	
Major landing craft	319	190
Minor Landing craft	715	510
Coastal craft	160	83

8 Operation code-names mentioned in the narrative

Avalanche	September	1943	Assault on Salerno
Corkscrew	June	1943	Assault on Pantellaria
Excess	January	1941	Convoy Gibraltar eastwards
Halberd	September	1941	Convoy Gibraltar-Malta
Harpoon	June	1942	Convoy Gibraltar-Malta
Herkules		1942	Planned German invasion of Malta
Hurry	August	1940	Hurricanes ferried to Malta
Husky	July	1943	Assault on Sicily
Landmark	November	1941	Diversion convoy from Malta
Musketeer			
Revise	October	1956	Assault on Suez Canal
Pedestal	August	1942	Convoy Gibraltar-Malta
Portcullis	December	1942	Convoy Alexandria-Malta
Quadrangle	December	1942	4 convoys, Alexandria-Malta
Retribution	April	1943	Attack on Axis forces escaping from North Africa
Rocket	June	1941	Hurricanes ferried to Malta
Shingle	January	1944	Assault on Anzio
Splice	May	1941	Hurricanes ferried to Malta
Stoneage	November	1942	Convoy Alexandria-Malta
Style	June	1941	Hurricanes ferried to Malta
Substance	July	1941	Convoy Gibraltar-Malta
Torch	November	1942	Assault on North Africa
Vigorous	June	1942	Convoy Alexandria-Malta
White	November	1940	Hurricanes ferried to Malta
Winch	April	1941	Hurricanes ferried to Malta

Bibliography

This has been listed by the six main periods. Primary sources throughout are those listed from the Public Record Office in London

General

Blouet, Brian: *The Story of Malta* (London, 1967).

Churchill, Sir W.S.: *The Second World War* (Cassell, 1948).

Clowes, W.L.: *The Royal Navy – a history* (London, 1900).

Cunningham, Admiral of the Fleet Lord: *A Sailor's Odyssey* (Hutchinson, 1951).

Harrison Smith, Professor: *The British in Malta* (Malta, 1953).

Hughes, Professor Quentin: *Fortress: Architectural and Military History in Malta* (Lund Humphries, 1969).

Jane's Fighting Ships: Various years (Macdonald & Janes).

Kininmonth, Christopher: *The Traveller's Guide to Malta* (Cape, 1967).

Laferla, Dr A.V.: *British Malta* (Malta, 1938).

Luke, Sir Harry: *Malta – an Account and Appreciation* (Harrap, 1949).

Monk, W.F.: *Britain in the Western Mediterranean* (Hutchinson, 1953).

Monsarrat, Nicholas: *The Kappilan of Malta* (Cassell, 1973).

Owen, Charles: *The Maltese Islands* (David & Charles, 1969).

The Times of Malta and *The Sunday Times of Malta:*
various dates.

Nelson's era

Hardman, D: *History of Malta During the French and British Occupations* (Longmans, 1909).

Howarth, David: *Trafalgar — the Nelson Touch* (Collins, 1969).

James William: *The Naval History of Great Britain* (6 vols) (Harding, Lepard, 1826).

Kennedy, Ludovic: *Nelson and his Captains* (Collins, 1951).

Kent, Alexander: *Form Line of Battle* (Hutchinson, 1969). *Signal — Close Action* (Hutchinson, 1974).

Lloyd, Christopher: *The Nile Campaign* (David & Charles, 1973).

Mahan, Captain A.T.: *The Influence of Sea Power upon the French Revolution and Empire* (1893).

Maps, Jim: *Menorca* (Tourbooks, 1975).

Padfield, Peter: *Nelson's War* (Granada, 1976).

Puges, F.T.: *Menorca* (Menorca, 1976).

ADM 51: Original Logs of Ships, 1797-1820 *(Vanguard, Foudroyant, Alexander, Success).*

ADM 180, 182-5: *List of Ships, 1756-1810.*

CO 158-5: *Vessels Admitted to Pratique in Malta, 1802.*

CO 158-19: *Report of Royal Commission on Malta, 1812.*

ADM 106-2043, etc: *In Letters from Malta Dockyard, 1800-1832.*

Victorian and Edwardian era

Febb & MacGowan: *The Victorian & Edwardian Navy* (Batsford, 1976).

Parkes, Oscar: *British Battleships, 1860-1950* (Seeley Service, 1960).

WO 33-8: *Report on the State of the Fortress of Malta* (June 3 1859).

WO 33-32: *Memorandum on the Defences of Malta* (February 22 1878).

WO 33-25: *Report on Malta by Brig General Adye* (December 15 1872).

CO 163: *Malta Times,* 1840-1855.

ADM 116-3089: *Mediterranean Strategy and Policy, 1887-1913.*

ADM 116-3099, 3493: *Mediterranean Strategy and Policy, 1912.*

The First World War

Chatterton, E. Keble: *Sea of Adventure — Minesweeping in the Mediterranean.*

Corbett, Sir Julian S.: *Naval Operations* (Longmans Green, 1931).

Hough, Richard: *The Chase — Goeben in the Mediterranean* (Warship International, 1969).

Mackinnon, Rev A.G.T.: *Malta — the Nurse of the Mediterranean* (1916).

Newbolt, Henry: *Naval Operations* (Longmans Green, 1931).

CAB 45-274: *Convoy System of Malta.*

ADM 116-1649: *Command of Allied Fleets in the Mediterranean.*

ADM 186-12: *Movements of Royal Naval Ships* (6 vols).

The inter-war years

Dawson, Captain Lionel: *Mediterranean Medley* (Rich & Cowan, 1933).

Poolman, Kenneth: *Ark Royal* (Kimber, 1956).

Roskill, S.W.: *Naval Policy Between the Wars* (NMM, 1978).

ADM 116-1660: *Self Government and the Economic Position, 1919-1922.*

ADM 116-3190: *Preparations Against a Turkish Attack, 1925.*

ADM 116-3134: *Preparations for War and Summer Cruises*, 1927.

ADM 116-2285: *Summer Cruise*, 1925.

ADM 116-2450: *Summer Cruise*, 1926.

ADM 116-3077: *Summer Cruise*, 1935.

ADM 116-3877: *Summer Cruises* 1936-1939.

ADM 116-3041, 3049, 3476: *Abyssinian Crisis*, 1935-1936.

ADM 116-3512: *Destroyer Flotillas in Spanish Civil War*, 1936.

ADM 116-3521: *Mining of HMS Hunter*, 1937.

ADM 116-3534: *Attacks on RN Ships near Spain*, 1937.

ADM 116-3845: *Albanian Crisis*, 1939.

The Second World War

Brookes, Ewart: *Destroyer* (Jarrolds, 1962).

Cameron, Ian: *Red Duster, White Ensign* (Muller, 1959).

Elliott, Peter: *Allied Minesweeping in World War 2* (Patrick Stephens, 1979).

Gerard, Francis: *Malta Magnificent* (Cassell, 1943).

Goosen, Commodore J.C.: *South Africa's Navy* (Flesch, 1973).

Gratton, Vice-Admiral Sir Peter: *Convoy Escort Commander* (Cassell, 1964).

HMSO: *The Air Battle of Malta* (1943).

HMSO: *Grand Strategy* (6 vols).

HMSO: *The Mediterranean Fleet — Greece to Tripoli* (1944).

HMSO: *The Mediterranean and Middle East* (5 vols).

Hart, Sydney: *Submarine Upholder* (Oldbourne, 1960).

Hay, Ian: *The Unconquered Isle* (1944).

Hill, Roger: *Destroyer Captain* (Kimber, 1975).

Hogan, George: *Malta — The Triumphant Years* (Hale, 1978).

Lloyd, Air Marshal Sir Hugh: *Briefed to Attack* (Hodder & Stoughton, 1949).

Macintyre, Captain Donald: *The Battle for the Mediterranean* (Batsford, 1964).

March, Edgar J.: *British Destroyers* (Seeley Service, 1966).

Mars, Alastair: *Unbroken* (Muller).

Morison, S.E.: *History of American Naval Operations in World War 2* – Vol. II: *Operations in North African Waters, 1942-1943.*

Vol. IX: *Sicily, Salerno, Anzio, 1943-1944.*

Poolman, Kenneth: *Illustrious* (Kimber, 1958).

Preston, Antony: *Navies of World War 2* (Bison, 1976).

Pugsley, Rear-Admiral A.F.: *Destroyer Man* (Weidenfeld & Nicholson, 1975).

Roskill, S.W.: *The War at Sea* (4 vols) (HMSO, 1956-61).

Roskill, S.W.: *HMS Warspite* (Collins, 1957).

Shankland, Peter and Hunter, Anthony: *Malta Convoy* (Collins, 1961).

Smith, Peter: *Pedestal – the Malta Convoy of 1942* (Kimber, 1970).

Winton, John: *Air Power at Sea, 1939-45* (Sidgwick & Jackson, 1976).

CAB 105-1-7: *Telegrams London-Washington.*

ADM 205-9, 48, 19, 22A: *First Sea Lord's Correspondence with US Navy.*

ADM 205-13, 14, 42, 69: *Loan of USS Wasp.*

PREM 3-266/4: *Flying in Spitfires, including USS Wasp.*

ADM 199: *Mediterranean War Diaries:* 389 (1939-40), 413-5(1941), 386-7, (1940), 651 (1942), 638-41 (1943), 1430-7 (1944), 1446-50 (1945), 424 (Vice-Admiral Malta, 1942).

Mediterranean Operations Reports:

General: 797-8 (1940-41), 806-10 (1941), 445-7 (1940-42) 258,600, 976-1002 (1943-44), 805 (1944-45).

Operation Halberd, 1941:831.

Operation Substance, 1941: 830.

Operation Vigorous, 1941: 1244.

Operation Pedestal, 1942: 1242-3.

Operation Lariat, 1942: 1-11979.

Operation Husky, 1943: Orders, 858-60, Reports, 943, 857.

Operation Shingle, 1943-44: 873.

Operation Avalanche, 1943: 861, 949.

Minesweeping Reports: Summaries, 1941-42, 1172, M/S trawlers at Malta 1-18858.

Submarine Operations: 10th. SMF reports, 1942-44, 1917, war diaries, 1923 etc.

Mediterranean Fleet daily state: 1942-44, 190-1, 1943, 200-2, 1944, 204-9, 1944-45, 1481.

Underground Warship Harbours: 1-12135, 18598.

Reestablishment of Repair Base: 1-13026.

Supplies for Malta, 1942: CAB 122-93.

Spare Parts Centre for Fleet, 1944: 1-15092.

Need for Big New Drydock: 1939-46, 1-17860, 1945-46, 1-17942.

Peacetime use of Malta's airfields: 1-17402, 17422.

Postwar requirements of Malta: 1944 1-16092, 16096, 16331.

Strike in Malta's dockyard, 1943: PREM 3-266/9.

Post 1945

Leggett, Eric: *The Corfu Incident* (Seeley Service, 1974).

Lloyd, Selwyn: *Suez, 1956* (Cape, 1978).

Malta Drydocks: *Dockyard News* (various dates).

Press cuttings: *The Times of Malta, The Sunday Times of Malta,* various British newspapers, over 25 years.

Sturton, I.A.: *HMS Malta (*Warship International, 1971).

United Nations: *Economic Adaptation and Development in Malta,* 1964.

ADM 205-694: *Long-term Policy in the Mediterranean,* 1948.

ADM 205-72: *Middle East Planning, Meetings with*

Americans, 1948.
ADM 1-19532: *Palestine Blockade Reports, 1946.*
ADM 1-19856: *Summary of Palestine Blockade, 1946.*
ADM 1-18855: *Postwar Minesweeping Reports.*
ADM 116-5791: *Mediterranean Zone Mine Clearance, 1945-51.*
ADM 1-16331: *Postwar Fleet Tug Requirements, 1944.*
ADM 1-19845: *Autumn Cruise, 1946.*
ADM 1-20692: *Spring Cruise, 1947.*
ADM 205-68: *Disposal of Italian Fleet, 1945.*
ADM 1-21433: *Food subsidies at Malta, 1949.*

Index